D1500042

WITHDRAWN

coach, athlete, and the sport psychologist

Edited by

Peter Klavora, PhD
Juri V Daniel, PhD

Illustrations

Hans Zander

UNIVERSITY OF TORONTO
SCHOOL OF PHYSICAL AND HEALTH EDUCATION

ISBN 0-7727-0100-8

Manufactured in Canada by the School of
Physical and Health Education, University
of Toronto, Toronto, Ontario M5S 1A1.

This book was designed and its production
supervised by Peter Klavora. Manuscript
editing by Mary McDougall Maude and
Paul Stevens; graphics and composition by
Igor Tuma, illustrations by Hans Zander;
typesetting by Tanya Klavora.

Distribution in Canada by
School of Physical and Health Education
University of Toronto, Toronto, Ontario M5S 1A1
and
Canadian Coaching Association
333 River Road
Ottawa, Ontario K1L 8B9

Distributed world wide except Canada by
Human Kinetics Publishers, Box 5076
Champaign, Illinois 61820.

The book was printed and bound by
Twin Offset Limited in Toronto, Canada.

preface

This book is the result of a fortunate modification of the intention to publish, in a modest way, the proceedings of the Applied Sciences Symposium, the second part of the 1978 Congress of the Canadian Society for Psychomotor Learning and Sport Psychology, held in Toronto, November 1978. In designing the Applied Sciences Symposium there was a clear commitment to the importance of the practical application of various aspects of sport psychology. At the conclusion of this largely successful attempt to "bridge the gap" between sport scientist and sport practitioner it was evident that, with the addition of a few carefully chosen papers and the slight modification of some symposium presentations, a modest proceedings could become an excellent book. This is that book; comprehensive in coverage and including information for athletes, coaches, sport technical planners and sport scientists.

The greatest strength of this publication is the contribution made by authors from five countries. They all are highly prominent sport psychologists who have been known for years for their unique and successful approaches in working with elite athletes and coaches. Throughout the book they are sharing unselfishly their invaluable experiences in collaborating with the Olympic athlete.

The major purpose of this book is to explore several important topics in the area of sport psychology which are of value to coach and athlete. Information is also presented for sport scientists as a means of strengthening the links between scientists and practitioners.

Structured into five parts, this work should provide something of value for the most critical reader. Part one includes articles which deal with the need for sport psychology in sport practice. Also emphasized is the continuing need for effort in bringing coaches, athletes, and sport scientists closer in the pursuit of a common goal. Part two concentrates upon the topics reflected in the title of the book: *Coach, Athlete, and the Sport Psychologist.* Several views are offered on the interrelationships and responsibilities of the three major actors listed in the title. Of particular significance in this regard is the case made by Rainer Martens for sport psychologists to move from essentially laboratory research to applied research in the real world of sport. This plea, coming from a man with an excellent reputation in his field, who is clearly indicating a personal change in direction, provides grounds for much optimism. The third part includes topics concerned with peak performance, and part four examines prediction of performance and the shaping of athletic behavior; these two sections will likely be the major areas of interest and value for the coach and the technical director. These two parts contain a wealth of information of sufficient breadth and depth to accommodate the needs of a range of practitioners in many sports. The final part offers descriptions of psychological programs in five countries which represent east European and western world approaches. This part will perhaps hold most interest for national level sports planners.

The rapid growth of the sport sciences is but one example of the knowledge explosion characteristic of the latter half of this century. However, this increase in knowledge has generally not been paralleled by appropriate translation and dissemination of the information to those who will benefit. "Bridging the gap" is an idiom describing the processes of the sport science community with the operational needs of the practicing sport community. This book will make a most valuable contribution to this important task.

Geoff R. Gowan
Technical Coordinator
Coaching Association of Canada

acknowledgement

This book is an outgrowth of the Applied Sciences Symposium of the 1978 Congress of the Canadian Society for Psychomotor Learning and Sport Psychology. Many hours went into the planning of this symposium which assembled prominent sport psychologists from various countries. Our sincere thanks must be extended to Drs Evelyn I. Bird and Vietta E. Wilson for their informed and sensitive advice in the crucial initial stages of designing the symposium. Furthermore, their moral support continued throughout the symposium and during the preparation of this book.

Our special thanks are given to all contributing authors, who in most cases prepared original contributions in which they revealed their unique and highly successful approaches to working with Olympic athletes.

Drs. Geoff R. Gowan and Cal B. Botterill from the Coaching Association of Canada, and Mr. Jack C. Lynch from the Canadian Olympic Association have all helped in their own ways. Particularly their encouragement and moral support are greatly appreciated.

And finally, acknowledgement is extended to all sponsors of the Applied Sciences Symposium and of this book. Without their continuous help this collection of papers would never have been possible. The sponsors were: Wintario and Sport and Fitness Division of the Ontario Ministry of Culture and Recreation, Sport Canada, Coaching Association of Canada, the Canadian Olympic Association, Canada Council, and the School of Physical and Health Education of the University of Toronto.

P.K.
J.V.D.

authors

Cameron J.R. Blimkie is a technical assistant with the Coaching Association of Canada and is responsible for working to bridge the gap between sport and sport science. He is in the process of completing a PhD in the Department of Physiology at the University of Western Ontario, London. He played hockey and football at university and is the Coaching Association's representative on the recently formed Sports Medicine Council of Canada. He has published several papers in the area of exercise cardio-respiratory physiology.

Cal Botterill is assistant technical coordinator of the Coaching Association of Canada where he is involved in education programs for coaches. In addition, he is acting as manager of new initiatives by the association aimed at bridging the gap between sport science and sport practice. He has a PhD in sport psychology from the University of Alberta, is a former national hockey team member, and has had considerable practical experience teaching and coaching. He is a co-author of *Every Kid Can Win* and a member of the editorial review board for the *Canadian Journal of Applied Sport Sciences* and *Coaching Review.*

Dorcas Susan Butt is an associate professor of psychology at the University of British Columbia where she has taught since completing her PhD at the University of Chicago in 1967. For several years she worked as a clinical psychologist. She has consulted for a variety of individual athletes, teams, and clubs and is currently involved in a cross-national study of sport motivation in Canada, Japan, and Great Britain. As an athlete she was ranked the number one tennis player in Canada, played the international tennis circuit and captained Canada's national tennis team in 1970, 1971, and

1972. She has published on personality measurement, delinquen-
cy, social values, and the psychology of sport. A recent publication, *Psychology of Sport: the Behavior, Motivation, Personality
and Performance of Athletes* (New York, 1976) has been translated into Japanese.

Geoff R. Gowan, PhD (University of Wisconsin), is technical
coordinator of the Coaching Association of Canada, a position he
has held since 1972. Previously he was associate professor and
associate chairman of the School of Physical Education at
McMaster University. He has had extensive international coaching
experience in track and field. He has contributed several chapters
for books on track and field, coaching, and scientific aspects of
sport training and has presented numerous papers at national and
international symposia on coaching and sport science.

Wayne R. Halliwell is a professor in the Department of Physical
Education at the University of Montreal. He has a PhD in sport
psychology and his work has emphasized the psycho-social factors
affecting athletic performance. As an athlete, Halliwell played
hockey and baseball at the intercollegiate and international levels,
and he has coached hockey teams from the university to minor
hockey levels. At present, he is serving as a consultant to various
national and provincial teams in Canada and abroad. He has
published several articles dealing with motivation and sport.

James L. Hickman is a research psychologist who specializes in
the investigation of extraordinary human capacities. For the past
four years he has been a research associate with the Esalen
Institute Sports Center investigating the range of extraordinary
experiences that arise in sport and developing training routines
which integrate mental and physical disciplines into athletics. He is
currently working at the Washington Research Center in San
Francisco developing a computerized archive of all existing literature on supernormal bodily functioning. His published research
includes articles on altered states of consciousness, psychic
healing, meditation and sport training, and Soviet approaches to
psychophysical skill development.

Bruce Kidd teaches track and field and the political economy of
sport in the School of Physical and Health Education at the
University of Toronto. A lifelong advocate of athletes' rights, he
won a gold medal in the 1962 Commonwealth Games and is a
member of Canada's Sports Hall of Fame. His publications include

The Death of Hockey (with John Macfarlane) and *The Political Economy of Sport,* recently published by CAHPER. He is sports editor of *Canadian Dimension.*

Walter Kroll is Commonwealth professor in the Department of Exercise Science, School of Physical Education, University of Massachusetts, where he teaches an undergraduate course in the psychology of coaching. His work in sport psychology has included the multivariate analysis of personality profiles and psychological scaling of sportsmanship values. He has coached wrestling at Fort Hays (Kansas) State College.

Rainer Martens, PhD, is professor of physical education at the University of Illinois, Urbana-Champaign. He is director of the Office of Youth Sports which publishes *Sportsline,* a newsletter for volunteer coaches, and conducts research on children's sports programs. Martens currently is a consulting sport psychologist with the U.S. Nordic Ski Team. He has written three books, edited two others, and published numerous articles in the field of sport psychology.

James D. McClements, PhD, is associate professor of physical education at the University of Saskatchewan. His current research interests are in psychological aspects of sport and physical activity. A former coach of university rugby, as well as age class and senior speedskating, he is currently assistant coach of track and field and cross-country for the University of Saskatchewan.

Harold A. Minden, PhD, is a registered clinical psychologist. He is a professor in the Department of Psychology and in Physical Education and Athletics, York University, Toronto. He has been a consultant to the Clarke Institute of Psychiatry in Toronto for ten years. Minden is at present the clinical and research sport psychologist to the Canadian Olympic Gymnastic Program and a consultant to the Defence and Civil Institute of Environmental Studies and Integra Foundation. His present research is in attitudes towards fitness, stress management, motivational styles, and weight control in Olympic-level athletes and he is currently developing assessment procedures for athletes and coaches.

William P. Morgan, PhD, is a professor in the Department of Physical Education and director of the Sport Psychology Laboratory, University of Wisconsin-Madison. He has served as a consulting psychologist to various Olympic and national teams and to government agencies and institutes in the United States and abroad. He has edited two volumes dealing with sport psychology and has published papers on personality, hypnosis, perception, and mental health. Until recently, he edited the "Hypnosis News-letter"of the American Psychological Association.

Robert M. Nideffer, PhD, is president of Enhanced Performance Associates in San Diego, California, where he provides consultation services to individual athletes and teams. From 1970 to 1977 he was an associate professor in the Department of Psychology at the University of Rochester. A former college diver, he has developed the Test of Attentional and Interpersonal Style and has published two books on sport psychology, *The Inner Athlete* (just translated into Russian) and *A.C.T.: Attention Control Training*, which describes techniques for improving concentration in highly competitive situations.

Bruce C. Ogilvie, PhD (University of London), is a professor of psychology at San Jose State University. He is a former director of the Institute for the Study of Sports Motivation and was a consultant to the 1964, 1968, 1972, and 1974 U.S. Olympic teams. He has worked as a consultant to twelve National Football League teams, five National Basketball Association teams, and thirteen National Baseball League teams, and is at present a consultant to the Portland Trail Blazers basketball team, Colorado Rockies hockey team, and the Toronto Blue Jays baseball team. He has published over 80 articles in the area of sports and stress.

Maurie D. Pressman, MD, is chairman of the Division of Psychiatry, Albert Einstein Medical Center, Northern Division, Philadelphia, and clinical professor of psychiatry, Temple University Health Sciences Center, Philadelphia. He is trained as an adult and child psychoanalyst. His interest in sports medicine has enabled him to work intensively with figure skaters, and he has been a regular member of the faculty of the North Atlantic Training Center, Lake Placid, N.Y. He has worked with amateur and professional athletes, including activities with the White Face Mountain Training Center, Lake Placid. His work with hypnosis and visualization has been receiving a good deal of attention.

Lee Pulos, PhD, is a clinical psychologist and clinical assistant professor, Department of Psychiatry, University of British Columbia. He has worked with a number of world-class and professional athletes and teams since 1967. In 1978 he was sport psychologist for Team Canada at the Commonwealth Games and will serve in the same capacity for the Pan American Games in 1979 in Puerto Rico. In addition, Pulos is the coowner and operations director of a large business corporation. His interest in high performance people extends to business executives for whom he conducts seminars and training workshops throughout North America.

Willi S. Railo, PhD, is an associate professor in the Norwegian College of Physical Education and Sport in Oslo, where he concentrates on sport psychology in his research and lecturing. During the last ten years he has taught a lot of people now coaching in Scandinavia, and he works closely with different sport federations. During these years he has also worked preparing top Scandinavian athletes for important competitions such as the Olympic Games and the world championships. He has written a book on the psychology of training and competition—practical applications (only Scandinavian versions available) that is used as a principal source by the Norwegian and Swedish national sport federations. At present he is preparing psychological training programs on cassettes for top athletes.

Anne L. Rothstein, PhD, is associate professor in the Department of Dance, Health, Physical Education, and Recreation at H. H. Lehman College, City University of New York. She is co-director of the Human Performance Laboratory and is currently developing an independent motor learning laboratory. Her research interests revolve around those factors which affect prediction of moving objects in sport. She is editor of the journal, *Motor Skills: Theory into Practice*, contributing editor in the area of research for the practitioner for the *Journal of Physical Education and Recreation*, and author of many papers and articles relating research to practice in the motor skills area.

Brent S. Rushall, PhD, is a professor in the School of Physical Education and Outdoor Recreation at Lakehead University, Thunder Bay, Ontario, where he is involved primarily in the theory of coaching program. He participated internationally in sports and more recently has served as psychologist for a number of Canadian national teams at Olympic and world competitions. He is the principal consultant for Sport Science Associates and has written ten books and over eighty articles dealing with sport psychology, elite athlete training, and coaching effectiveness and procedures.

John H. Salmela, PhD from University of Alberta, is an associate professor of physical education at the University of Montreal where his research is concentrated in the area of the psychology of sport learning and performance. At present, he is research chairman of the Canadian Gymnastics Federation. He has edited two books in sport psychology and gymnastics and has just written another on competitive behavior of Olympic gymnasts.

N. Norman Shneidman is associate professor of Slavic languages and literatures at the University of Toronto. He graduated from the Belorussian State Institute for Physical Culture, Minsk, in 1954 and did graduate work in Moscow. He also received a MPHE in Warsaw, Poland. In 1971 he received a PhD in Russian literature from the University of Toronto. While in the Soviet Union, Shneidman was a leading athlete in hockey, basketball, and boxing, and he coached boxing at the Olympic level. He also worked in the Soviet sport administration and did extensive research in different aspects of the tactical preparation of superior athletes. He has published a number of articles on problems of physical education, education, and literature in Europe and in North America, which have appeared in the *Canadian Family Physician*, the *CAHPER Journal,* and other journals. He is the author of *Literature and Ideology in Soviet Education* and *The Soviet Road to Olympus: Theory and Practice of Soviet Physical Culture.*

Richard M. Suinn, PhD, is professor and head of the Department of Psychology at Colorado State University. He served as the psychologist for the U.S. Nordic Ski Teams and the U.S. Biathlon Teams at the 1976 Winter Olympics, is a psychology coordinator for U.S. Women's Track and Field, and has consulted with the U.S. Modern Pentathlon Team and the U.S. Marksmanship Unit, as well as individual athletes in swimming, diving, wrestling, football, and tennis. He has edited a book on sport psychology techniques, four other major books, and nearly one hundred papers on behavior modification, stress, and heart disease. He serves on the editorial boards of six professional journals in psychology and behavioral medicine.

Thomas A. Tutko, PhD, is a professor in the Department of Psychology, San Jose State University. As a consultant he has worked with numerous professional, college, high school, and youth organizations in a number of different sports. Tutko has consulted and lectured in seven different countries including China. He has co-authored six books and written numerous chapters and articles for a number of publications, all dealing with sport psychology. He is sport psychology editor for the *Journal of Sport Behavior* published by the United States Sports Academy, University of South Alabama, Mobile.

Lars-Eric V. Unestahl, PhD, is an associate professor in the Department of Psychology at the University of Orebro, Sweden, and is head of research in the Department of Physical Education. The author of two books about clinical and experimental hypnosis and one about mental training in sport, he is responsible for the Swedish courses in clinical hypnosis for psychologists, dentists, and physicians. He took part in the Montreal Olympics as a psychologist for the Swedish team and has since then served as a consultant to various national teams.

Tom Watt, MEd (University of Toronto), is assistant professor of physical education at the University of Toronto and has been its hockey coach since 1965. Since that time his teams have won nine national and eleven provincial intercollegiate championships. He has been appointed to the coaching staff of the next Canadian Olympic hockey team. A television hockey commentator, he is the author of *How to Play Hockey.*

Vietta E. "Sue" Wilson, PhD from the University of Oregon, is associate professor in the Department of Physical Education and Athletics, York University, Toronto. As an athlete she played a number of team sports; she has coached team and individual sports and has acted as a sport psychology consultant since 1972. She has published many articles on a variety of subjects relating to sport psychology and has presented numerous papers at workshops and conferences.

contents

*   *   *

PART ONE
THE NEED FOR SPORT PSYCHOLOGY IN SPORT PRACTICE

PART TWO
COACH, ATHLETE, AND THE SPORT PSYCHOLOGIST

PART THREE
THE PSYCHOLOGY OF PEAK PERFORMANCE

PART FIVE
PSYCHOLOGICAL PROGRAMS FOR
ATHLETES AS PRACTICED IN VARIOUS COUNTRIES

*   *   *

my first encounter with the sport psychologist

Peter Klavora

My first encounter with the sport psychologist was a complete disaster. It happened in 1964 in my native Yugoslavia, a country where after the Second World War sport became a major concern of the society. I was only 25 at the time and the national rowing coach. I had worked with the squad for only a year before it achieved a series of splendid successes in international competition including a bronze medal at the European championships and a fourth place finish at the 1964 Tokyo Olympic Games. Suddenly I was allowed the luxury of inviting a team of scientists from a sport institute to my training camp; their services in various fields were to improve the quality of crew preparation for the upcoming rowing season.

The team of scientists included a medical doctor, an exercise physiologist, a sport psychologist, and a number of their support staff. The team started working enthusiastically immediately upon arrival at the camp—this was their first encounter with a rowing squad. The athletes underwent a number of tests including a paper-and-pencil personality test which took about an hour to complete. After busying themselves with the athletes for a couple of days, the scientists left the camp with the promise to return as soon as the results became known.

They returned three weeks later. I met with each scientist separately and the athletes' profiles were discussed in detail. I held a university degree in economics, but my understanding of the physiological, medical, and physical aspects of training was very good. I had gathered the information at various coaching seminars, by studying on my own, by discussions with other coaches, by trial-and-error, and, notably, by using common sense. It looked like the exercise would be a worthwhile experience—until it was time for the psychologist's interview with me. "This athlete is low on Factor A or sizothymia but high on Factor Q2 which is acceptable for a sculler but perhaps undesirable for a member of an eight- or a four-oared crew," the psychologist started. Then he went on for a couple of hours talking about "oarsmen who were high on Factor B, and others who scored low on threctia and harria, which was acceptable, but were in the normal range as far as alaxia was concerned." I was shocked after the first few minutes—later my feelings changed to humiliation and embarrassment. I felt thwarted by an expert who knew *so much* about human personality. My usual self-confidence was thrown off balance. How was I going to gather the information I considered vitally important in coaching?

The sport psychologist was not invited back to my training camp—we had had our first and last encounter. There was nothing else for me to do but to resort to my "common sense psychology" again. It worked remarkably well throughout the remainder of my tenure as the national coach. However, to this day, I get a strange sensation at the mention of the terms such as harria, praxemia, alaxia . . ..

This first encounter with the sport psychologist turned out to be one of the major reasons for concentrating my studies on sport psychology when I decided (already in Canada, having coached for a while) to return to university for a graduate degree in physical education. My search for the usefulness of psychology in athletic training and competition also began at that time.

It did not take me very long in my studies to come across the Cattell 16 Personality Factors Inventory which was the test applied to my athletes in 1964. The test measures 16 personality traits. Each trait has two names—one set of names uses popular language to be used in speaking to persons not trained in psychology and the other set are the terms used by trained psychologists. Now I was able to ponder my first encounter with the sport psychologist better equipped. However, why he chose the technical language when he spoke to me, as well as some other questions related to the episode, is still unknown to me.

After several years of intensive study I realized that for the pscyhologist, only the technical terms have the power to convey the richness of predictive connotation. However, everyday adjectives are essential for effective communication with the layman and should be used when the personality profiles of athletes are explained.

During my graduate studies I also realized that most of the contents of graduate programs in sport psychology on the North American continent today have a basically theoretical orientation and little or no relevance to sport practice. Having gone through the mill myself, I also realize the immense, as yet untapped, potential psychology harbors for athletics. All that is needed is that the psychologists who have excellent sport background put a conscious effort into using it. Scattered efforts by a handful of psychologists in the western world have demonstrated this and time and again these psychologists have been asked by coaches and athletes to come back and render their valuable services. My own experience tells me they must have offered invaluable knowledge. A further indication of the success of the application of psychology to sport is the work of sport psychologists in eastern European countries. They have successfully assisted athletes and athletic teams in international competition for several decades. My own dual experience as a former international athlete and coach, coupled with an academic background in sport psychology, further strengthened my belief that the assistance of the sport psychologist is absolutely essential for the athlete and the coach.

ABOUT THE BOOK

As the organizer of the tenth Congress of the Canadian Society for Psychomotor Learning and Sport Psychology I had the unique opportunity to assemble the most prominent western and Soviet psychologists who have had extensive experience in assisting Olympic athletes. Without exception, they came to Toronto with great interest to present their work. For two days they generously shared their experiences in formal sessions as well as in several informal dialogues with Canadian national coaches and sport consultants. During a panel discussion they expressed their opinions on the development and several other important aspects of applied sport psychology.

This book summarizes the Applied Sciences Symposium. In addition, several other papers were included which strengthened Parts Three and Five. The book is offered as a timely summary and explication of the best methods of applied psychology for athletic training and competition. The methods are not final and complete but the underlying principles are quite clear and substantiated. The book offers new hope for the application of psychology to sport practice in the western world. It brings together in one volume the present state of the art.

part I

the need
for sport psychology
in sport practice

ZANDER

INTRODUCTION

Part One is about the need for sport psychology in sport practice. The three articles herein focus respectively on bridging the gap between sport science and sport practice, on a coach's subjective views about what he wants from sport psychology, and on the importance, yet difficulty, of applying research findings to sport practice.

In "Bridging the Gap between Sport Science and Sport Practice," the authors remind us of the conceptual biases that exist about the sport scientist on one hand and the coach and sport administrator on the other. They point to the need and the increasing practice of cooperation between the coach and the scientist. They delineate the responsibilities of each and, supported by survey results, suggest ways of increasing better understanding and cooperation with resultant benefits to better performance by the athlete.

In the second article Tom Watt presents his personal views as a coach on what he feels he needs from sport psychologists. He suggests that better dissemination of learning, motivation, modelling (role), and leadership theories, and information on psychological aspects of conditioning would help him to be more effective in the team coaching situation.

John Salmela in the last article, "Psychology and Sport: Fear of Applying," points out that the psychologist and the coach and athlete have long been uneasy partners. Yet, the importance of the notion of a holistic approach to the process of improving performance by giving greater credence and attention to sport psychology in general, and to the sport psychologist in particular, is shown as a much needed development. This movement is not without some major problems, among which the conflict between the sport practitioner's desire to resolve specific, practical problems and the scholar's need to build theories is one to which the author refers. The author gives a comprehensive picture of trends in sport psychology and motor learning research, and the major needs in the field, indicating where the research trends meet the practical needs. His point about individualization of learning, for example, projects the intricacy and complexity of dealing with high level performance. In the light of this generalizations and thus general theories are less likely to be satisfactory. Models which integrate particular information from various disciplines specifically to the individual athlete-coach process are what is most needed.

bridging the gap between sport science and sport practice

Geoff R. Gowan
Cal B. Botterill
Cameron J.R. Blimkie

INTRODUCTION

Attribution is defined as *an ascribed quality, character or right.* The qualities we ascribe to people influence the ways in which we deal with them. Unfortunately, many ascribed qualities are not based upon fact but are the result of hearsay or association. Attribution has undoubtedly played a part in maintaining the present gulf between sport science and sport practice.

In the recent past it seems reasonable to state that when the words *sport scientist* were introduced, the qualities ascribed and the images which sprang to mind may have included:

> Studious, intellectually superior.
> No coaching ability.
> Unaware of sport needs.
> White lab coat and stethoscope.
> Theoretically strong, practically weak.
> Rats and calculators.
> Treadmill and Douglas bags.
> Field work with athletes.

Similarly, introduction of the word *coach* or *technical director* may have resulted in ascribed qualities and images like:

> No research abilities.
> Invalid coaching techniques.
> Stopwatch and sweat.
> Tactical talks.
> Inferior scientific background.
> Olympic Games and world travel.
> Tough talk and TV interviews.
> Insecure, unwilling to learn.
> Track suit and whistle.
> Work with record holders.

Although these qualities and images may represent somewhat

extreme attributions, there can be little doubt that they have all been used at some time. Their existence has not encouraged the formation of a group which should be combining individual skills and talents to assist athletes to perform effectively.

The rationale behind the plea for one unified group assumes the sharing of a major interest which can be stated in two words—*athletic performance.* This performance, at high levels of competition, is very much concerned with winning.

MISSION POSSIBLE: COOPERATION OF COACH AND SCIENTIST

It seems clear that with growing numbers of nations engaged in various forms of sport, for various reasons, more and more effort is required to win events. In an increasing number of sports, the athletes who stand on the podium and who finish in the final eight of the competition represent a larger number of nations than twenty or even ten years ago. The more advanced sporting nations are increasingly utilizing a team approach to prepare athletes. That is to say, the coach is no longer the only individual concerned with the many facets of athlete preparation. It is, however, generally true that the coach is the captain or leader of the support group, which consists of medical doctors, physiotherapists, trainers, psychologists, nutritionists, and sport scientists from several disciplines. That this leadership role of the coach demands increased understanding of and empathy for the major facets of sport science is widely acknowledged. That there are too many coaches working with top level athletes who are insufficiently prepared for this leadership role is also acknowledged. The slowly evolving coaching education programs represent a serious attempt to rectify this weakness. These programs require the cooperation of sport scientists, not primarily to produce practicing coaches who are as expert as they in every discipline related to coaching, but to provide sufficient depth of knowledge to ensure the degree of understanding and insight that results in intelligent communication with the scientists in striving for the enhancement of performance.

Responsibility of the Sport Practitioner

The solution of the problem requires a clear commitment on the part of coaches and sport technical personnel to accept responsibility for increasing their knowledge in the important disciplines associated with the preparation of athletes. Numerous formal and

Coach's ascribed qualities are stopwatch and sweat, lack of security and un-willingness to learn, invalid coaching techniques, and so on.

informal opportunities are available for the acquisition of information. Conferences are one example, and they offer the advantage of allowing personal contact with individuals who can offer much valuable advice on the latest developments in their field. As the sport practitioners increase their knowledge in the sport science area, their confidence will increase and with it their ability to question the sport scientists about applied sports research. This then represents a responsibility which has to be accepted by the sport practitioner if we are to move closer to more effective utilization of the talent and knowledge that is available at present.

Responsibility of the Sport Scientist

The sport scientists must accept the second major responsibility. They must make greater efforts to talk with sport practitioners to discover their major concerns and needs and to attempt to answer their questions on athletic performance. Although there has been a pleasing move in this direction in recent years and by certain individuals from the scientific ranks, it is still true that much room remains for improvement. There are still many research projects that have been initiated by sport scientists in splendid isolation and that do not begin to attend to some of the basic and important questions of sport practitioners. In many areas, sport science findings are still merely confirming the validity of practices that coaches have been using for many years. It is valuable to verify that the coach has been selecting good training activities and utilizing sound techniques, but it hardly suggests that sport science is in the vanguard of the athletic performance procession.

Use of Conferences

Recent conferences have indicated by title and program content that there is an increased desire to bridge the gap between scientist and practitioner. However, title and content alone represent only a small step forward along a lengthy and difficult path. The Post Olympic Games Symposium at Montebello in 1976 brought together a good mix of hand-picked sport scientists, technical directors, and coaches. Much useful information was exchanged, good contacts were made, and the participants came away with ideas for future projects. The weakness of this conference lay in the follow-up or, more precisely, the lack of action thereafter. Many speakers at Montebello stressed the necessity of the team approach and their suggestions met general agreement and much enthusiasm. The logical corollary would have been for Sport Canada to adopt a policy of ensuring that there would be carefully selected support teams for future training camps, international tours, and major games. This did not happen in any systematic manner and the good examples we have seen since 1976 are largely or entirely the result of the initiative demonstrated by sport scientists and personnel from sport governing bodies. The example of the swimming team is one which should be generally encouraged as a development principle. It should be examined critically by other sports.

The International Congress of Sports Sciences, Edmonton, July 1978, had as its title *Bridge the Gap.* This title certainly indicated a positive attitude concerning the importance of closer ties between two groups with a common aim. Some stimulating presentations were made but there were two major weaknesses. One was the large number of people presenting papers who quite clearly had not considered the implications of their work for sport practitioners and athletes. The second was the extremely low percentage of sport practitioners present as delegates. Doubtless, there are many reasons for this low number; however, the fact remains that on this occasion sport scientists were essentially talking to one another and the potential for more valuable dialogue was not fully realized. This poses questions that conference organizers must attempt to answer if there is a concern for good representation from all major groups who have influence on athletic performance. On certain occasions and for certain topics one of these major groupings should be athletes.

Research Possibilities

Few would dispute the advantage to be gained from pursuing sport research using athletes as subjects rather than physical education students or psychology majors. The greater the liaison between sport scientists and sport practitioners, the more opportunities there will be for more meaningful studies using athletes. Certainly our counterparts in many other countries enjoy the advantages of working closely with high-calibre athletes of various ages and both sexes over prolonged periods of time. This situation depends on mutual trust and an understanding of the tasks to be done in the pursuit of a common goal. A start has already been made but there is the potential for much greater progress following the establishment of sound guidelines and appropriate project support.

SURVEY OF SPORT SCIENCE NEEDS

There has been tremendous interest shown in the booklet *Information on Faculty, Facilities and Programmes in Canadian Universities,* a recent publication of the Coaching Association of Canada, and the National Sport Governing Bodies (NSGBs) are becoming increasingly aware of the potential role of the sport scientist. The

Table 1. Current importance of sport science disciplines to NSGBs.

Sport Science Discipline	Ascribed Importance Score*	Rank
Sport Psychology	2.1	1st
Physiology	2.5	2nd
Biomechanics	2.7	3rd
Sports Medicine	3.0	4th
Motor Learning	3.3	5th
Growth and Development	3.9	6th
Sociology of Sport	4.4	7th

* Scores are averaged values and are based on a scale of 1-7, with 1 denoting most importance.

Coaching Association of Canada in cooperation with the Technical Directors' Council conducted a survey of the National Sport Governing Bodies to try to establish their present practices in the sport science area, as well as their future needs. Forty-one replied and the results of the survey are analyzed in Tables 1-3. As shown in Table 1, sport psychology, physiology, and biomechanics were cited as the three most frequently used sport science disciplines, followed by sport medicine. There appears to be limited use at present of sport science expertise and knowledge in the areas of motor learning, sociology of sport, and growth and development.

Table 2. Important ways in which sport science specialists are currently being utilized by NSGBs.

Ways to Utilize Sport Science Specialists	Ascribed Importance Score*	Rank
Education of Coaches	1.9	1st
Preparation of Athletes	2.3	2nd
Talent Identification	2.7	3rd
Interpreting Existing Research	2.9	4th
Carrying Out New Research	3.0	5th

* Scores are averaged values and are based on a scale of 1-7, with 1 denoting most importance.

Table 2 indicates how sport science specialists are currently being used. Approximately half the National Sport Governing Bodies surveyed are using specialists in the education of their coaches. This fact probably reflects to some extent the development of the Coaching Certification Program. With time and further implementation of these programs, it is likely that greater demands will be made of sport science specialists in this area. Preparation of athletes was the second most common area of use. It is evident that the National Sport Governing Bodies would like to make better use of sport scientists in the preparation of their athletes, in the form of short- or long-term support programs, special seminars and clinics, or assistance at training camps and competition.

As indicated in Table 3 the National Sport Governing Bodies feel the need for more applied sport science research, particularly in sport psychology. Motivation, peaking, and anxiety or stress management were the specific areas of concern most frequently mentioned. Interest in sport specific fitness testing and training programs in the general area of exercise physiology were next in importance. Equal numbers of respondents felt that sport scientists should become more actively involved in coaching development and training and in research on equipment design and sport injuries. These results may lend some direction to sport scientists by indicating the specific types of problems the National Sport Governing Bodies would like researched.

Table 3. Key areas of concern requiring sport science assistance.

Areas of Concern General	Rank	Specifics
Sport Psychology	1st	Motivation Peaking Stress management
Exercise Physiology	2nd	Sport specific fitness testing Sport specific training programs
Sports Medicine	3rd	Equipment design Sport specific injuries: prevention and treatmen

CONCLUSION

The results of the survey confirm that the National Sport Governing Bodies are aware of the importance of sport sciences and sport science specialists and it appears that there will be greater need for sport science assistance in future programs. However, fulfilment of this need will depend on the degree of sport administrative and sport scientific commitment to these programs. We hope that this survey will provide some challenges for both scientists and practitioners and help to narrow the gulf between them. We urge that scientists and practitioners alike take the initiative, make contacts with one another, and contribute to making the mission of a coordinated effort in sport a reality.

what I want from sport psychology

Tom Watt

I enjoy everything about sport, and I have worked for over 20 years as a coach, primarily in hockey. I coached gymnastics for six years at the high school level and I have worked a little in track and field. I have some background in individual sport, therefore, but my main interest is in group activity. We have perhaps a million participants in hockey in Canada, but there are only about twenty or twenty-five people involved in coaching it on a full-time basis. In fact coaching hockey is really not accepted here as a legitimate occupation, and perhaps because of that fact coaches do not get the kind of help they might from what is being done in sport psychology. I am going to outline what I as a coach would like to know from sport psychology.

Learning theory and good coaching. There are certain areas I want to learn more about in order to be a more effective coach in group activity. I would like to find out more about learning theory, first of all. We have taught hockey for years in this country by playing more and more games, following the example of the professionals. Instead of concentrating on the skills of the game we teach by a trial and error method: the kids play games and the coach corrects their mistakes as they go along. I would like to know more about reinforcement of learning and about whole and part teaching. I want to know when to teach a child to shoot the puck, for instance, and I want to know whether I should teach the whole or whether I should break it down into parts. I would also like to know what the elements of good coaching are. More articles such as the one on John Wooden (Tharp and Gallimore, 1976) and his learning techniques would be welcome. What do great coaches do? How do they instruct? How do they run practices? These are questions that could be answered.

Social psychology axioms. I would also like to know more about the axioms of social psychology that will help me work with the group I am coaching. For instance, I would welcome information on how individual achievement within groups can hamper the functioning of the group. Does the fact that an athlete may be trying to achieve a personal goal (which could be a certain number

There are certain areas I want to learn more about in order to be a more effective coach in group activity.

of points for the season in hockey) interfere with the team's achievement?

Motivational theory. As a hockey coach faced with a long schedule I need to know more about motivational theory. How can you maintain the players' motivation over a long period of time? It is a problem for us at the university level with a season of 35 or 40 games, but it must be a greater problem in professional sport with 80 or 100 games played in a season.

Team selection and leadership theory. Team selection is another area with which sport psychology could help. One of the toughest jobs that I have to do is to cut someone from the team—to tell them that they are not good enough to make the team. Few people really ever believe that they should be cut, and I would like suggestions from psychologists about how I can do this job more effectively and in a more humane way. Leadership theory is also a subject of interest to me. I know that to have a great hockey club you must have a great captain, but I want to know what makes a great captain and how he should be selected. My method is to be quite autocratic and to choose the captain for various reasons. But I do not know if this is the best way or if a more democratic method might be in order.

Staleness and conditioning. People tell us that staleness in an athlete is psychological and not physiological. I accept that this is generally true but I am not sure that all staleness is psychological; from my experience I think that some is more physiological than one might think. I would like to have more research done on this problem, which is of particular concern to those in hockey because of the length of the season. Another area that I would like to know more of is the psychological advantages of great physical conditioning.

The coach as a model. I would like to know how important the coach is as a model for the members of a team. Certainly based on my own experience I think he is very important, more so than he often realizes. I once coached lacrosse for a season although I really knew nothing about the game. It was a great experience. I had a lot of dead-end kids; I was a social worker really, not a coach. I knew the importance of the coach as model, and all season I kept my cool and acted as an example. Near the end of the season we were in a tough game one night in the play-offs, and things were going badly for us. I got pretty excited with the officials and in the end was thrown out of the game. It was the only time it has ever happened to me, and I was ashamed of myself really. We went on to win the game and afterwards the captain said to me: "It was great that you were thrown out. Now we really know you care." His perception of my actions when I had been trying to be a model was that I really did not care about the outcome of the contest, which could not have been farther from the truth.

There are a couple of other points I would like to make in terms of sport psychology. I do not think that I need extensive psychological testing of my athletes. The athletes resent it. I have always explained that as members of an educational institution we have a responsibility to further learning, but they do not accept this argument. They would not object to psychological testing to help them as hockey players, but they do not wish to be used as subjects for abstract research.

Furthermore, I for one would like to see less criticism of competition. There are positive as well as negative values to competition, and in the sport and in the area that I work, competition is very important.

CONCLUSION

Sport psychologists are but one part of a growing army of specialists, including physiologists, physicians, and so on, who have made a study of sport and developed a body of accurate scientific information. This information takes much of the guess work out of training, skill development, and the creation of competitive attitudes. And this kind of information, if the coach accepts it and makes use of it, can make coaching much easier and far more effective.

psychology and sport: fear of applying

John H. Salmela

The psychologist and the athlete or coach have always been un-easy partners. Neither the psychologist or the athlete/coach has had much understanding of the long-term concerns of the other, and hence they have had little respect for each other. Too often in the past psychological researchers (perhaps concentrating on graduate theses or academic advancement) have borrowed inap-propriate tools from experimental psychology and applied them indiscriminately to problems in sport. The coach and athlete have legitimately complained that psychologists have made use of them with no concern for their long-range needs. But before laying all the blame on the psychological researchers it must be said that until recently a clear statement of the needs of coach and athlete was wanting.

In working with the Canadian Gymnastic Federation I have learned that this sport federation, along with many others, has a genuine desire to know more about the psychological parameters of the problems of human well-being and excellence in perform-ance. As noted in chapter 1, the National Sport Governing Bodies in Ottawa have expressed a strong desire for collaboration in the area of sport psychology. Researchers in the areas of skill acquisi-tion and sport psychology are also, I believe, becoming more con-cerned with the problems of sportspeople.

In this chapter it is my aim to analyze the potential utility of the research that has already been done in the psychology of sport and physical activity by North American scientists, to attempt to evaluate the possibility of a successful partnership between the coach and/or athlete and the researcher, and to propose some ways of bringing the academic disciplines and the field of applica-tion closer together. To do so I have examined the legacy of the research published by the Canadian Society for Psychomotor Learning and Sport Psychology in its proceedings and by its American counterpart, the North American Society for the Psychology of Sport and Physical Activity. Brent Rushall, former president of the Canadian society, did a similar survey of the literature and reported on the sport psychology area at the society's fifth symposium in Montreal in 1973; at that time he indicated that there were only a few sport psychologists working in the applied area in Canada.

I have analyzed the content of the research articles of the Canadian proceedings (Williams and Wankel, 1973; Rushall, 1975; Bard *et al.,* 1975; Kerr, 1977; Landry and Orban, 1978), as well as those of the American society (Wade and Martens, 1974; Landers, 1975, Christina and Landers, 1978; Landers and Christina, 1978; Roberts and Newell, 1979) so that this information can be compared with the projected needs of coaches and athletes. The content of the ten publications within the broad categories of motor learning and motor performance is outlined in Table 1 and within the areas of sport psychology and social psychology of physical activity in Table 2.

Results

Overall, there are 2.8 times as many studies in motor performance as in motor learning. The motor performance research has mainly been in the area of information processing in motor skills in which man's perceptual, decision-making, and response capacities have been evaluated experimentally. For the most part, attention has been on the execution of the response, using short-term motor memory and motor control paradigms. Whiting (1978), in a recent paper, questioned the disproportionate attention directed towards response execution, when in reality a great deal of the variance in motor skill results from perceptual and intellectual processes. In publications surveyed here, 54.5 per cent of the performance research was in either motor memory or control. Only a small number of papers were directly related to the application of skill learning in sport, although it could be said that some of the non-applied papers would contribute to the eventual understanding of the theory underlying these phenomena. Finally, it should be noted that the predominant research vehicle in both the motor learning area (feedback theory and practice of simple tasks) and the research in motor performance (motor short-term memory and motor control) was a simple motor task, often involving a movement of only a few centimeters.

Papers in sport psychology and the social psychology of physical activity are analyzed in Table 2. The total number of papers in these two disciplines (144) is slightly lower than in the motor learning and performance field (188). However, the field of study is related to sport activity to a greater degree, by definition perhaps. The topics of personality of athletes, sport attitudes,

Table 1. Distribution of motor learning and motor performance research papers in recent North American sport psychology proceedings.

Subject Category	Frequency
Motor Learning	
Feedback theory for discrete movements	15
Practice for simple tasks	10
Learning of complex tasks	9
Transfer of training	4
Long-term practice	3
Fatigue effects on learning	2
Movement organization	2
Performance decrements	2
Schema theory of learning	2
Total	50
Motor Performance	
Motor short-term memory	50
Motor control	25
Motor reactivity	12
Long-term memory and motor programs	11
Motor abilities	8
Attention demands of motor tasks	8
Velocity prediction in sport	7
Measurement	6
Decision-making in sport	5
Sport taxonomies	6
Total	138

competitive anxiety, achievement, motivation, and aggression make up 60.4 per cent of the total. The area of personality was studied most frequently, a finding that was also reported by Groves, Heekin, and Banks (1978) for articles published in the *International Journal of Sport Psychology.* The great majority of these articles were experimental in nature and dealt with issues related to human well-being; a smaller number were concerned with the application of research and the pursuit of athletic excellence. Rushall (1973) pointed out a similar finding in his earlier survey of this research in Canada. The research in these areas was predominantly concerned with sport activity, however, an orientation found only in isolated instances in the motor learning and performance research.

Research in the social psychology of physical activity was not as abundant as in sport psychology. The topic of social facilitation was most common, accounting for 39.4 per cent of the total production. Again, sport is the focus of attention of most of these studies.

Table 2. Distribution of sport psychology and social psychology of physical activity research papers in recent North American sport psychology proceedings.

Subject Category	Frequency
Sport Psychology	
Personality of athletes	16
Attitudes toward sport	14
Competitive anxiety	14
Achievement and motivation in sport	10
Aggression in sport	9
Satisfaction in sport	6
Behavioral assessment in sport	6
Coping in sport	6
Intrinsic motivation	4
Roles and attitudes of women in sport	4
Competition	4
Self-control in physical activity	4
Meaning in sport	3
Cooperation in sport	3
Cognitive styles	3
Leadership in sport	2
Preparation for excellence	2
Superstition in sport	1
Total	111
Social Psychology of Physical Activity	
Social facilitation	13
Group structure and performance	6
Attributions for success and failure	5
Stereotypes in sport	4
Socialization in sport	3
Social motives	2
Total	33

Discussion

Most of the research undertaken in the area of motor learning and performance has not used sport as a focal point; the reverse is true for the areas of sport psychology and the social psychology of physical activity. Probably because of the concern of the two latter with sport, athletes and coaches have cooperated in advanced study in this area. Although we have not seen a concerted thrust in terms of athlete preparation and training as occurs in Europe (Groves *et al.,* 1978), researchers in these areas put considerable emphasis on attitudes, feelings, self-control, and other phenomena related to sport performance. It is probably because of this emphasis on what are some of the essential issues in sport that the directors of the different sport governing bodies indicated that sport psychology was the area of greatest importance to their programs.

At the same time the sport governing bodies ranked motor learning fifth in importance to their programs, behind sport psychology, physiology, biomechanics, and sports medicine. This low ranking of motor learning may be due in part to the fact that little of the published research can be remotely related to sport or learning but is concerned with the testing of performance models of a theoretical nature. Defending this approach, Jack Adams (1971, p. 112) justified the search for broad general principles of skill acquisition when he said: "The villain that has robbed skills of its precision is applied research that investigates an activity to solve a particular problem, like kicking a football, flying an airplane or operating a lathe. . . . " Such a viewpoint has helped to keep motor skill researchers in their comfortable labs studying their subjects pushing buttons, moving levers, and pursuing rotors. Adams does, however, continue to say that "the task centered approach is justified when practical reasons require us to know about tasks and efficiency in them, but it is a limited way of achieving the larger scientific goals of law and theory." The question now becomes, whether it is more important at this moment in time to pursue applied solutions to specific sport problems, or continue the search for theory until all variables are understood?

Certain indications in Canada suggest that energies should be applied to the resolution of specific sport problems. The first is the strong leadership role that the Coaching Association of Canada has taken towards "bridging the gap" between theory and practice by its recent hiring of an individual to try to do just that. Another indication is the ambitious research program initiated by the federal government in conjunction with the sport governing bodies and directed towards the search for performance excellence. It seems that the moment may now be ripe for applied research in order to understand better "tasks and efficiency in them," as Adams suggested.

A recent analysis of motor skill practices in mainland China demonstrated that much of the gymnastic skill that the Chinese have recently developed was not due to secret procedures or innovative theoretical development but to the application of principles that we have known for years, such as specificity of practice, matching task demands to performer ability, and the overlearning of motor skills.

It is my personal opinion that there already exists an abundance of usable information on motor learning that can be applied to specific sport problems. A recent analysis of motor skill practices in mainland China (Salmela, 1979) demonstrated that much of the gymnastic skill that the Chinese have recently developed was not due to secret procedures or innovative theoretical development but to the application of principles that we have known for years, such as the specificity of practice, matching task demands to performer ability, and the overlearning of motor skills.

It seems that there is but Crossman's classic study (1959) on cigar rolling that can be referred to when performance is considered across years of practice. Are the apparently constant increments of learning of cigar rolling across a ten-year period similar to those found in sport? Can the voluminous quantity of literature on performance decrements based on Hullian theory remain buried forever, or can parts of it be resurrected for application in practical situations?

CONCLUSION

Although I am by no means attempting to be exhaustive in outlining the projected needs of Canadian coaches and athletes, it seems apparent that research endeavors being undertaken at present may not be related even to their major preoccupations. Yet, there seems to be an abundance of areas to which sport scientists could turn their attention. The needs of the specific sport federations should provide the direction, if researchers decide to commit themselves to sport.

In summary, it seems that sport researchers, especially in the area of motor learning and performance, must change their attitudes if an attempt to bridge the gap between theory and practice is to succeed. The sports bodies also must actively search out the information they need to improve their programs, and when such information is unavailable they must be ready to identify their most urgent needs and to secure research funding. The sport psychology researcher, whether in the psycho-social or motor skill area, must also be willing to shift his priorities and look at research areas that may not be in fashion in the higher circles of the American Psychological Association, but may be of utmost importance to the athlete or coach. It goes without saying that the active support of government in funding applied research would help many scientists overcome the stigma attached to these endeavors. Only through this type of collaboration of athlete, coach, and researcher can we be confident of the development of performance excellence and personal development based upon sound psychological principles.

Research in sport psychology seems to be serving the needs of sport technicians in Canada to a certain extent. However, if a projection of the needs of the majority of Canada's coaches in the motor skill area was made at this moment, I do not think it would resemble the profile of published research that I have presented in Table 1. It is my belief that many of the old "chestnut" topics that were studied in the past regarding learning would surface and might read like the following.

Practice schedules. The research on massed versus distributed practice was beaten to death in the 1950s and 1960s in psycho-motor learning research. Nevertheless, it is still an essential question for coaches and athletes in relation to the efficient distribution of their time. What can now be added to the age-old findings is how to dissect a motor task in terms of its information processing demands, so that more appropriate means of skill acquisition can be used. Given that high level performances are attained only after long periods of time, it would appear that more research on the learning of skills over extended practice periods is essential. Of course, such projects are not favored by graduate students who are looking for studies that are "fast and dirty."

Most of the research undertaken in the area of motor learning and performance has not used sport as a focal point.

Modes of learning. The incredible complexity of the motor skills that occur in sport has for the most part been ignored as a focus of interest in research, possibly because of the lack of conceptual models to deal with this variability (Salmela, 1976). Only recently has the work of such individuals as Nideffer in *The Inner Athlete* suggested that there may be different attention styles and, therefore, various means of learning tasks. This individualization of learning can be related back to whether the athlete conceptualizes the skill in whole or parts, and then related to the manner in which he attempts to acquire the skill. The information processing demands of the specific tasks could then be matched with the preferred mode of learning of the individual, whether it be visual, auditive, or kinesthetic.

Amount of learning. Like practice schedules, the issue of amount of learning is an area believed to be important to athletes and coaches but no longer to researchers. The studies that are at present being done on the attention demands of motor tasks could well be directed towards the question of overlearning and the automation of task components. When can attention be directed to new dimensions and when should efforts be sustained on previously, partially acquired ones?

coach, athlete,
& the sport
psychologist

INTRODUCTION

Part Two deals with various views on the interrelationships and responsibilities in the theme "Coach, Athlete, and the Sport Psychologist." In the first chapter Bruce Kidd treats the rights of the athlete vis-a-vis the coach, the sports governing processes and structures, and the sport psychologist. He argues that the sport psychologist's responsibility is primarily to the athlete, not to the coach or the team. Another important aspect of Kidd's paper is his attention to the question of deviant behavior not only by athletes but also by coaches on national teams.

Thomas Tutko discusses the persistent lack of clear definition of the field of sport psychology and those who practice in it. He defines sport psychology as the study of behavior as it relates to sport and athletics, and the sport psychologist should not favor any single group but should be committed to assist the individual and the team reach their maximum potential.

Bruce Ogilvie draws attention to the problems of credibility of sport psychologists in professional sport. He bases his comments on extensive experience as a clinical psychologist with various professional teams in crisis situations at management, coaching, and player levels. He presents some of the major problems of credibility encountered by sport psychologists in professional sport and offers guidelines for increasing the effectiveness of the sport psychologist in this setting.

Rainer Martens makes a strong case for sport psychology to move from what has essentially been laboratory research to applied and field research in the sport setting. He proposes that rather than testing general psychological theories what is needed is the empirical observation of sport behavior in order to build and test theories peculiar to sport.

Brent Rushall and Dorcas Butt present their experiences about working in sport practice on two levels of participation. Rushall on one hand demonstrates that psychological support services can most effectively assist elite sport teams by providing information on coaching through sporting scales and interviews, by measuring effects, by constructing programs, and by performing counseling and clinical functions. Butt, on the other hand, argues that if human growth is the primary goal in sport, then motivational categories such as aggression, conflict, and competition should be discouraged in favor of those of competence and cooperation.

The last chapter of this section presents the viewpoints of several prominent sport psychologists on what are the best ways to solve psychological problems contracted by a a team or an athlete.

athlete's rights, the coach, and the sport psychologist

Bruce Kidd

There has been much comment in recent years about the need to humanize children's sport. Parents, teachers, sport psychologists, government inquiries, and sports governing bodies have all emphasized the importance of creating a supportive, pleasurable environment for the young athlete. The new emphasis is upon the right of every boy or girl to participate at whatever level of ability or ambition he or she chooses. In the words of the National Coaching Development Program (1976), "sport is for happiness," "the coach's main job is to help his athletes define and achieve their goals," and "losing can be triumph when you've given your best."

Many school and community programs have been changed as a result. In hockey leagues in Edmonton, Windsor, and Quebec, for example, game scores are not kept in an effort to emphasize skill development, enjoyment, and sportsmanship. These attempts to minimize the trauma of children's sport have grown out of earlier, more broadly defined efforts to humanize the institution of schooling, of which the Hall-Dennis Report is the best known example in Ontario. These efforts have not been completely successful, for violence and "cutting" are still widespread in youngster's sport, but the battle to humanize it has been squarely joined.

Yet when it comes to high performance sport, whether the athletes be teenagers or adults with children of their own, the humanistic approach is almost always discarded in the interests of "producing winners." Winning gold medals was the only definition of excellence put forward by the federal sports minister in her Green Paper on Sport (Campagnolo, 1977) and most sports reflect this singlemindedness. As a result, training has become more work than play, characterized by long hours and endlessly repetitive movements. Janet Morrissey, the 1979 Canadian figure skating champion, reports she trains 56 hours a week in summer, 35 in winter. National television advertisements by Loto Canada tell us sport has to be that way. In efforts to psych up athletes to better performances, nationally acclaimed coaches resort to public humiliation and sexual repression. Compulsory physical tests and "training" by such mechanical means as Faradic (electro-muscle) stimulation have almost become commonplace. The result is that the champion athlete loses control over what sport means. He ceases to be a self-directing "subject" of the activity, but is gradually transformed into the "object" of an increasingly rationalized national system, the raw material of coaches, scientists, bureaucrats, and politicians. In the winner's spotlight, he may smile and jump for joy, but what has happened to the quality of day-to-day experience? And what about the "losers?"

In this chapter, I will argue that the humanist approach encouraged for children's sport is just as essential for adult athletes in national and international competitions and that sport psychologists and coaches must be mindful of it in their practice. This approach is hardly new—it was first articulated in the gymnasium of ancient Greece and in our own century it has been the subject of novels, plays and films, as well as statements by athletes and physical educators. Few coaches and sport scientists may actually disagree with it in *principle*, but the growing rationalization of Canadian sport makes it urgent that its message be reflected in *practice*.

THE ATHLETE AS HUMAN BEING

My starting point is the belief that the proper objective for any high performance sports program should be the provision of opportunity for athletes to develop their human powers to the full, with a minimum of economic, physical, or psychological hardship. The goal should be to provide as many of these opportunities as possible. Although it may be reflected in championships and "winning" performances opportunity should not be dependent upon them, nor upon attendance at university, the provision of construction jobs, or the sale of sugared water or beer. A jumper who may rank "only" 100th in the world can experience extraordinary possibilities for self-expression and growth through sport. At the same time, he can delight and inspire those who have the opportunity to watch him. There are thousands of Canadians who have been moved by the performances of the 100th best hockey player in the world, but we rarely question his worth because his status is legitimated by our society.

Implicit in this approach is the right of athletes, individually and collectively, to participate in the formulation of what we mean by "excellence." In modern industrial societies where the belief in scientific progress borders on the superstitious, "excellence" in sport has increasingly been defined in terms of victories and records. As a result, most athletes tend to measure what they do in quantitative terms—personal best performances and world rankings. But not every society has valued sport in these terms. In the caneball games of Burma, for instance, the grace. with which the players hit the ball is just as important in the final outcome as the number of goals scored. Even in our own sporting tradition, we have stressed non-quantifiable measures of excellence. The preservation of sportsmanship used to be one such norm, the integration of one's athletic career with other social responsibilities another. The point is that if an athlete is to develop his talent to the full, he must be able to contribute to—and contest, if necessary—the *meaning* of sport, even in *qualitative* ways. The case of Toller Cranston, who concentrated on the articulation of dramatic new forms of skating to the neglect of his compulsory program, provides an example that is easy to understand and accept. But it is necessary for every athlete in every sport.

This humanist perspective can be traced to the 18th-century Enlightenment and 19th-century liberalism. "The end of man," John Stuart Mill wrote in his famous essay, *On Liberty,* "is the highest and most harmonious development of his powers to a complete and consistent whole." (1952, p. 295) These ideas were taken up by Pierre de Coubertin and other leaders of the Olympic movement and international sport. "The most important thing in the Olympic Games," Coubertin said at the opening of the 1908 Games in London, "is not to win but to take part, just as the most important thing in life is not the triumph but the struggle." These words are now heard by the entire world every four years during the opening ceremonies of the Games and most of us can recite them by heart.

The emphasis of the humanist tradition in sport is on the possibility it affords for human development and pleasure. "Sport is education," Rene Maheu, UNESCO's director-general, once wrote.

> [It is] the most concrete and the truest kind of education—that of character. Sport is knowledge because it is only by patient study and self-revelation that a sportsman can go from strength to strength.
>
> Sport is also a truce. In our technological way of life, ruled by an inexorable law of toil, in which we are only what we have, and have only what we earn, sport is the hallowed pastime, a princely gift to enrich our hours of leisure. In an era of antagonisms and conflicts, dominated by the drive for power and by pride, it is the respite of the gods in which fair play competition ends in respect and friendship.

> Sport is culture because the transient movements it traces in time and space—for nothing but the sheer pleasure of doing so, as Plato has it—illuminate with dramatic meaning the essential and therefore the deepest and widest values of different peoples and of the human race itself; it is culture, too, because it creates beauty, and above all for those who usually have the least opportunity to feast upon it.

In recent years, the developmental approach has been reaffirmed by sport psychologists who have investigated the harmful effects of the solely instrumental approach to sport. The clinical work of Dorcas Susan Butt, for example, suggests that those athletes who are motivated by the need to overcome others or to gain external rewards, that is, to win for winning's sake, often end up with deep psychological problems.

> The athlete whose sport is an expression of external support, such as winning, money, or gaining status, will show signs of disintegration upon losing that are manifested in anger, weeping, sulking, and self-imposed isolation. Other defenses are rationalization (attributing the loss to external factors such as injury), projection (blaming someone else such as an umpire or an opponent), denial (pretending one didn't really want to win), and compensation (escaping from feelings of failure by excesses such as drinking or sexual exploits). . . . Immature behavior, whether it is an expression of negative feeling (fighting, spitting, swearing, crying, screaming, vomiting) or positive feeling (hugging, kissing, holding of hands, pouring champagne over heads) is tolerated in sports far more than elsewhere. The social behavior expected of an athlete resembles in many ways that expected of a young, ill, or irresponsible person. Athletes are rewarded to an extreme for good behavior (winning) and punished (often inconsistently) for misbehavior. The athlete is not expected to appreciate and internalize the rules and regulations; he functions under a system of fines and penalties levied against him, that force him like a child, to behave. This is not a sound way to develop children and it is an even poorer way to develop athletes. (1976, p. 54.)

Butt also argues that the social structures which encourage the definition of "excellence" in terms of winning are largely to blame for the neuroses of individual athletes. She says that the only healthy approach to sport is to view it in intrinsic terms such as skill mastery or physical satisfaction.

In concrete terms, the humanist perspective means that athletes and programs should not be evaluated solely by the medal count at one or two major championships every four years. We should develop more qualitative measures of the success of our programs. One yardstick could be the number of athletes who can pursue their goals without financial hardship, injury, or neurosis. Another could be the number of Canadian communities who can be excited by their performances and exhibitions. (Sport Canada could have a touring office like that of the Canada Council to show off our best performers in exhibitions and clinics across the country.) Since far too many Canadian athletes retire prematurely, an immediate goal (and measure) could be the number who are helped to train and compete until they reach their prime. In individual cases, athletes should be judged by their performances and commitment over a long period of time, and relative to their own previous perform-ances and the best previous performances by Canadians, as well as those of the rest of the world. Athletes and their representatives should enjoy parity on all selection bodies, as in the case of the Canada Council. When an Abby Hoffman breaks the Olympic record and her own national record placing eighth in the Olympic final, there should be widespread rejoicing about a superb race by all participants, not accusations of failure. When a Debbie Brill is only beaten by a new Commonwealth record, we should send her flowers, not grumble about "letting us down." (I do not believe for an instant that Canadian athletes will become less ambitious if we adopt this approach.)

A jumper who may rank "only" 100th in the world can experience extra-ordinary possibilities for self-expression and growth through sport.

THE CANADIAN CONTEXT

As I have already noted, athletes are losing what little control they once enjoyed over their sporting lives and "excellence" is increasingly defined for them in quantifiable terms: medals, world rankings, and along the way, training mileage, maximal VO_2s, and percentage fast-twitch fibres. A recent example is the decision by Sport Canada and the Canadian Olympic Association to send only those athletes who rank 16th or higher in the world to the 1980 Olympics. An athlete may be a popular and inspirational national champion, but if he ranks less than 16th, he will have to watch the Games on television.

The disappearance of the humanist approach to high performance sport has been accelerated in Canada by four circumstances which I will describe below.

1. The monopolies enjoyed by the sports governing bodies.

In virtually every internationally organized sport, an athlete must join and obey the rules and regulations of the appropriate federation. Such registration and regulation provide a necessary order to competitions, but they also leave the athlete vulnerable to exploitation. If he wants a federal or provincial training grant, he must be recommended by his federation. These bodies also have the power to discipline and suspend. Although other "natural" monopolies which wield tremendous power over people's lives, like the telephone and gas companies, have been brought under public regulation, the power of the sports governing body remains largely unchecked. In 1973, an Albertan inquiry found with respect to the Canadian Amateur Hockey Association and its Alberta affiliates as follows:

> i   that in declaring itself the final and absolute authority in the establishment of hockey policy and in the control of hockey players, the Association has attempted to remove itself from public accountability and to deny the possibility of external arbitration and review mechanisms;
>
> ii   that in many of its by-laws and regulations, the Association does, in fact, impose invalid restraints upon the rights and freedoms of individuals;
>
> iii that in its assignment of powers and duties, the Association vests in individuals and committees far more discretionary power over other individuals than any free society should tolerate; and

iv   that by its prohibitions against appeals to the courts and its specifications of the sanctions to be applied if and when individuals do appeal to the courts, the Association, in fact, denies hockey players their rights to natural justice. (Downey, 1973, p. 4.)

The report recommended that the Alberta government enact legislation to correct these abuses. I feel that other sports governing bodies are not significantly different. Although some now allow a modicum of athletes' rights, the balance of power is largely unchanged.

2. The rationalization of Canadian sport.
The athlete is no longer guided or assisted by a single coach, but by a team of specialists, and a hierarchy of bureaucrats, all of whom have access to information about the athlete's activity by means of standardized training diaries, copiers, and perhaps a computer. All competitors in the 1979 Canadian Winter Games, for example, were required to provide their Social Insurance Numbers (see *Hansard,* 31 Jan. 1979). For the athlete, the consequences of these developments are ambiguous: on the one hand the new sport professionals may be able to offer some helpful advice, on the other they represent as a team a formidable means of control. They are generally older, more experienced and they work at it full time. If they define excellence strictly in terms of winning medals, the athlete has little choice but to go along or quit.

3. The oversimplified positivism which has accompanied this rationalization and the popularization of sport science.
The dominant approach to sport sociology and sport psychology in Canada operates on the false assumption that human beings act according to natural laws as predictable and verifiable as the laws established in the physical sciences and that these laws are independent of any human apprehension. The psychological inventories published by Thomas Tutko (1975) and Brent Rushall (1975) provide examples of this approach: despite their brief disclaimers, their publications suggest there is a definite personality type in each sport which leads to successful performance and to which coaches should try to mold their athletes. They ignore as phenomena for analysis the *ever-changing* social circumstances and definitions of "excellence" which shape attitudes, and they wrongly assume that the attitudes they have studied have always existed. One unfortunate consequence is that they encourage coaches to impose an abstracted average on the diverse range of people who

want to play any sport.

There are too many problems inherent in this approach for full discussion here. The reader is invited to read articles by Scott (1970), Gruneau (1978), and Whitson (1978) if he wishes to pursue the question further. But two points should be made. If the national sport system is considered to be "scientifically objective," then the only thing open to debate is the best strategy for rationalizing the activity—the feelings of athletes have little place. Secondly, the appearance of "rationality" serves to legitimate the stamp of inferiority given to those who fail to measure up according to quantitative standards.

4. The growing use of sport as a means of ideological control.

Sport is particularly suited to express and reinforce the ideas of the dominant social class. According to the British sociologist John Hargreaves (1975, p. 60),

> there is an inherent limitation in the potentiality of sport to act as a focus of opposition to power. The point can be made concretely by a comparison of sport as a dramatic form with "purer" forms, like the cinema and theatre. The latter have always functioned in some ways as powerful media of social criticism, for they are inherently capable of being used to express and communicate . . . critical ideas about the society. . . . Sport lacks this potential to express and convey a wide range of ideas and feelings. In being more narrowly limited, sport is far more amenable to domination by the powerful, and therefore is much more likely to mystify its adherents than to function as a means of mastering one's fate.

As Canada's sense of "national purpose" is eroded by Quebec's aspirations for independence, by regional disparities, continuing unemployment and inflation, and the Americanization of Canadian cultural institutions, it seems we are increasingly turning to sport "for the image we have of ourselves and for our national spirit" (Campagnolo, 1977). To ensure that this image is a good one, Sport Canada is more and more tying its grants and programs to winning medals, and there seems to be little room for another definition of "excellence," nor for a more developmental measure of the success of the program.

There are some who would argue that the humanist approach is no longer realistic in high performance sport. Canadian Olympic Association president Richard Pound recently told a panel at Queen's University that today's athlete should accept sport for what it is and try to do his best. Another to argue this position is William J. L'Heureux, a former chairman of the National

I have a highly developed sense of competitiveness. On the one hand it helped me enormously as an athlete, but until I learned—painfully and still incompletely—to keep it under control in other situations, it made it difficult, if not impossible, to function cooperatively or to provide emotional support for friends and loved ones. I have now come to realize that athletes do not have to have the "killer instinct" to be successful. Psychologists could help us become more civilized human beings.

Advisory Council for Fitness and Amateur Sport and a prominent university physical educator. L'Heureux (1973) makes the distinction between Sport as Play (SAP) and Sport as Work (SAW), and includes Olympic competition in the latter: ". . . enjoyment is seen to be a necessary condition of SAP. But it cannot be so in SAW, any more than it can be a necessary condition in the work of a postman, accountant, housewife or teacher. No doubt some athletes like other workers find pleasure in their work; it may even seem desirable to find it so, but it is not essential. So there can be no natural right nor any appeal to equity as a moral rule preserving the joy of playing in SAW." Such arguments encourage athletes to resign themselves to the alienation that necessarily occurs if they abdicate control over their energy and creativity when they are forced to sell their labour to compete, or to eat. Professionals, such as doctors, lawyers, and university professors do not relinquish control over what they do or the ethics within which they practice—nor should workers or athletes.

As long as these attitudes and the practices they condone persist, the athlete's ability to realize his full human potential is reduced. Many of us have completely forgotten how much modern sport compromises its possibilities. One coach who has not is Howard Slusher (1967, p. 175).

> I need to stress, in the sport situation all is potentialized. The "molding" needs to be accomplished by the participant. At the heart of the process of actualization is the necessity of "freedom of choice." When this freedom is reduced, so is the potentiality for fulfillment. Thus, one has to question the place of sport, within this process, if this freedom is negated. The calling of plays by the football coach, instead of the quarterback, is an example of limiting the potential of each man. . . .
>   Perhaps the height of prostitution of humanity is symbolized in the rather strange phenomenon of track's "human rabbit." . . . a "rabbit" in track, is a *man* placed into a race for the sole purpose of setting a fast pace so that other more talented performers will be able to run a fast race. Not only does man no longer run with man, now he runs against an artificial standard *using* man to assist his efforts. Is this not the height of human decay? Man *uses* another. And perhaps what is worse, man allows and offers himself to be used. Perhaps one might argue that man is not being used. But rather the "rabbit" is cooperating with his fellow man. To argue this way is to admit human sacrifice as a form of desired human action; and to deny the basic motivation for the race. It is not enough for man to run for the sake of running or even for victory. Man now becomes the tool and even the slave instrument of measurement. Man is not important. Records are important.

THE SPORT PSYCHOLOGIST

The sport psychologist can contribute enormously to the creation of conditions where the athlete can develop his energies and find his own meaning in sport. The psychologist can become an invaluable confidant and ally. He can help the athlete in the following areas:

1. To prepare for particularly stressful competitive situations, like a first race before a large home-town crowd, or a meet in another country.

2. To deal with a highly publicized and media-defin⎯
The psychologist could also help the athlete understand⎯
not unquestioningly accept—other external pressures which
he must face, such as the requirement in many sports that
athletes pay most of their training expenses and living costs
themselves.

3. To communicate more openly and honestly with his coach
and teammates.

4. To understand his motivations in sport, particularly if they
spring from circumstances or relationships external to the
sport environment, such as parental pressure. In some circumstances, a psychologist could actually help an athlete end a
sports career without guilt or self-doubt, in situations where
intrinsic motivation is no longer present.

5. To understand the destructiveness of certain character traits
that are encouraged by the sport system. Thomas Tutko has
said that an athlete who scores highly on his Athletic Motivation Inventory may be successful in sport, but he is often
"the meanest son-of-a-bitch in the valley." I know this in myself. I have a highly developed sense of competitiveness. On
the one hand it helped me enormously as an athlete, but until
I learned—painfully and still incompletely—to keep it under
control in other situations, it made it difficult, if not impossible, to function cooperatively or to provide emotional
support for friends and loved ones. I have now come to
realize that athletes do not have to have the "killer instinct"
to be successful. Psychologists could help us become more
civilized human beings.

6. Finally, if so many of the problems of contemporary sport
are caused by the *structure* of sport programs, psychologists,
both individually and collectively, must organize to change
some of these conditions.

In each of these cases, the psychologist's primary responsibility
is to the athlete, his general health and well-being and *his* goal
definition. At all times, he must be committed to the belief that
the athlete's human worth cannot be judged by whether he wins
or loses. If the psychologist is willing to help the athlete in this
way, the athlete will be happier, healthier, and in most cases will
perform better. But the psychologist must be prepared to perform
this role *regardless of the consequences for athletic performance.*

If he ties his responsibility to performance, the psychologist
may do great harm.

1. He may reinforce attitudes and habits that could inhibit full
and humane maturation. If the emphasis upon external

motivation or interpersonal aggression can lead to serious psychological problems, he should help coaches, athletes, and officials learn to define what they do in more intrinsic terms. Yet when the psychologist hires himself out to improve performance, he may be led to exploit and exaggerate many of these harmful attitudes. The manipulation of nationalism at the Commonwealth Games pool in Edmonton provides a recent example (Rushall, 1978). As much as we can admire and encourage a community's independence, flag-waving nationalism is not a substitute for motivating an athlete in terms of his own competence and power.

2. The psychologist might recommend that athletes who do not measure up on psychological tests be cut from the team. I have no incontrovertible evidence that this has occurred, but I know several athletes who believe it happened to them. In one case, a swimmer was ordered to take and pay for regular counseling from the psychologist. When she refused, she was dropped from the team.

3. The psychologist might provide coaches with a new basis of power over athletes that could be used unfairly. Some coaches use public humiliation as a means of "psyching up" athletes. The psychologist who sees his role as aiding overall performance might give the coach confidential information for this purpose. Such practice completely perverts the purpose of sport.

If the psychologist is to contribute to the developmental goals of sport, his commitment must be to the athlete alone—not the coach or the team. I am uncompromising about this. The psychologist who believes he can serve both "will be tightrope-walking on a laser beam" (Ogilvie, 1977). That is simply impossible.

Thomas Tutko, in his book *Winning is Everything and Other American Myths* (1976), has proposed a bill of rights for young athletes. Many of his suggestions should be adopted by Canadian sports governing bodies. The following should be added.

All athletes should enjoy:

1. The right to refuse any psychological test or counseling proposed by a coach or sports governing body. Parental permission must be obtained in the case of athletes under the age of 18.

2. The right to a full report of the results.

3. The right to confidentiality. No information obtained from psychological testing or counseling should be shared with anyone else without the written permission of the athlete.

4. The right to seek psychological guidance of his own choosing.

Some psychologists have told me that these rights are already implicit in the ethical codes of all certified professionals. If such is the case, then they will not mind repeating and emphasizing them. These safeguards are similar to those established for psychological testing in schools by the Ontario Ministry of Education and enacted in regulation 191 of the Ontario Education Act of 1974.

THE COACH AND DISCIPLINE

In recent years, there has been a growing number of cases where athletes have lost training, competitive opportunities, and sometimes economic benefits as a result of arbitrary disciplinary suspensions by a coach or sports governing body. In 1975, three speedskaters were sent home from Europe immediately prior to the World Championships. In 1976, two skijumpers lost their opportunity to compete in the Olympics in similar circumstances. In 1978, a wrestler was dropped from the national team to the World Championships and two swimmers were sent home from their World Championships. In the wrestler's case, his only offense seems to have been that the coach didn't like him. In the other cases, the "crime" involved the consumption of alcohol. In all cases, athletes were disciplined without due process—without a fair hearing. Although the wrestling association has established an appeal procedure for suspensions, the athlete in question was not informed of it at the time.

There are some who believe that the coach must have the discretion to select and cut athletes at will. The Canadian Amateur Wrestling Association recently wrote: "Any coach must have the right to select the best team available for any given competition based upon the athlete's performance, physical condition, and attitude. If we were to take this right away, then there would be no need for a coach" (*Canadian Wrestler*, January 1979). But such absolute discretion is incompatible with the developmental approach to athletics argued here, and it leaves the athlete vulnerable to the sport governing body's monopoly power. Nor is there any evidence that authoritarian coaching is the only road to success, as those experiments with collective team decision-making have clearly shown (Kidd, 1971).

The whole question of "delinquent" or "deviant" behavior on national teams is extremely complex. In my view it involves the following questions.

1. What constitutes delinquent or unethical behavior? Should it be equated with the moral standard of the coach or the

parents and businessmen who sit on national executives? Should it be limited to behavior that harms others, including unfair or unsportsmanlike competitive practices, and property damage? Should there be different definitions for age-class and adult athletes?

2. Who should define delinquent behavior and what procedures should be established for defining it?
3. Once it has been defined, how should it be identified and what procedures should be established for "trying" an accused person?
4. Who should define punishment and what procedures should be established for meting it out?

I have always felt that most of the problems that fall under the category of team discipline can be handled by open and frank discussion among the persons involved. If a member of a team does something out of character on a national team, an effort should be made to understand the full circumstances, including the tremendous pressures under which team members must operate. A psychologist operating in the way I have suggested could greatly facilitate this process.

But if formal procedures are necessary, they should:

1. Be decided on democratically by all participating athletes, coaches, and officials. This is easier for teams that are together for longer periods of time, but it could be done quickly at the beginning of a training camp. Just as in any college residence where the rules of acceptable behavior vary widely from floor to floor, house to house, I would expect that athletic codes of behavior would vary with the composition of teams. Democratic rule-making assumes, of course, that athletes are self-directing adults who care more passionately than anyone else about their own performance. It is an assumption that too few coaches and officials in Canada are prepared to make.
2. Include full due process, such as
   a. the right to a hearing;
   b. the right to hear one's accusers;
   c. the right to cross-examination;
   d. the right to representation;
   e. the right to appeal.

There are some who argue that such procedures are too cumbersome for the hurly-burly of a major competition. Not so. In other areas of public policy, such as pollution and epidemic control, procedures exist for quick but fair decisions. The same should be developed for sport. The overriding concern should be the career of the *athletes* involved.

3. Include rules (and where applicable, penalties) for coaches and officials. If drunken coaches and officials were suspended as often as imbibing athletes, the turnover on some of our national teams would be high indeed. These rules, too, should be democratically determined. If I were still on a national team, I would insist that coaches who publicly degrade athletes be sent home immediately. Other athletes have their own list.

These recommendations could be translated into practice in one of two ways. The sports governing bodies can do us all a service and implement them from the top, or athletes can band together—perhaps even forming an Olympic athletes' union—and fight for them from below. The professional athletes' unions have led the way. In 1977, for example, the National Football League Players' Association won a clause in its collective agreement which states: "No psychological or personality tests will be given to any player after he signs his first contract with an NFL club. A player is entitled to review the results of his (previously taken) psychological or personality tests upon request." There is also precedent among Canadian amateur athletes. The Canadian Olympic Association likes to take full credit for the Athletes' Assistance Program which in 1975-76 chanelled 1.5 million dollars in additional living grants to athletes. But if a number of us had not threatened political action, up to and including a strike of the Montreal Games, if more funds were not made available, that money would never have been granted. I am not altogether happy about the development of an adversary system in sport, but for the athlete it may be necessary. It all springs from the belief that opportunity for self-development in high performance sport is a basic human right.

the identity of the sport psychologist

Thomas A. Tutko

WHAT IS SPORT PSYCHOLOGY?

Over the last two decades interest in sport psychology has mushroomed and many people seem to be trying to get into a field that has not been clearly defined. Colleges and universities in the United States and Canada have developed courses in the field, and in some instances offer advanced degrees, and yet what constitutes the field is not clear. It is one of the growing pains a new profession must face.

Several examples reflecting the lack of a clear definition of the field come to mind. At many of the meetings (conventions, symposia, clinics) papers cover a wide spectrum not only in topics but in basic orientation. There are position papers, theoretical papers, pure research, practical research, academic treatises, practical papers, and how-to-do-it, sock 'em in the jock papers. Moreover, they may express only ideas, show valid data, manipulate pure statistics, work with animals, work with athletes, work with amateur or professional athletes, and so on.

To add to the confusion these papers are being given by physical educators, educators, sociologists, recreation specialists, psychologists, psychiatrists, coaches, athletic officials, administrative officials from athletic teams, athletes, and in some instances people from fields totally unrelated to sport (for example, politicians). It is no wonder that when someone in the field is asked what a sport psychologist is, the answer is frequently a long one.

The major growing pain of sport psychology, as I see it, is trying to organize and clarify the field. The wide diversity of papers as well as people presenting them is not a disadvantage but a marked advantage. It only attests to the need for organization. It is a testimony that the field of sport psychology is needed.

/ As a basic definition I would suggest that sport psychology is a study of behavior as it relates to sports and athletics./ It does not even have to be human behavior; intensive studies on such areas as horse racing are fascinating. From this definition one can see why the field is so broad.

When Dr Ogilvie and I first started in this profession we were continually seen as "shrinks," people who worked with the "crazies." In fact in one instance we were advised to change our titles from psychologists to behavioral scientists to become more acceptable to athletes and coaches.

We are in fact talking about three fields—physical education, athletics, and psychology—each of which is vast. It is because of this wide range that any course taught or degree offered becomes an idiosyncratic one often dependent upon the developer's background.

One final point needs to be clarified, and it has to do with other related areas of study. Sport psychology should not be confused with two other fields: sport sociology and sport psychiatry. Whereas sport psychology deals with the individual's behavior in sport and athletics, sport sociology is more interested in the behavior of the group as related to sport and athletics, and sport psychiatry is concerned with mental health or the psychopathological aspects of sport and athletics. Too often these three fields are not understood to be entirely separate domains, especially by the lay person.

A SPORT PSYCHOLOGIST'S WORK

Now that we have defined the field, we might as well describe what a sport psychologist does. This provides our greatest dilemma because the work is not narrowly circumscribed. As I see it, there are actually five different fields under the umbrella called sport psychology. At the risk of being presumptious I would like to outline a potential working format organizing these various fields.

Experimental sport psychology. The work in this area involves both theoretical testing as well as pure research as it relates to sport and athletics. As examples we may think of mathematical models or physiological research and how each is related to sport behavior, directly or indirectly.

Measurement in sport psychology. The assessment methods as well as psychometric measures used would fall within this category. Various methods from traditional instruments to test development to behavioral modification approaches would be included here.

Social sport psychology. The influence of the individual on the group and the group's influence on the individual fall in this area. Prejudice, team cohesion, and group comparison could be included. Communication poses as one of the major concerns here.

Personality and sport psychology. Various personality theories as well as personality characteristics and how they influence performance are what is explored in this sub-field. Motivation would fall in this area but its assessment would be under measurement.

Clinical sport psychology. The work done in this area involves working with athletes and coaches on an individual basis. It involves a knowledge of counseling as well as therapeutic techniques. This would be the only area requiring further training and an internship, after graduation from a program.

The organization set forth here is not original. Others have suggested a similar breakdown, including Dr Robert Singer of Florida State University.

RESPONSIBILITY OF THE SPORT PSYCHOLOGIST

Several comments need to be made about the identity of the sport psychologist. The first of these is a question raised by Dr Jack Scott in his book *The Athletic Revolution* (1970) and that is the question: "Who is the sport psychologist an agent of?" Is he an agent of the owner, coach, school administration, athlete, or parent? This is a tough question to answer since we are often agents of those who hire us. Perhaps the best way to answer the question is to put it on a professional basis and compare our work to that of the physician. The physician is not in a position to favor any single group. His job is to see that the individual is in good physical condition so that he might reach his maximum potential.

The same holds true for the sport psychologist. It is to help each individual and the team reach its maximum potential. It is easy for us to slip into a role other than that. If we see ourselves as only producing winners, or as agents of owners or coaches, the profession is short-lived. That is why it is important in the work we do to make it clear that we have certain training and our area of expertise has a certain range. To go beyond that can only damage not only the people we are working with but the profession as well. Bruce Kidd and Bruce Ogilvie have also discussed this point in chapters 4 and 6.

As an example of what I am saying, I recently talked to an individual who is to set up a sport psychology program. The program involves his working with individual athletes, teams, and coaches, setting up research programs, and teaching sport psychology.

We cannot assume that because someone has training in sport psychology or takes a few courses in psychology and gives himself the title of sport psychologist that he is capable of dealing with equal ability in every area. I consider it unethical for anyone to work on an individual basis when any form of personal counseling is necessary, if he is not a clinical psychologist and thus not trained in counseling procedures. Without specialized training he can do harm that goes beyond the sports area. All sport psychologists should know their specialty, and any problem they are not trained to handle should be referred to the appropriate professional.

CONCLUSION

Finally, a word of concern and caution. I regularly receive mail and telephone calls asking how to become a sport psychologist. When I inquire about the interests of the student, the reply is usually the same. They are in the field of physical education or athletics and want to help a coach or an athlete on a team win.

We must be careful not to use the profession to work out our own desires for success. If we have feelings of frustration because we do not feel like winners, or if we see our job as producing winners, we will be trapped by a professional model that can only serve to undermine the true meaning of the work in sport psychology, which is to gain knowledge and to act as a helping agent. The aim is not to produce super bowl winners. This aim can only lead to frustration.

It is natural that most people wanting to get into the field are from physical education. They are nearer the problems and can see the need for help. But anyone developing a course or a program should try to get across the critical point of the meaning of the work. Otherwise we will be like alchemists trying to turn everything into gold (or, in our case, winning).

I see a bright future for this infant field. It can be a science and it can be of great help. It is heart-warming to see it finally reach acceptance.

the sport psychologist and his professional credibility

Bruce C. Ogilvie

INTRODUCTION

In this chapter I will present the background and some of the significant experiences that I have had in the world of professional sports. It is my hope that by sharing some of the problems I have faced as well as some of the experimental approaches I have tried I may give direction to the training necessary for the sport psychologist. I have chosen to outline the most predictable problems faced in professional sport, based on those with which I was confronted during my more than 20 years as a consultant. The fact that those of us who have sought to work in this capacity are essentially "self taught" has both positive and negative aspects. On the one hand we have known the excitement and joy of being a pioneer. On the other we are continually struggling to be effective in a world that is alien, that is highly conservative, and that often mistrusts the behavioral scientist.

MY TRAINING EXPERIENCES

My training is that of a psychotherapist, and a significant portion of my professional energy has been invested in law enforcement personnel selection and executive stress factors, as well as in the sport setting. My research interest centres on the problems of human stress and methods of managing stress. Based upon my analysis of the research findings from these areas of investigation as well as considerable consultation experience I believe that there is a striking overlap in terms of environmental, social, psychological, and physical stress within these career areas.

The psychologist also faces the same kinds of challenges when he seeks to be of service in these areas. As with the professional athlete law enforcement personnel are individuals who choose to live on the fine edge of existence, and are not likely to welcome the offerings of any "head shrinker." Men like these want to judge your credibility and trustworthiness for themselves.

In the field of sport my primary identification is that of a clinical psychologist applying my training as a psychotherapist. Specifically I have tried to apply mental hygiene techniques where indicated in sports situations. Whether conflicts were at the management, coaching, or player level the goal was always increased emotional freedom and enhanced performance.

My training in psychodiagnostics and individual and group therapy has been of inestimable value. The learning and insight I gained from police and management research have been essential. Subjecting thousands of athletes to psychological study has also made an important contribution to my knowledge, but more important than the psychological findings has been what I have learned in private meetings with great numbers of competitors. This review of the psychological data provided for more open, trusting communication.

As a consultant to a number of police departments, I was able to gain increased insight as to the defensiveness that exists towards psychologists. This training has had unusual transfer value in terms of consultation in professional sport. In both situations one is confronted with a rigid command structure populated by highly competitive people with little respect for psychology. Those in charge in the two areas show similar personality traits. Their survival in highly stressed occupations has depended to an extent upon their capacity to confront harsh reality, for instance. They are authoritarian, and as a group they measure quite low in those personality variables that would incline them to want to take care of other people. They set the same high goals for others as for themselves.

MAJOR PROBLEMS ENCOUNTERED
IN PROFESSIONAL ATHLETICS

As a sport psychologist in professional sport, your first and foremost problem will be to establish your credibility and the credibility of the behavioral sciences. The young consultant's first responsibility is that of an educator; he must dispel misperceptions, ignorance, and prejudice. The neophyte consultant is obliged to become a salesman for his discipline. In no particular order here are some of the most prevalent problems that generate resistance to the discipline.

1. Many in the sports world see the psychologist as a mystical and even mysterious kind of professional and feel threatened.
2. A significant number of individuals within every organization

will have feelings bordering on paranoia when they are forced to interact with psychologists.

3. Credibility is rarely established in terms of total acceptance of the profession; therefore, the consultant must always be aware that he can never assume he has been accepted.

4. The consultant must learn to be aware that acceptance of him as a professional is offered tentatively and may be withdrawn without warning.

5. Because of the nature of the stress within the professional sports environment you may be expected to wear too many "professional hats." Unreasonable expectations can produce insurmountable problems.

6. Because the sport psychologist must practice in a similar role to that of the community worker or crisis interventionist he may be expected to be available to anyone in the organization.

7. A most challenging problem that occurred relatively frequently was being placed in a position of competing loyalties. It is imperative that the young professional be trained to anticipate when and where this situation may arise.

8. Problems are created by the consultant's conscious or unconscious need to identify with the conflicts presented by certain individuals within the organization.

9. A problem area fraught with complexities and conflicts is that of working in an environment where there is a rigidly hierarchical power structure. The challenge for the consultant is to function effectively without threatening the status of any member of the chain of command. Between team president, general manager, and head coach there resides a middle-management hierarchy that expects a degree of deference.

10. There will be the problems of establishing a good working relationship with other professionals who are providing overlapping services such as the team trainer, team physician, or the exercise physiologist.

11. The problem of continuing to be effective in an environment that is continually changing personnel is a severe one. This can involve new management, publicity director, coach, or general manager.

12. A problem area which has enormous significance for me is establishing credibility with minority group team members. One of the great challenges is to earn a high enough level of trust that these athletes will seek to use your services.

From this extremely limited sample of special concerns it would be possible to structure a specific number of training experiences.

The professional coaches are highly ambitious, achievement-oriented men who see themselves as leaders. They are highly organized, assertive, dominant, and aggressive. They take a hard-nosed view of life and express great self-confidence. They measure slightly above average in emotional maturity and super-ego formation. They enjoy above average physical health and love to take risks. This is not the type of personality that would be inclined to defer to anyone. Titles, status, roles will have little impact upon such men. What does have impact is the evidence you can present to substantiate that you can contribute to their success.

PROFESSIONAL SPORT AS AN ENTERTAINMENT BUSINESS: CONSEQUENCES AND CHALLENGES

Survival in this world is totally dependent upon economic factors. The ebb and flow of the fans will dictate much about the stability of the world the consultant is seeking to serve. It is not possible to describe the levels of tension and anxiety that are the consequences of a losing season. It will be during these periods of unbearable stress that the tendency to find answers by projecting blame or using scapegoats will begin to arise. This world is comprised of men of great pride and large egos whose lives have been blessed with more success than most. When they find themselves trapped in a no-win situation they are prone to make quick judgements to try to find solutions.

High turnover of personnel is endemic to professional sports, not just of players but of managers and coaches as well. It becomes extremely important that the young consultant anticipate this probability to maintain his credibility. He must face the reality that he may have to begin again the process that has gained him the respect and trust of the personnel who have been released. It will be extremely rare for the consultant to be able to rest on previously established credibility; more typically the quest is end-less.

You may wish some documentation to justify my selecting this problem as such a high priority concern. In the years in which we provided consultation services to four National Football League teams, the San Francisco 49ers, Los Angeles Rams, New Orleans Saints, and Dallas Cowboys there were the following changes in staffs: the 49ers had four changes in head coach, Rams three, Saints four, with only the Cowboys in a stable situation under Tom Landry. In addition, I have been a consultant for the Portland Trail Blazers of the National Basketball Association since their inception seven years ago. In that period I have had to establish a professional relationship with four head coaches and three assistant coaches.

Opening Communication

In order to reinforce an important recommendation with respect to training, I have gone back to my files and reviewed a portion of my services in the world of professional sport for the year 1974. During that year I had personal interviews with over 60 coaches each of whom I had subjected to psychological study. Between February and July, I subjected 280 professional athletes to study and met two thirds of them personally. The opportunity to review the psychological findings with each coach proved to be one of the most positive contributions to open communication. When the coach is able to compare the psychological findings with coaching norms and see the potential for generating useful insights which can further his career, his trust and acceptance of the psychologist are generally enhanced.

This meeting with the coach will also provide an opportunity for the psychologist to define his role and explain his limitations. Primary emphasis must be placed upon responsibility to the coach. He must be assured that your services will not impinge in any way upon his role as coach but will only be employed at his request as a complement to his role as teacher. When it seems appropriate, inform him that you will be available should any of his athletes present problems he cannot fully understand. Should the opportunity present itself explore with him the meaning of privileged communication and define the boundaries within which you must operate. Reassure him that the same privilege will be extended to him should he so desire.

Continuity of Relationship
Upon Hiring a New Coach

Whether or not you will be able to function with a new coach will depend almost entirely upon how you are seen by that coach. From my experience, if you are imposed upon the new coach simply because the general manager wishes the service to continue, your career with that team will generally be at an end. Should you as a professional be unknown to the new head man, or if he is totally unaware of the application of behavioral sciences in sport you suffer great risk. Ideally you should be introduced to the new coach privately with the general manager outlining what you have contributed to the organization. He should let the new coach decide whether he finds your services of value. After you offer evidence of what you have done, based upon positive or constructive intervention during the past season, he can make his own evaluation. I have always taken this initial meeting as the right time to admit my limitations. I have found it of particular value to admit openly that I know nothing about coaching and less about motor skills acquisition.

The new commander generally prefers to clean house. Each new leader seems to be obsessed with the need to erase any reminders of past failure, and in some cases this attitude has extended to the boy in the towel room as well as to the team physician. Such was the case when George Allen replaced Harlon Savare as head coach of the Los Angeles Rams, and inherited me as a professional staff member in an organization that was failing.

Based upon psychological study of the personality structure of men who are coaches, this obsessive need to start afresh might be anticipated. The traits of personality that seem to support their aptitude in the coaching field may produce such behavior. They measure as highly ambitious, achievement-oriented men who see themselves as leaders. They are highly organized, assertive, dominant, and aggressive. They take a hard-nosed view of life and express great self-confidence. They measure slightly above average in emotional maturity and super-ego formation. They enjoy above average physical health and love to take risks. This is not the type of personality that would be inclined to defer to anyone. Titles, status, roles will have little impact upon such men. What does have impact is the evidence you can present to substantiate that you can contribute to their success.

Crisis of the New Identity of the Leader

The consultant must be prepared to appreciate and relate effectively to the important survival need "the transfer of loyalty." It is a basic requirement of such significance that the consultant should contribute in every way to its occurrence. The coach will have only days or weeks to establish his identity with his players and convince them that he is the type of leader in which they can place their faith. The veterans will present the greatest challenge depending on their emotional attachment to the former coach. If they are relieved to see him go, the problem of transferring loyalty is lessened. If he has been an inspirational leader, the problem is magnified.

The consultant can make an important contribution in this area if given the opportunity. Having experimented with a number of approaches to the problem, I will use only one example to reinforce this point. In one situation the coaching change was not made until three weeks before the team was to report to training camp. This was psychologically unsound judgment on the part of the administration because of the timing and because they had literally dumped a much loved coach. In spite of a disastrous season, no player had expressed a loss of faith in him as a leader. The veterans voiced angry hurt feelings, and many felt that they had been deceived. It was evident from the previous season that the leadership of the team resided in three veterans; two had been with the team five years or more, one only a year. We arranged to meet for an entire weekend in a private resort-like setting to discuss what had occurred and to see if we could find the most effective way of reducing its impact. Space does not permit me to give all the alternatives and approaches that were forthcoming from these veterans, but three basic strategies were developed, each of which would be employed to find the one with the most positive effect.

One of the most fortunate spinoffs of the veterans' actions was the effect on the new leader; he saw their commitment as an initial sign of loyalty that provided support for him while he worked to earn the respect of the rest of the team. With the irrational threats reduced, everyone had more of an opportunity to form a working relationship.

ETHICS AND RELIABILITY IN
THE PROFESSIONAL SPORT SETTING

Your ability to function effectively in the highly stressed environment of professional sport depends on your capacity to establish and maintain trust. Your ethical standards will be subjected to an unusual number of tests. Because tenure and retention of team and staff members is so dependent upon producing a winning unit, there is always an undercurrent of fear. This fear leads to almost paranoid feelings on the part of an athlete who is referred to you by the coach. The reference to you as the "head doctor" early in your relationship with the club is not one of endearment. Each consultant must find through his own experience, based upon his own personality, the means of breaking through such stereotyping, but these will be the areas in which both your ethics and professional reliability will be tested by the professional athlete.

1. Are you acting as a consultant specific to his needs or are you an agent of management?
2. Will the psychological information you derive by subjecting him to study or interview be used to determine his worth as an athlete?
3. Will you share your clinical insights or information in a form that could cause him to be devalued as a human being?
4. Will information be shared with members of the organization that could be used to manipulate him?
5. Will he be able to trust you to live up to your stated obligation to him: "I will use every aspect of my training and experience to enhance the possibility of your continuing your career as an athlete?"

I have found that I can be most effective by keeping a low profile and being available on planes, buses, or in my hotel room. An open-door policy based upon a genuine interest in each player has proven to be the most productive approach for me.

The following selection of negative player reactions arose from the threats to their survival that occurred in training camp.

1. Number one draft choice suffers classic anxiety panic reaction after an exceedingly traumatic experience.
2. High draft choice develops phobia reaction and finds he is unable to throw the ball back to the pitchers mound.
3. Important infielder wants to discuss his fear that his specialty coach is racist and that he will not be given a fair chance.
4. Three pitchers want to explore ways of increasing their pain tolerance.
5. A number of athletes wish to explore their confusion about

marital conflicts.
6. Starting pitcher wants to uncover the reasons for his total loss of control.

Based upon this selection from a single team it becomes most apparent that the counselor will require training as a crisis interventionist. Most important will be his skill in making appropriate referrals.

Management and the Sport Psychologist

Many of the same problems of ethics and professional reliability arise when dealing with management. To help improve the effectiveness of the sport psychologist I will list some of the priority concerns of management.

1. If you gain privileged information about his club, will it be used to undermine his decision-making capacity? This knowledge may be about a contract dispute with a superstar, a possible coaching change, medical care, knowledge of drug use, and so on.
2. Will research or what you learn from interviews of subordinates in the organization diminish your respect for him?
3. Will your opportunity to study his administrative style result in your judging him as a person?
4. In your role as a behavioral scientist will you have a tendency to identify more with the problems of his subordinates than with his own?
5. Should he choose to share personal conflicts with you will you honor this privileged communication?
6. Will you ever violate your relationship by publishing or relating to the press sensitive information?

As the organization begins to open up to you as a reliable professional, you may be called upon by any of its members who are experiencing unfulfilled needs. It may be the general manager who feels ignored by the team owner. It may be the team trainer who has been demoralized by the players' decision as to his share of the championship money. It may be the team physician who wishes to consult about emotional factors that seem to have limited the physical recovery of the team superstar. Because the demands in this world of entertainment are so often out of touch with reality, problems are frequently stress related.

The men who have reached the top of this profession have large egos nourished by great drives for success. Dominant, aggressive, tough-minded, and assertive like their coaches, they are not inclined to defer to others. By their own admission, they do not like to depend on others and are most impatient with those who seek to form dependency relationships with them. They feel they have gotten through life by being self-sufficient and independent. The approach of our profession, therefore, often seems unnatural or strange to them. As we examine the causal chain seeking alternative explanations before selecting the most rational choice they lose interest. They would prefer that we define the problem and recommend action that leads to problem resolution. The fact that our training forces us to be cautious and tentative in defining problems or stipulating actions can be a source of irritation to them. It becomes important therefore that the consultant think through and spell out as precisely as possible the modification program he has evolved. I have found a written plan of action, no matter what the problem, has the best effect upon the executive and increases its chances for success.

The men (managers of professional teams) who have reached the top of professional athletics have large egos nourished by great drives for success. Dominant, aggressive, tough-minded, and assertive like their coaches, they are not inclined to defer to others. By their own admission, they do not like to depend on others and are most impatient with those who seek to form dependency relationships with them. They feel they have gotten through life by being self-sufficient and independent. The approach of our profession, therefore, often seems unnatural or strange to them.

GUIDELINES FOR
INCREASED EFFECTIVENESS

To be most effective in the professional sports setting it is essential that you set firm lines of demarcation in terms of accepted areas of responsibility. You will be wise to define your role as precisely as possible. Based on my personal experience I would recommend the following as essential boundary statements.

1. Define your area(s) of responsibility precisely in your contract.

2. Admit openly and directly the limitations that are imposed upon the behavioral scientist when he seeks to help an individual change his behavior.

3. At no time allow your service to be equated with winning. Your role is that of freeing the individaul to utilize his potential.

4. Try to resist the tendency to form loyalties that will limit your effectiveness with others within the organization. The problems that follow such a commitment are many, for example, when the team president, general manager, coach, or superstar become a villain in your mind, communication can be impaired.

5. Spell out to media people, public relations men, and others why your communication about the organization or players is privileged. Any statement, no matter how innocuous, can be distorted by a media person and destroy your credibility.

6. If you are called upon to do crisis intervention work, have the procedure for referral spelled out. The other professionals should be made known to the appropriate management person.

7. Whenever the opportunity presents itself teach staff members that it is not your role to judge. This will help you to avoid contributing to negative stereotypes. Take care that your use of jargon does not lead to labeling. "Paranoid feelings," "tender-minded," "depression-prone," are all excellent clinical shorthand but they can be misrepresented by those not trained in their use.

8. There will be times when you must appeal to someone in the organization because an important decision is necessary. Be absolutely certain that when this moment arrives this person will have the authority to take the desired action. If possible get that assurance in writing. For example, should you on the basis of your clinical judgement be convinced that medical intervention or hospitalization is imperative, you

must be assured of the support of someone in authority. No matter how good your intentions you will be helpless without someone in power to take responsibility.

FINAL REMARKS

As I drift into the sunset I have but one word of wisdom. Steel yourself against the time when you will be sacrificed to the god called "winning." When the fans thin out in the stands and the board of directors begins to become uneasy while reviewing the bottom line of the financial statement, you will face a harsh truth. As panic sets in, you will find you are valued somewhere between the janitor and the towel boy. The sign that you should take your Rorschach cards and run will be when you go to the box office for your free tickets to the game and find that the attendant has forgotten your name.

from /mock/ to jock/: a new adventure for /port p/ychologi/t/

Rainer Martens

A LOSS OF FAITH

I would like to begin by sharing with you what I find wanting about my own past research and much of sport psychology research in general. For me, there have been gaps greater than tolerable between my aspirations and realizations, both with respect to theoretical synthesis and applicability to important problems in sport. I am concerned about the failures in replication abilities of sport psychology research. I have doubts about the snapshot model of linear causation so fundamental to laboratory experimentation; doubts indeed that the categories of ANOVA with its neatly isolated independent and dependent variables can provide a useful model of what goes on in the personal and social world of sport. I have misgivings about the use and deception, and more generally with the manipulations used in laboratory studies. In fact, I have grave doubts about the utility of laboratory research for most of sport psychology. And I am disturbed about the gulf between those who do sport psychology research and those who interpret sport psychology research to practitioners.

Just when I was convinced something was seriously wrong with me for having such doubts and concerns, I began to learn about the "great crisis" in social psychology. Social psychologists for the past five or six years have been engaging in intensive soul searching, discussing such issues as: (a) whether social psychological research is merely a recording of history, (b) the need for a new research paradigm, (c) the direction in which the field is and should be moving, and (d) the relevance of the research to the social problems of the day. These fundamental questions about the science of psychology have paralleled my own concerns within the field of sport psychology.

Arising first from an analysis of my personal research, and then from my reading on the crisis in social psychology, my faith has been seriously shaken in logical positivism,* operationalism as specified by behaviorism, and laboratory experimentation. These principles of research learned in graduate school, the very canons of science, are being doubted by an increasing number of behavioral scientists, including me. I know it is sacrilegious to think that principles so hallowed in the "hard" sciences cannot be used satisfactorily to explain human behavior and that such heresy surely deserves excommunication from the scientific community.

I have been reticent in discussing these concerns with others in sport psychology. When making reference to some of these issues with colleagues, I have sensed an uneasiness to discuss it, an almost I-don't-want-to-think-about-it attitude. You see, these concerns are the very pillars of the faith upon which the practice of our science is built. If we were to find these canons of science wanting, what would we do?

Yet somehow I doubt that I am alone in my concern about these issues. I suspect more than a few sport psychologists have dared to risk some introspective analysis, flirting dangerously with such thoughts as: Am I participating in a big intellectual and academic game in which, in the "name of the game," problems are being manufactured rather than formulated, methodological tools are being used because they have the "good scientific stamp of approval" rather than because they have been logically and theoretically derived from a problem, and quantification is to be achieved at any cost, even at the understanding of a problem?

Have you not wondered why sport psychology, as we know it, has had little or no influence on the world of sport? It is not because the coaches and athletes are unreceptive to information from our field. Indeed, they are eager for such information. But unfortunately our insights have not been challenging, the issues studied have not been critical, and our data are not convincing to the vital issues in sport. Thus, experiential knowledge and common sense, though certainly sometimes erroneous, have been more appealing, and usually more beneficial than knowledge from sport psychology research.

---

* Logical positivism asserts the primacy of observation in assessing the truth of statements of fact and holding that metaphysical and subjective arguments not based on observable data are meaningless.

I believe that if we continue to follow the traditional path so deeply cut by our graduate programs, the major journals of our related fields, and our borrowed research paradigm, it will result in a sport psychology of predictive impotence and theoretical irrelevance.

CHANGING PARADIGMS

Space does not permit me to elaborate on all my concerns about the way we practice science in sport psychology, but if you would like to consider these issues further, you should read about the crisis in social psychology (e.g., Gergen, 1973, 1976; Helmreich, 1975; McGuire, 1973; Schlenkar, 1974), and think about the metapsychology of sport. Personally, I believe that the existing paradigm of social psychology, which many of us in sport psychology have borrowed, is inadequate for understanding human behavior. This paradigm directs us to select our hypotheses for their relevance to broad theoretical formulations and then to test them by *laboratory* manipulational experiments. I believe that a radically new paradigm is needed—in Kuhn's terms, a scientific revolution.

But here is where I begin to have difficulty. While it is clear that a new paradigm is needed, I do not know, nor it seems, does anyone else know fully how to create this new paradigm. It seems unlikely that this new paradigm is suddenly going to be created. Instead it will evolve gradually, emerging from continued modifications of the existing paradigm.

Compared to my earlier research, I have incorporated what I

think are some of these modifications into my own recent research. I would like to describe some of these changes, suggesting that they are characteristic of an emerging paradigm which has special significance to sport psychology.

The most significant change in my research is the switch from laboratory to field settings. Rather than testing my notions on college sophomores recruited at random and corralled into laboratories, I am observing and describing behavior, and probing for cognitions of people who are actually participating in sport. In fact, I no longer have a laboratory at the University of Illinois; it has been replaced by playing fields, gymnasia, and natatoriums everywhere. I have exchanged my smock for a jock when necessary, to observe and understand the real world of sport.

I would judge my recent research to have more relevance to sport. Much of it is more applied, but even some of what I consider to be basic research is more pertinent than my previous research. The hypotheses I now investigate are formulated for their relevance to sport, but at the same time are formulated with a consideration of existing theory and a view to constructing theory specific to sport. I do not believe that socially relevant, applied, field-based research need be divorced from theory.

I now use a wider array of methods in my research. My loss of faith in the canons of positivism and operationalism, which restrict inquiry into only those areas capable of technical manipulation, has freed me to investigate phenomena that I felt in the past were impossible to study. Part of this new freedom emanates from my rediscovery that much of what man does is determined by his thoughts. And thus, I am enthusiastic about the reception being given to cognitive orientation in psychology. I applaud the radical proposal of dialectical social psychology which states that we should treat people, for scientific purposes, as if they were human beings, capable not only of reacting to, but also interacting with and at times even changing their environment.

Such a view of people as active agents produces a greater acceptance of self-report information. Such a view places greater significance on the observation of behavior as it occurs naturally within the social context of sport. Sport psychology will surely be a healthier field when we recognize that the internal psychological processes that occur when people engage in sport must be understood within the social context of sport. Thus, rather than making war with sport sociologists, we must make love.

I believe that if we continue to follow the traditional path so deeply cut by our graduate programs, the major journals of our related fields, and our borrowed research paradigm, it will result

The most significant change in my research is the switch from laboratory to field settings.

in a sport psychology of predictive impotence and theoretical irrelevance. Certainly today sport psychology trades more on promise than on performance, but I think that promise is great, if we undertake some change. I would like to elaborate briefly on how I think sport psychology can become a more relevant science. In this regard, I will reinforce several suggestions made by Professor Alderman (1979) in his keynote address at the 1978 Congress of the Canadian Society for Psychomotor Learning and Sport Psychology.

Should we pay more attention to theory building?

We have been so eager to test theories of the larger field of psychology in order to confirm our scientific respectability that we have not adequately observed, described, and theorized about our own thing—*sport!* We have been so enamored with our operational definitions, clever manipulations, and high-powered statistics that we are in danger of losing sight of the phenomenon these instruments were designed to illuminate. We clearly need to spend more time observing behavior in sport and building our own theories unique to sport. Then we can test them!

Should we pay less attention to laboratory research?

Somehow I suspect you have sensed my disenchantment with the laboratory. I am not opposed to laboratory research; there is a place and time for it. I just think it has occupied too big a place and been used before we have adequately identified the important variables of sport psychology. Consequently, we have often taken less relevant variables into the laboratory. It has produced a tremendous amount of chaff and few golden kernels; it threatens to suffocate us under a paper avalanche of little worth.

I am sure we all recognize the weaknesses of descriptive, observational methods—the weaknesses of self-report data. But I am not sure we all know the inadequacies of the laboratory study. Fear not if you do not, I shall tick off a few.

1. I have grave doubts that isolated psychological studies which manipulate a few variables, attempting to uncover the effects of X on Y, can accumulate to form a coherent picture of human behavior. I sense that the elegant control achieved in laboratory research is such that all meaning is drained from the experimental situation. The validity of laboratory studies is at best limited to predicting behavior in other laboratories.

2. The population sampled in laboratory research most often continue to be unrepresentative of those to whom we wish to make application. We all acknowledge this failing, but for pragmatic reasons continue its practice.

3. Somehow there continues to be an implicit assumed equivalence between laboratory and life situations, even though we know better. We, of course, never create the richness of social situations in the laboratory; in fact we strive not to, because we want to gain control over the situation. Thus, laboratory research almost always forces a kind of reductionism, reducing a multivariate universe to a bivariate or trivariate model usually factorial in design. Such models may frequently isolate significant effects, but account for negligible amounts of variance.

4. Laboratory studies also frequently lead to an erroneous specification of causality. We assume if we manipulate X and it significantly affects Y, then X caused Y to change. Laboratory studies, however, usually impose a directional model of causality. In unconstrained natural settings Y may also cause X or X and Y may cause changes in each other. An excellent example of this occurring in sport is the relationship between group cohesion and performance.

THE WHY OF IT ALL

After only six weeks of studying sport psychology, one of my students asked me the question: Why do sport psychologists spend so little time studying *sport?* Can you answer that question? And if you can, can you answer these? Why have we done so little *applied* research? And so little *field* research?

One reason, I believe, is that there is an attitude that applied research conducted in the field is nonscientific. Others consider this type of research to be unresponsive to theory, assuming that theory development and testing can proceed only through research that is conducted in artificial and contrived settings. But it seems to me to be the contrary. I think there is a greater probability that the best theories of sport psychology will grow from field research on applied problems. Involvement with practical problems in sport should be a never-failing source of theoretical ideas and knowledge of fundamental psychological relationships in sport. Indeed, applied field research in sport psychology need not be restricted to a methodology made uniform by theoretical concerns.

To be sure, I am not saying that sport relevant field research is the complete and final solution to the serious problems facing behavioral scientists in constructing new or modified paradigms for the study of human behavior. But I do believe it is an important step in the right direction, especially for the field of sport psychology as it currently functions.

CONCLUSION

To get at the complexities of human behavior in sport, much of our field research will need to be large-scale, long-term, and multivariate. Our new paradigm will consist of theoretical models of cognitive and social systems of sport in their true multivariate complexity, involving a great deal of parallel processing, bidirectional relationships, and feedback circuits. Such theoretical models will emerge from and be tested through field methods, and will thus merge practical and theoretical relevance. Yet I am well aware of the problems inhibiting the undertaking of such research—lack of money, existing university reward systems, and the mobility of the population, to name a few. But the outcome of such research will be a healthy diversity in the subject matter of our field. While research will likely be more difficult to do, more problematical, and occasionally a pain in the ass, I also feel it will be more valid, much more useful, and surely more fun to do. For me, the asking of more sport relevant questions and attempting to answer them through field research has aborted much of my disenchantment with the sport psychology of the past.

ob/ervation/ of
p/ychological /upport /ervice/
for elite /port team/

Brent S. Rushall

This chapter is based on the experience of my association with the Canadian National Swimming Teams since the 1976 Olympic Games, and my observations of the Canadian National Wrestling Team before and during those Games. The interactions and responsibilities enjoyed during these past few years have proved to be enlightening, while at the same time both rewarding and frustrating. It is hoped that these observations on my experience and their possible implications for the future will be of value, especially in view of the recent increase in associations between psychological support personnel and national teams (swimming, gymnastics, and wrestling).

The supply of psychological support services for elite sport teams is especially challenging, because each team and occasion is unique. The coaches and staff, team personnel, duration of association, and the nature of the competition and its environment all differ with each international competition. Thus, the opportunities for learning and adaptation for everybody concerned are difficult and full of stress. A further complicating factor, one which determines the scope of a psychologists' potential influence, is the length of time that the team is intact. This time period can range from a few days, as at the Canada-USSR dual swimming meet, to as much as a year, as when the national wrestling team had its training headquarters at Lakehead University from 1975 to 1976. This produces difficulties. It stands to reason that the shorter the duration of interaction the more limited the possible influence of the psychologist will be. However, the effectiveness of support personnel is usually gauged without this time factor being taken into consideration.

The varying circumstances which surround national elite teams require an adaptability and degree of preparation by support personnel that extends beyond normal expectations. It is this requirement that sets apart the attendant sport psychologist who demonstrates effects from traditional and self-professed sport psychologists.

PERSONAL INTERACTIONS WITHIN THE TEAM

The roles that a team psychologist can perform effectively are directly influenced by the constituency of the team coaches, staff, and athletes. The scope of activities is limited by the coaching staff in structures where the supporting psychologist is subordinate to at least the head coach. This means that the potential for effect is limited by personal biases towards support personnel, organizational inertia, or the degree of unawareness of a psychologist's function. To further complicate the matter the singular coaching model (Rushall, 1977) produces behavioral delusions of omniscience in many head coaches and coaching staffs when they are subject to measurement and criteria for accountability. This reaction is understandable when the stresses of international competitions are also encountered. It appears to me that it will only be avoided when the educational influences and programs for coaching development exceed the traditional powerful modelling influences for learning the coaching "trade." It is rarely the case that teams function without ego-dependent restrictions and deficiencies generated by one or more members of a coaching staff. In this context, the primary concerns of sport psychologists who are capable of performing technical and medical support functions should be (1) to make the elite coaching fraternity aware of the valuable and measurable contributions that can be made, (2) to gain credibility through demonstrated effectiveness, and (3) to perform supporting roles rather than competing with coaching activities.

The effectiveness of a supporting psychologist is equally limited by the individual himself. A number of criteria for viable sport psychologists have been suggested by Rushall (1977):

1. The psychologist's analysis capabilities must provide valid, useful, and accurate information.
2. The interest of the individual in the problems of the sport should be clearly evident.
3. The psychologist should have qualifications and experiences in both psychology and the sport.
4. A capacity to objectively evaluate the sporting environment must be demonstrated.
5. An in-depth appreciation of *elite* athletes must be shown.
6. An acknowledged restriction of capacity for input should be

demonstrated.

7. Consultations need to be balanced and multi-disciplinary.
8. Individual differences and common characteristics should be sought among tested athletes.

The psychologist should also be prepared to have his own functions, contributions, and effectiveness evaluated.

In my opinion, another major obstacle in the way of establishing psychological support services is produced by those psychologists who are involved with teams without really understanding what they require. Teams can boast that they have team psychologists, but cannot detail their effectiveness. Athletes can attend "sessions," but cannot react with anything other than negative candor, when counseling turns out to have little or no relevance to the sport environment. One such instance of an ineffectual presence can retard the advances achieved by all those who promote a more cautious and accountable involvement.

Unfortunately, the relative functions of coaches, athletes, and support psychologists at the moment is so vague and non-directed that one can reasonably anticipate little improvement in future years. Drastic changes in the athlete development system will have to be invoked to alter this prospect.

SOME DEMONSTRATED FUNCTIONS

Perhaps the best way to describe a sport psychologist's role would be to describe the functions that have been performed. Instances of these functions will be limited to those that have occurred within my own experience.

The Provision of Information

Coaching decisions are more accurate and appropriate when based on the knowledge of athletes' behavior in specific situations. This is usually facilitated when coaches work with athletes over a long period of time and where trial-and-error encounters gradually build coaching competence. However, in situations where teams are formed for a short period of time, the knowledge necessary to create an appropriate interaction between coaches and athletes is extremely limited. Consequently, poor associations and relationships develop and inappropriate competition preparations are pursued. Problems such as these are not conducive to elevating performance. The psychologist's task then becomes one of generating valid and reliable information that can be used to advantage

My interactions and responsibilities with the Canadian National Wrestling and Swimming Teams during the past few years have proved to be enlightening, while at the same time both rewarding and frustrating. It is hoped that these observations on my experience and their possible implications for the future will be of value, especially in view of the recent increase in associations between psychological support personnel and national teams (swimming, gymnastics, and wrestling).

by a coaching staff and athletes.

The use of sporting scales. It has been my impression that coaches become openly critical of the commonly promoted, vague trait descriptions of athletes. General trait personality tests, which are valid for only about five per cent of the behavior in specific environments (Endler and Hunt, 1969), in a practical sense provide trivial information. Partly for this reason and, more importantly, for scholarly purposes, sport environment-specific behavior inventories have been developed over the past six years (Ebeze, 1975; Pound, 1977, Rushall, 1974, 1975d, 1978a). The commercially available computer analyses of the responses to these tests provide coaches with vast amounts of information and coaching directives, concerning social, interactional, pre-competition, and competition behavior, motivational events, and stress symptoms. The intentions behind the use of these tests and services have not been fully realized. Coaches acknowledge the plausible and specific nature of the information content of the environmental behavior inventories and are enthusiastic about "having an analysis done." However, providing information alone has little impact on changing coaching behavior. When the information is provided by an attendant and vigilant support psychologist some coaching behavior changes do occur, but not to any significant degree. This produces a dilemma. If important information can be provided which, if used properly, would enhance coaching effects, but is not used by a coach or staff, then the effort is all in vain. This is a major problem which is still to be overcome. When psychological information of value can be provided how does one change the behavioral inertia displayed by elite coaches? Even coaches with the best of intentions fail to construct circumstances to produce the flexible and adaptive behavior necessary to elevate performance in unique international competitions. It would appear that one procedure that is a possibility is the study and discussion of this information, and the development and implementation of strategies to advance the standard of coaching. It is not difficult to envisage work days, similar to those demonstrated in the preparation of professional football teams, that require 14 to 16 hours of intense planning and evaluation as a coordinated coaching staff. Unfortunately, such dedication and precision have been rarely, if ever, seen in Canadian amateur sport systems.

Two sporting scales, Achievement Motivations Scales (Fox, 1977) and the Sport Internal-External Scales (Strauss, 1975), do provide useful information. At the recent Commonwealth Games, an outstanding swimmer was not performing to capabilities. Fox's Achievement Motivations Scale indicated that the swimmer had a very high degree of approach response to competition. This indicated that the behavioral cues of the athlete, which showed reticence and withdrawal, particularly before competition, were specific to the situation which existed at the Games. Fortunately, steps were eventually taken to alleviate the athlete's problem, which contributed to a final gold medal performance. Similarly, the internal-external scale indicates individuals who need external team commitments and pressures to produce maximum performances. Situations can be constructed to produce elevations in performance for externally controlled individuals. This information supplements the environment-specific responses.

Interviews. A further source of information stems from the conduct of interviews with athletes. Interviews are the most difficult interaction to execute. It is in this encounter that a psychologist can establish or destroy his credibility. A simple strategy is to concentrate questions on the athlete's satisfaction with training, coaching, the training program, meals, living circumstances, competition preparation plans, associations with other athletes, and concerns for family. Any negative options should be further investigated by asking the athletes what they would like done to remove the troublesome feature. Although this is a standard interview strategy, it has been my experience that such an approach provides one of the few occasions on which athletes are asked their opinions about their sporting situation. It appears that getting athletes to air their frustrations and ideas is such a change from the normal coach-directed environment that the psychologist gains a heightened degree of credibility. Information obtained in interviews is confidential. The athlete should be asked what can and cannot be communicated to the coach. The next step, communicating the information to the coach, is very difficult. Some coaches react in the most negative and sometimes violent manner, others are extremely adept at rationalizing the information so as to maintain their behavioral inertia, and others do attempt to use the information.

Behavioral information can be generated from the two sources mentioned above. Used wisely and implemented appropriately, the effects of coaching can be elevated dramatically. However, at the present time it is my contention that the major hurdle to achieving this improvement resides in the coaches assigned to teams and athletes.

The Measurement of Effects

In situations where behavioral information is used and program changes are attempted, the two measurement techniques mentioned above can be repeated to see if responses have been altered. This repeated measurement is advisable, particularly after a training camp when athletes have adapted to unusual circumstances and personnel. Initial information which is obtained mostly at the commencement of camp can become outmoded. Thus, reevaluations are necessary to determine new statuses of athletes, even if the coaches do not wish to know whether the changes have been affected by them.

Further techniques for evaluating coaching effectiveness from a psychological viewpoint have been described elsewhere (Rushall, 1973). Only when coaches are willing to have their effectiveness and behavior analyzed will these suggestions be fully used.

The Construction of Programs

Periodically, the psychologist is requested to construct specific programs. Mr Don Talbot, head coach of the Canadian Men's

Swimming Team for 1978, was concerned about team unity and national pride in his team. With the enthusiastic support of the coaching staff and manager, various experiences were devised to generate the behavior appropriate to these concepts. The program was constructed with the psychologist having major input and control over its implementation. It was effective in that it produced user satisfaction and significant changes in objective measures (Rushall, 1978b).

A further program that was implemented for both the Canadian Men's and Women's Commonwealth Games Swimming Teams was the provision of periodic information about the swimmers' responses to training. The Women's Team logged their stress reaction symptoms in the Daily Analyses of Life Demands for Swimmers (Rushall, 1975b). Both swimmers and coaches were able to assess the reactions in a meaningful and common manner. Periodic assessments of physiological parameters were also instituted. The results of these tests often needed to be interpreted and described. This demonstrated a further requirement of the support psychologist. He must have a considerable degree of expertise in both physiology and biomechanics, as well as applied psychology. The performances and training responses of elite athletes are difficult to separate into only one area of sport science. A failure to understand the contributions of physiology and biomechanics to performance could lead to serious errors of omission and judgement by the psychologist.

As the coaching staffs and national sport governing bodies become more confident in their technical support personnel, the requests for the development of specific programs should increase. Such requests will act as a measure of value of those concerned.

Counseling

An obvious function of a team psychologist would be counseling. However, in my experience with the 1976 Canadian Olympic Swimming Team, athlete interactions were limited to structured sessions concerning the development of competition strategies. Since these sessions were voluntary, eventually only half of the team participated. Poor attendance was in some measure due to specific directions given by some coaches not to participate in the program. The fact that the credibility of the psychologist was low and the insecurity of some coaches was high most probably caused this reticence of the athletes and coaches. Cases of adventitious counseling were non-existent in this situation.

It was felt that the source of the problem was the novelty of the team psychologist's role and presence.

After two years of involvement, the psychologist for the Canadian National Swimming Team has become an accepted position for both athletes and coaches. Consequently, credibility has increased and threat has been reduced. In the preparations for and during the recent Commonwealth Games, both structured and unstructured counseling sessions were frequently held. It is believed that these were important, as problems and suggestions for system improvement were uncovered. The major difficulty with these interactions is the confidentiality of the content. Using one's own judgement, the athlete should be asked if important content can be communicated to the coaches or staff. It was extremely gratifying to see the positive attitude of both the athletes and coaches to these communications in the two Commonwealth Games teams.

Coaches also need counseling. Attempts to cope with the stresses that are placed on coaches, coaching conflicts, jealousies, family problems, these are some of the difficulties which arise during a training camp and competition. Valuable contributions can be made by locating the sources of these problems and expediting their solutions. This problem concerning coach reactions is greater than one would expect and is worthy of considerable attention, when planning for future international games.

In my opinion, confidential counseling becomes an integral part of the support service, when the psychologist has achieved both credibility and acceptance. Counseling is valuable for both athletes and coaches.

Competition Preparation

A major role of the psychologist can be the preparation of athletes for competition. There is a science of competition preparation that indicates a variety of skills and knowledge necessary to control effectively an athlete's development in order to produce a maximum performance. Coaches usually monopolize this task. It seems to me, however, that coaches cannot perform the necessary functions because of certain inadequacies:

1. They fail to develop in the athletes primary and coping competition strategies, structured in the most efficient manner.
2. They fail to rehearse and develop competition behavior in athletes as part of their training regimen.
3. They become so emotionally involved in the competition

outcomes that behavior changes in them due to the stress affect the athletes prior to competition.

4. Insufficient attention is given to pre-competition control.

It would appear that competition preparation, its development and integration into training, and its control during competitions, would best be supervised by a skilled psychologist. This involvement would include the development of various strategies for competition day and competition control, the appropriate behavior modification techniques necessary to facilitate the implementation of the devised behavior, and the manipulation of the competition site atmosphere. The details of these interactions are too lengthy to be described here. However, they revolve around producing a competitive milieu, where the scope of an athlete's behavior is self-generated, coping-oriented, and predictable.

The above statements are claims and have yet to be verified by a complete test of their effects. In 1976 those swimmers at the Olympics who were controlled by the psychologist in less than optimal circumstances reacted favorably to the attention and performed extremely well in competition (Jamieson, Rushall, and Talbot, 1976). In the recent Commonwealth Games, pre-race interactions were a standard feature of the men's team's preparations. That team performed better than the women's team which did not employ standardized, deliberate race preparations. On the few occasions that a psychologist did prepare women for their races, the head coach, Mr Dave Johnson, remarked that he noticed an elevation in each athlete's performance. Similar assumed effects have been observed in individual wrestlers at the 1976 World Cup and the 1976 Olympic Games Wrestling Trials.

It should be emphasized that the failure to use such expertise cannot be blamed on the individual coaches concerned. This is a new development which is slowly emerging throughout the world. At the recent World Swimming Championships the USSR Team employed a psychologist for race preparations in a manner similar to that described above. Eventually, coaches and organizations will realize the benefits that can be produced by using highly trained support personnel for specific functions. It is hoped that when this realization is fulfilled there will be a sufficient number of psychologists with the appropriate expertise to be able to satisfy the demands of Canadian sports organizations.

Clinical Functions

The length of time and the logistics of the support function will

Periodically, the psychologist is requested to construct specific programs. Mr Don Talbot, head coach of the Canadian Men's Swimming Team for 1978, was concerned about team unity and national pride in his team. With the enthusiastic support of the coaching staff and manager, various experiences were devised to generate the behavior appropriate to these concepts. The program was constructed with the psychologist having major input and control over its implementation. It was effective in that it produced user satisfaction and significant changes in objective measures.

determine the scope of clinical practices that can be used. Occasionally, there are problems which require considerable time to solve and are not within the capacity of any treatment to effect miracle cures. Most phobias about ensuing competitions or specific situations which are unique to camp or Games can be alleviated by "flooding" or implosion therapy procedures. A common practice with many athletes has been to teach self-relaxation and sleep techniques. These allow athletes to get their rest and sleep as well as combat anxieties. Other techniques are available, but my own experience has been limited to the above practices.

In some circumstances it is of advantage to refer athletes to another psychologist. In Edmonton one swimmer was treated by the Canadian team psychologist, Dr Lee Pulos. The problem could not be solved for competitions in Edmonton, but the imagery therapy used by the athlete facilitated a successful performance at the World Swimming Championships in Berlin. There is every reason to believe that other Canadian athletes in Edmonton could have benefited from the competent medical and support staff that was provided. However, there is still a great deal to do in educating coaches before the available services can be used to their best advantage.

CONCLUSION

The use of sport psychologists with teams is in its earliest infancy. At this time, possible uses appear to be limited by the adaptability of coaches. For myself, I have been fortunate enough to work with Mr Don Talbot and Mr Gordon Garvie, who have explored the integration of psychological procedures and the development and control of athletes. There is still a long way to go before the full effect of a total psychological package of involvement can be demonstrated or evaluated. Unfortunately, it appears that Canada is not yet ready to expand its coaching involvement in the direction of support staff. Perhaps this may be overcome as the result of an educational program. The change in coaching trends in the direction advocated is being demonstrated by other nations, notably the Soviet Union and the United States. Perhaps Canada could at least endeavor to maintain pace with the sport science developments of those nations.

This chapter has related anecdotes and opinions. It was intended to provoke thought and to gain attention, particularly through its pointed criticisms of present coaching trends. For those who react negatively, apologies are extended, for those who react positively, cooperation is offered in the most sincere sense.

the psychologist's contribution to sport organization and the athlete:an example

Dorcas S. Butt

In order to indicate how the application of the theory and study of sport psychology may be of use to the athlete and coach, I intend to present a particular example of such an application. I intend to lead you through the theory involved, the data base for the theory, and its actual application in examining the profiles of two individual athletes.

THEORY

A schematic representation of sport motivation, the details of which have been outlined elsewhere (Butt, 1973; 1976), is presented in Figure 1. Briefly it is suggested that there are four levels of sport motivation: a biological, a psychological, a social, and a secondary reinforcement level which may be external or internal. The basic life energy of the biological level may be chanelled into the service of aggression, conflict, or competence motivation on the psychological level and these will be present to a greater or lesser extent in any individual. Each of these energy models of psychological motivation (aggression, conflict, and competence) has extensive theorizing behind it in the works of Konrad Lorenz (1963), Sigmund Freud (1923), and Robert White (1963) respectively, and in turn each has been modified and extended, but remains essential to an understanding of motivation.

We have theorized, in considering the third level of social motivation, that competitive motivations will tend to evolve from patterns of aggression and conflict on the psychological level, while cooperative motivations will tend to evolve from competence on the psychological level. Both competitive and cooperative motivations are also heavily influenced by social reinforcements (level four). That is, the competitively motivated will want to win at any costs in order to achieve external rewards such as money,

74

recognition, and status, while the cooperatively motivated will be rewarded more by feelings of self-fulfillment, confidence, and well-being. However, as the dominant social values of many of our institutions endorse and foster competitions in which there are only winners and losers, even the competence oriented athlete must force himself to be somewhat competitive. On the other hand, the aggressive and conflict oriented person must gain some competence feedback from performance or become even more frustrated. Thus strong relationships are expected between aggression and competition, conflict and competition, and competence and cooperation. Lesser or moderate relationships are expected between aggression and cooperation, conflict and cooperation, and competence and competition. The solid lines in Figure 1 predict where the strongest relationships should lie.

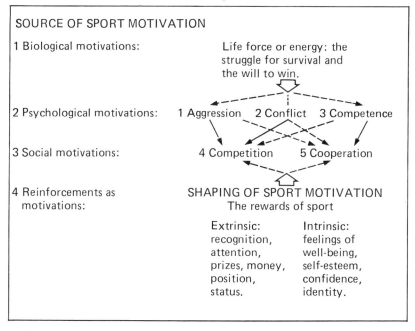

Figure 1. The motivational components of sport as adapted from Butt, 1976, p. 2.

Motivation in sport evolves from two major sources or influences: biological motivation and the reinforcements conferred through the sport enterprise. Psychological motivation is represented in the three basic energy models of aggression, conflict, and competence. The solid and dotted arrows indicate the greater and lesser degree of a connection thereafter. Aggressive motivation and conflict are most likely to lead to competitive, social motivation and, to a lesser extent, to cooperation. Competence motivation is most likely to lead to cooperative, social motivation. Both the competitively and cooperatively motivated will be affected by the reinforcements of sport. The external rewards will usually be most important to the competitor, however, and the internal rewards to the cooperator.

DATA BASE

In order to test the merits of this descriptive model of sport motivation, a 50-item scale was constructed to measure the three psychological and two social motivations for sport. Participants in the study were asked to use a sport of leisure activity as a base and to answer whether during the last month while participating or competing they had ever felt: strong (expression of aggression), guilty for not doing better (expression of conflict), happier than they have ever been (expression of competence), like trying to win a prize (expression of competition), or like sharing ideas or strategies with someone (expression of cooperation). There were ten such items for each scale to which participants answered yes or no. Item content was based upon behavioral descriptions (Butt, 1976, pp. 1-60) of athletes representing high levels of each motivational component. The items were finally reduced by half in number, selections being based upon test and item statistics.

The preceding analyses resulted in the conclusion that the motivational constructs could be measured reliably and this allowed us to proceed with the testing of the descriptive model. Correlations between the scales are reported in Figure 2. The results are based upon the answers to the questions of 67 males

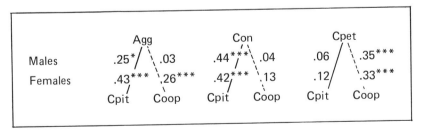

Figure 2. Testing the descriptive model of sport motivation.

Product-moment correlations followed by one-tailed tests of significance test the descriptive merits of the motivational model. Abbreviations are: Aggression (Agg), Conflict (Con), Competence (Cpet), Competition (Cpit), and Cooperation (Coop). Asterisks indicate levels of significance: *(p < .05), **(p < .01), ***(p < .005) for one-tailed tests. Ns are 67 males and 121 females.

and 121 females about half of whom were university students and half members of a competitive swimming club. The results are clearly in support of the theoretical model proposed.

By examining the correlations of the motivations with other measures, one may gain further information about them. In order to keep the present chapter concise, I will summarize the significant correlations which occurred across both sexes with the motivational measures.

Aggression. Aggression as a sport motivation was significantly related to general unhappiness, male sex-role typing, and lack of concern about protecting oneself from physical harm.

Conflict. The individual who scores high on conflict as a sport motivation describes himself as generally unhappy, insecure, and lacking in self-confidence.

Competition. Skipping to competition because of its association with the preceding two motivations, one finds what is hypothesized to be social expression of the foregoing styles. Those high on competition also describe themselves as insecure, lacking in self-confidence, and feeling that they must defend themselves from other people in their environment.

Competence. Both males and females scoring high on competence motivation describe themselves as generally happy. Since there were no other parallel relationships for both sexes, we will report the highest for each. In males the highest relationship was with the need for social recognition, while in females it was with not being fearful of her environment.

Cooperation. Similarly, there were no mutual patterns for males and females on cooperation. However, the strongest relationships for males were with the need to be understood by others, and the need for variety. In females the three strong relationships were with the need to explain and understand events, the need for social recognition, and the need for affiliation.

I should point out that these results are only descriptive and are abridged. However, it has been our contention that aggression, conflict, and competition should be discouraged as sport motivations in preference to competence and cooperation. The participants in the study seem to support such assertions by what is generally a negative self-description for those high on aggression, conflict, and competition and generally a positive or neutral description for those high on competence and cooperation. Thus we may still contend that the latter are most likely to encourage the psychological growth and health of both individuals and groups.

The foregoing results are all based on self-report measures.

For the swimming club in the study, three indices were reported from quite different methods of assessment. The first was the swimmer's performance rating from one to five for his own age group, while the second and third were the independent ratings from one to seven by two coaches of the swimmer's future potential. Although the trends were weak, they again supported the theory proposed. Actual achievement in performance was related to competence in the female swimmers. The coaches showed trends in their ratings which may be sex related. The male coach's ratings show little of significance in relationship to the female swimmer's motivations, but in the motivations of the male swimmers they relate to cooperation. Similarly, there is little of significance in the female coach's ratings of male swimmers, but her ratings of female swimmers show associations with competence and competition (a finding we explain by noting the coach's heavy exposure to national competitions as a former athlete). When the data are combined for males and females, performance and potential are clearly demonstrated to relate to competence. Here is preliminary evidence that competence and perhaps cooperation as sport motivations are associated with excellence in sport.

APPLICATIONS

We have proceeded with the application of these results, always giving psychological information and opinions to coaches and athletes in the form of "ideas" with which they might experiment rather than in the form of "facts" with proven success. The variations in the needs of athletes in training and their relationships with coaches are infinite. Every case is unique. Therefore, psychological measures will never replace the coach's or the athlete's continual need to evaluate and experiment with their own attitudes, goals, and training procedures. Psychological measures can, however, open areas for discussion and thought, so that athlete and coach can work more closely and effectively together.

We have administered the *Sports Protocol,* which contains measures of the constructs previously described and others, to athletes representing various sports, age levels, and abilities in Canada and in Great Britain (in collaboration with Dr June Redgrove of Middlesex Polytechnic). We are currently preparing for work in Japan (with Dr Yoshiyuki Matsuda of Tsukuba University and the Leisure Research Centre). The profiles of two

Dr Butt is one of the few sport psychologists who have excelled as athletes. She played twice in the All-England Championships at Wimbledon and was Canada's number one ranked player in 1960, 1961, and 1967.

female athletes follow for discussion purposes. They have been altered in order to make individual identification impossible without altering the actual scores of the participants.

Profile 1

Profile 1 highlights conflict and competition. The athlete has very unhappy feelings when participating in sport (guilt, weeping, fatigue, moods, nervousness) and at the same time feels competitive pressure to outdistance others. As might be expected, she also feels aggressive towards her fellow team members and opponents, while competence, although endorsed, is lower. The endorsement of cooperation is a very positive feature, because the girl identifies with her sport group. The low experience of competence is, however, a serious concern. The athlete's family background provides an explanation for the profile. It features a broken parental relationship of much concern to the girl, while at the same time both parents are perceived as pushing her to succeed in sport. In general mood, the girl describes herself as unhappy. Such a profile, in a girl of recognized high athletic ability, would suggest a coaching strategy which would concentrate upon developing the girl's awareness of feelings of competence in sport, personal acceptance, and a genuine lessening of pressure to perform, while at the same time supporting her ability and achievements. Discussion with the athlete should be directed towards the high endorsement of conflict, that is, why are unhappy feelings experienced in sport and what can be done to lessen them while increasing more positive ones? Can the coach help? Can the team help? It is likely both could alleviate the pressure this girl feels, in that sport is already compensating in her life for the disappointment she feels over the failure of the parental relationship.

Profile 2

Profile 2 belongs to a 12-year-old girl, who withdrew from her club shortly after responding to the *Sports Protocol* (but before intervention) and raises some interesting questions for coaches. When such an individual is identified as a likely withdrawal, how much time should or can a coach give towards keeping the athlete motivated and in the program? This girl said that she was going to give up because her coach gave her a hard time, and her parents, especially her mother, were pushing her to do well. She was rated by her coach as of moderate ability. She endorsed many unhappy feelings in her sport motivation (conflict). She was somewhat angry (aggression) and expressed few experiences of competence in her sport. She was not very competitive, but was high on cooperation, evidently satisfying some of her needs for affiliation through the other members of her club whom she enjoyed and cared for. Such an athlete should have the opportunity for weekly discussions in a group with a coach during which individual and group goals are discussed. If this girl's needs for affiliation were satisfied through the club, it may be that over time new horizons of intrinsic feedback (competence) from her own performance could be opened up for her. She might therefore be saved from dropping out of the program and might become an important source of support to other members of the club (even though she was not of high ability). However, if such an athlete should choose to drop out of her sport after self-examination, then such a decision should be supported by all with the understanding that the program will again be available to her if she feels she can benefit from it in the future.

CONCLUSION

In this chapter our comments have been restricted to the consideration of individual athletes. Group consultation was omitted, although it is quite possible to use these methods to examine and to discuss group or team trends. Underlying this work are two assumptions. The first is that the achievement of athletic performance should never take precedence over the psychological and personal growth of the athlete. The second is that the psychologist should complement and never supplement the existing roles within the sports field (trainer, coach, or manager). The psychologist's unique contribution is in opening new horizons and possibilities for the coach and athlete. The decision to use or explore these possibilities always belongs to them.

who is doing what: viewpoints on psychological treatments for athletes

T.A. Tutko, M.D. Pressman,
D.S. Butt, R.M. Nideffer,
R.M. Suinn, B.C. Ogilvie

This chapter offers some viewpoints of the prominent sport psychologists on how may psychological problems contracted by a team or an athlete be solved. The psychologists addressed themselves to two categories of questions. The first category deals with "How do we identify athletes who develop psychological problems?" "Who is supposed to treat these athletes or how to go about treating them?" "What is the success rate of these treatments?" The second category deals with such basic questions as "What can the coach do himself?" "When does he need help from a sport psychologist?" "When does he need support from a clinical psychologist?" and "When the psychiatrist has to be approached?"

Tutko

To say that an athlete is undergoing some form of psychological treatment immediately suggests to most people a form of pathology, or to put it bluntly, "He's nuts." This is the most common mistake made by the lay person in athletics. When Dr Ogilvie and I first started in this profession we were continually seen as "shrinks," people who worked with the "crazies." In fact in one instance we were advised to change our titles from psychologists to behavioral scientists to become more acceptable.

We are involved with two kinds of work at present. One is the use of the Athletic Motivation Inventory (AMI) to help coaches and athletes communicate more effectively in the area of motivation. Coach and athlete can use the results of the inventory to discuss various aspects of performance. Each may present a viewpoint, and areas of improvement or change can be agreed upon after discussion. In addition to being a communication tool the

AMI enables the coach and athlete to be more specific about motivation and to relate it to exact on-the-field behavior which can be changed to enhance performance.

The other kind is one that I believe is more apropos to this discussion. It is dealing with anxiety and determining its effects on the athlete. Anxiety can cause many different reactions, some of which are normal and some of which are disturbed. The sport psychologist must be able to recognize the differences and know what to do about them.

Anxiety is a natural phenomenon. The stress of competition creates a threat and results in anxiety. To the athlete the source of the threat may be concern about the evaluation by others, loss of self-esteem, a sense of guilt, lack of confidence, and so on. Nor is anxiety a bad thing. It is a motivation—it produces action and results—and in most cases the athlete is capable of dealing with it effectively.

Everyone has a different way of handling anxiety. Some ways are productive and some disruptive. Some athletes deny they are anxious; some even fall asleep—a form of complete denial. A common method is to become more active—some athletes go through continued warm-up exercises and rehearsals of the forthcoming event. Some want to be left alone; some need reassurance. The way each individual responds is a result of a long-standing pattern and should not be interfered with.

Symptoms are common at this stage. Agitated activity, rigid rituals, and superstitious actions, sweaty palms, dry mouth, frequent trips to the bathroom, and so on are all normal reactions. Treatment can be optional since most athletes prefer to repeat their personalized habits and rituals. Some athletes, however, may wish to change, for example the athlete who ruminates on failure and does not feel he is being productive. There are simple techniques to reduce anxiety and produce positive imagery. Controlled breathing exercises and muscle relaxation exercises were developed in the 1930s by A. D. Jacobson. I have written a book with Nino Tosi entitled *Sports Psyching* (1976) where some common problems and simple ways of coping with them are described.

There are athletes, however, that are less capable of dealing with anxiety. They lack what is called ego control or ego strength. If the anxiety is intense or prolonged, they begin to exhibit symptoms that go beyond the "normal." This type of anxiety might best be described as neurotic anxiety. In such cases the way the athletes handle anxiety is counterproductive. Their habits become dysfunctional and non-productive. For example, there are athletes who become so involved in their workouts that they exhaust

Everyone has a different way of handling anxiety. Some ways are productive and some disruptive. Some athletes deny they are anxious; some even fall asleep—a form of complete denial. A common method is to become more active—some athletes go through continued warm-up exercises and rehearsals of the forthcoming event. Some want to be left alone; some need reassurance. The way each individual responds is a result of a long-standing pattern and should not be interfered with.

themselves. The only way they can reduce their anxiety is by working out and as a result they either burn themselves out or do not have enough stamina to put forth effort when it is required. A second common neurotic response to anxiety is for the athletes to become so involved in rituals that they are extremely upset if they cannot be performed. In fact a number of athletes get "psyched out" because their ritual is disrupted. I know an athlete who had a ritual so rigid that it started from the moment he woke in the morning and continued until the game started. More often than not a disruption would occur and his performance would suffer. Bruce Ogilvie and I have written a book describing some such cases. The title of the book, *Problem Athletes and How to*

Handle Them (1966), gives an indication of the common problems faced by coaches and their difficulty in understanding such behavior. Although not severely disturbed the neurotic has a rigid belief and ritual system which he cannot abandon. At the core of this system are often more deeply seated problems which the stress of the athletic contest brings to the fore. Working with such an athlete requires clinical training since the athlete may wish to explore the cause of his behavior and do something about it. In severe cases a sport psychiatrist may need to prescribe tranquilizers.

It is useless to try to use logic to talk these individuals out of the "off-beat behavior." They are aware of it and often embarrassed by it, but can do little to change it. It is extremely important that sport psychologists not qualified in clinical work avoid working with such people. They can work with a trained person but to attempt to go it alone is unethical. The title of sport psychologist does not automatically give one the skill and knowledge.

It is also important that you refer the individual to a clinical psychologist or psychiatrist who has some knowledge of sport. The athlete wants to be understood and he will not feel that he is if the psychologist or psychiatrist lacks knowledge of sport.

In extreme and rare cases anxiety may cause athletes to manifest bizarre symptoms, such as delusions, hallucinations, and so on. These individuals are clearly in need of a psychiatrist, the only one who can prescribe drugs and recommend hospitalization. Despite the rarity of such cases a sport psychologist should be prepared to recognize the early signs in order to head off future trouble. If you detect such signs, the best approach is to try to establish personal rapport. You can become the contact the athlete might want under extreme pressure.

It is critical not to ignore the signs. Of even greater significance is that the athlete be supported, not ostracized (which often happens because others are either made anxious by his behavior or embarrassed by him) or made fun of. It is devastating to make such an athlete the brunt of jokes. It can only cause his performance to deteriorate further.

The sport psychologist is quite capable of dealing with routine stress and the anxiety that results. With some training he may be able to work with those who begin to show more serious symptoms. If he suspects something more serious, it is critical that he refer the individual as quickly as possible. The sooner the athlete has help, the better.

Pressman

Although Dr Tutko and I are very much of a mind in terms of our understanding of the neurotic process, I would like to undertake a somewhat different approach to the question of neuroticism and the need for treatment in the athlete. I believe that we can adhere to some simple important truths when we speak about neuroticism. I believe that there is an easy way to measure whether neuroticism requires treatment or not and that is in terms of the interference, or lack of interference, with the athlete's functioning. Everything else can be dismissed. For example, if the athlete has all of the equipment to perform well in his particular sport, but for mysterious reasons does not, then some hidden psychological factor is at work. A neurosis is really an adaptation that was once useful and is now misapplied and operating without the athlete's or patient's awareness of its hold and its activity. If the athlete is not able to use his resources well to achieve his conscious goals, then the hidden factor, the neurotic factor, must be addressed. Our best formula would be in terms of applying simple techniques for the management of this hidden factor. If they do not work, we can go to more specialized techniques which may require a professional, a psychologist or a psychiatrist.

I would like to go on to note that the qualities of aggression and anxiety are neither good nor bad. It is rather a matter of how these qualities are used. Anxiety can be an interference, or it can be a motivator. A helpful use of anxiety can produce a good result; on the other hand, anxiety may become excessive, in which case it can inhibit, even paralyze. Under these circumstances, it is not operating in the service of the individual and needs some specialized attention. The same is true for the use of aggression. Aggression is instinctive; as long as we are alive, we are going to be manufacturing aggression. If we use it to produce harm, we are misusing it. If we use it for healthy competition, for example, or for the exchange of ideas and discussion in the face of opposition, we are using it well. It is important, I believe, that we not fear the aggressive factor because of social acculturation and that we cultivate the helpful use of aggression in our athletes.

Finally, I would like to return to the theme of the coach and his usefulness. Our efforts should be directed towards bringing out the best in the final product, the athlete, but to do this I believe that the most important resource that we professionals have is the coach. The coach is the family practitioner of the sports world. As such, he has a tremendous amount of information about the athlete, he has a tremendous amount of power and influence that the sport psychologist will never acquire, and he has time with the athlete at a formative period in the athlete's life. If we can provide the coach with correct information, then not only can we improve his ability to create a better product and a better life for his students, but we can increase our ability to do good, and at the same time we can learn from the rich and broad experience of the coaching world.

Butt

We are discussing *psychological treatments* for athletes, but more often than not, the athlete does not need psychological treatment or any artificial aid to help increase performance. The athlete needs *education.* What does need *treatment* is much of the social organization of sport because of the negative values and purposes which are allowed to continue there.

I like to look at sports performance as an expression of, or a growth of, *self.* Self-confidence, self-esteem, and the ability to perform grow out of each individual's response to new and varied challenges on the sports field over months and years. This seems very simple. But when sport organizations and structures place the individual under stress because of extraneous values and pressures that have little to do with competence development, it is no wonder that the athlete falters. Freedom to experiment and freedom of choice are necessary for growth, yet for the athlete they are often limited. What the athlete must do is ignore the extraneous pressures as far as possible and concentrate on developing his competence. The athlete must seek challenges and accomplishments while avoiding those pressures that alienate one from the *experiencing of intrinsic rewards.* Intrinsic reward and feedback are essential for continued motivation.

Psychology can contribute by educating athletes to become more aware of some of the problems lying ahead and by teaching them how to deal with the problems. This involves offering suggestions on how to cope and how to withstand competitive pressures. At the same time the psychologist can help remove the organizational pitfalls widespread in sport by working with government, coaches, and various sporting bodies. The psychologist can do none of these things, however, unless individuals and groups are receptive to new ideas. I find increasing readiness within sports groups for new ideas. Some of the old ones have not served us well and almost everyone knows it.

I think it is better if the athlete and the coach at all levels of sport can operate without clinical services. Thus the process of education to which I refer should take place long before the heat of the contest draws near. To my mind, the area of the contest is entirely the territory of the coach and of the athlete, and not that of the psychologist. The psychologist assists the athlete, coach, and organization to deal with their problems long before they enter the arena. Only in a few cases, when problems have grown beyond the effectiveness of such intervention, are *clinical services* called for.

The two levels of need for psychological services in sport, for education and for clinical help, bring up the important question of how sport involves the psychologist and how the psychologist chooses to be involved. Sometimes people in sport have relatively small yet bothersome problems. They are irritating rather than debilitating. Once identified, such problems or interferences can usually be solved relatively simply by opening up communications, by rearranging group structures, by examining interpersonal relationships, by suggesting changes in training techniques, that is, by education. Participants become aware of some of the non-obvious processes influencing sport at all levels which the psychologist is trained to understand and to interpret. In other more unusual cases, individuals may need special help because they are unable to cope and sport plays a central role in that inability. Such a case is as complicated to handle as any other clinical case not involving sport. All the tools available to clinicians must be considered. These are wide and varied and no clinician is master of them all. Referrals often take place.

Let me give you one example of each approach or level of *psychological service.* The first is on the educational level and is a very simple technique we have used successfully as part of a series of questions which make up a written interview for athletes. In one question each athlete is asked to write down candidly what they would like their coach to do differently. When we have used this question, athletes have responded with a variety of reactions that coaches have found valuable. Some have become more aware of features in their behavior that are affecting the motivations and performances of their athletes. Others have altered a personal style with an individual athlete. Sometimes the information has been used by coaches as a basis for discussion with an athlete or a group of athletes. "Some of this is so simple we could do it ourselves," coaches have commented. Of course they could and if they do, the process of education, in providing a new idea, has been effective.

An example of a more serious problem occurred when a young man, who strongly stated that he wanted to become a champion in his sport, asked for counseling. He was lacking motivation in practices, had a tendency to fall apart after building up large leads in competitions, and thought that coaches and other athletes were avoiding him because his talent threatened them. After only a few sessions he was able to decide to leave his sport, for an unspecified time, to work on other areas of his development and education. He came to see his sport aspirations as external to his natural wishes and needs because they were dependent upon compensation for feelings of inferiority and denial of personal needs (to affiliate rather than to dominate). There was no joy for this man in competing and little experience of competence from sport. He decided to seek the rewards of competence elsewhere in his life.

Other contributions to sport from psychology include the explanation of how general principles might be applied by athletes and coaches. These fall under the education category. For example, sports people should know about the superiority of part over whole learning (frequent short training sessions are usually more effective than long, extended sessions). Most athletes train too hard and do not know it. Another is the interesting area of mental imagery, rehearsal, and cognition as applied to sport. Others come from the application of sociometric principles to teams and the discussion of individual goals, purposes, and motivations in sport.

A vast area is opening for athletes and coaches in the psychology of sport—if they have the time and the inclination to partake of it. However, putting complex information together in the service of self-expression through sport requires talent, maturity, and practice. It takes time. *I do not know of any quick and easy method from psychology that will increase performance.* And that is just as well because increased performance is not what sport is all about. Sport is about growth and expression in individuals and groups which may or may not surpass previous performances and which may or may not inspire others and win medals or money through artistry, skill, and control. *Sport is an adventure in self.* Social reform is needed in sport so that we do not lead every child into thinking that he should become a champion. That is a false goal for anyone because it involves external validation of self and it will mean little unless accompanied by feelings of efficacy and competence.

Nideffer

One of the issues that has been brought into focus is the fact that we need to define what we mean by "psychological treatment" of athletes. One side argues that a coach should be the service provider, that clinicians are not needed. Another side maintains that coaches are not trained clinically and cannot deal with the problems that athletes present. Without defining what is meant by the term "treatment" it is impossible to resolve these differences. What I would like to do here is offer my own personal opinion. I realize that it may not be shared by many of my colleagues.

First, I would like to say that I do not feel that the interventions of coaches, sport psychologists, clinical psychologists, or psychiatrists need to be limited to "problems." In fact, I believe that the major contribution psychology has to make involves making the good better, helping athletes integrate mental and physical functioning so they perform at higher, more consistent levels. An athlete can be mentally and physically healthy, functioning as a "superstar," and still benefit from psychological techniques. Treatment in this sense is a far cry from what we typically view as psychological interventions. Obviously there are times when athletes become depressed, go into a "slump," become suicidal, have a "nervous breakdown," or develop fears and mental and emotional blocks. On these occasions athletes are performing below their normal level, and treatment refers to the more traditional clinical interventions.

Given these two extremes let me define what I believe is the role of the coach, sport psychologist, and clinical psychologist. To begin with, most of the psychological techniques (progressive relaxation, mental rehearsal, meditation, operant programs, and so on) that are used to improve performance do not require a great deal of training. You can learn self-hypnosis or how to meditate in a few minutes. The most important aspects of successful application of techniques involve: (1) timing, knowing when to use a technique, and (2) motivation, developing trust and the belief of the athlete in the procedure.

It is my belief that coaches *who have the time,* and a close relationship with an athlete, are often in a better position to motivate and to pick an appropriate time to intervene. I would hasten to limit this intervention by coaches to working to improve performance. I believe it would be a mistake for a coach to attempt to deal with more clinical issues.

For me, the sport psychologist is an individual whose primary responsibilities are to develop programs to help improve perform-

You can learn self-hypnosis or how to meditate in a few minutes.

ance. This may involve working out reinforcement contingencies to increase motivation, team building, evaluation and management of competitive anxiety, developing communication skills, and so on. It is also the role of the sport psychologist to train and supervise others (trainers, coaches) to implement these programs.

I think it is a mistake for the sport psychologist (even if he is clinically trained) to attempt to do traditional psychotherapy or to deal with problems that are not directly tied to performance (marital difficulties, addictions, personality problems, neurotic conflicts). Most often the sport psychologist is paid by management and has a primary responsibility for seeing that everyone functions at their best level on the field. The needs of the team can conflict with the needs of an athlete who is involved in psychotherapy. The sport psychologist may be caught in a conflict of interest especially if his therapy results in a further deterioration of performance, in the athletes leaving the team, or in management dropping the player. The sport psychologist should be capable of personal crisis intervention and should be sensitive enough to recognize when an athlete needs to be referred to a clinical psychologist or psychiatrist. Both of these skills can be developed fairly quickly.

The clinical psychologist and the psychiatrist are trained to deal with severe emotional problems. Their education has a clinical focus. Both are capable of providing some type of psychotherapy. The psychologist may be better trained to use psychological tests either to gain an understanding of underlying clinical problems, or to provide a treatment focus. The psychiatrist is trained to be able to administer drugs and may hospitalize the athlete if necessary. Both need to have a strong identity with athletes to be able to empathize with the individual, to understand the realities of the athlete's life, and to ensure that their treatment interventions fit with the athlete's needs. In the same way that sport psychologists should not get involved in therapy with an athlete, clinicians should make sure that they are not involved clinically with any of the members of a team, should they decide to start functioning as a sport psychologist with that team.

Suinn

I am very much in agreement with Bob Nideffer's statement about the important distinction to be made between clinical psychologists and therapy treatment on the one hand, and sport psychologists and enhancement of performance in healthy functioning people on the other. In my own consulting work in sport I have used some psychological test instruments; I did not select those instruments that were pertinent to identifying pathology, but instead selected a battery of tests that had been constructed on the basis of normally functioning people. Although I happen to be a clinical psychologist I do not feel I can make the best contribution in a sport setting in this role. I function in sport as a psychologist to help enhance athletic performance and as a professional who is interested in, has specialized in, and has some experience in that field. I think that sport psychologists should be utilized in a training—or retraining—capacity rather than in a therapeutic capacity. There are lots of clinical psychologists available to handle the treatment responsibility and the two roles should be distinguished.

I would like to turn now to stress reactions. I find it useful to look at stress in terms of the variety of responses that are possible. For one individual, the stress response may appear in terms of an emotional, an autonomic physiological reaction. In another person it may appear in a behavioral response; stuttering would be an example. A third possibility is a cognitive response, such as having certain kinds of negative thoughts or doubts—a lack of confidence is usually expressed in that way. I think the retraining program or the way of handling the stress responses depends on which responses or patterns you are finding in the athletes.

One of the interesting things about elite world class competition is the fact that stress responses are occurring because of the unique and unexpected conditions. The circumstances are totally unfamiliar. Athletes have to put up with waiting, with not having anything to do, and with not having enough time for recreational activities. Roommate selection is sometimes a source of stress.

I function in sport as a psychologist to help enhance athletic performance and as a professional who is interested in, has specialized in, and has some experience in that field.

More serious can be cultural factors such as language differences, and so on. Some have been trying to prepare their competitors by working out with them through role playing exactly what will happen in the competition.

Another area of concern for the psychologist relates to the individual who spends four years preparing to compete in a single event of the Olympics. What happens to that person when the Olympics are over? How do you prepare the individual for a different kind of life? Another aspect of the stress arising from this kind of dedication is whether or to what degree a competitor is acceptable to peers who are not competitors, particularly if the athlete's specialty is one of the more obscure of the Olympic events. Yet another source of stress to the athlete is the perception of being taken advantage of by the media or by a sponsoring institution, being treated as an object rather than a person and individual. Finally, I think the issue of depersonalization—when an athlete becomes a piece of machinery that is trained to run faster or shoot more accurately—should be one of our most pressing concerns as psychologists today.

Ogilvie

At sports clinics and congresses I am continually asked the question, "If you, as a motivational consultant, could have only a single insight into the personality of an athlete, which trait would you select as most basic for helping him attain his athletic goals?" Consultation experience forces me to focus immediately upon the athlete's capacity for trust. Faith in others is so fundamental to all forms of learning that when an individual loses it the emotional barrier he then constructs must be considered as the most dramatic inhibitor of human communication.

More than twenty years of seeking to provide psychological services to competitors performing at every level from age nine to professional has made it abundantly clear that when an athlete admits the loss of his capacity for trust, most valuable insights can be gained. Let us examine what he is telling us when he shares this feeling, and then explore the implication of the disclosure for you as a coach, teacher, trainer, or physician. In exposing his true feeling, he permits us to see the degree to which he has lost his faith in others. Generally this will be tied to specific negative learning experiences within his early life in which he was conditioned to expect frequent or consistent betrayal, and his feelings limit his ability to relate in a non-defensive manner to others, to teammates, coach, trainer, and even in certain cases to the team physician.

Behind the wall the individual has created to protect himself against further emotional hurt is often a deep wish that somewhere there is one person who is completely honest and trustworthy. These feelings are often so covert, however, that it may take years to realize why communication has been limited or blocked entirely. Frequently the youngsters who feel this way have turned to sport because they see the world of athletics as a bastion of justice and fair play. This is the one area where they are measured in terms of worth by their motor skills.

The implications of such expectations for the helping professional are so considerable that we must examine the essence of our responsibility to these emotionally scarred individuals. First and foremost we must be aware that our ego may be threatened to a degree by the withholding of trust on the part of anyone we are seeking to serve, and our initial reaction may be defensive or angry when greeted by resistance or subtle rebellion. This is a natural human response, but the focus should be directed to the source of such resistance. The best protection for your ego is to remain constantly mindful of the causes for the athlete's reaction.

What is most important will be how you apply your insight as a helping person. Because directness and openness are such basic requirements for these emotionally limited persons it is suggested that you meet with the individual in private and present him with what he has revealed about himself concerning his capacity to trust. The entire mood of the meeting should be one of gentle inquiry. An ideal opening statement might take the following form: "Harry, the attitudes you expressed by the way you answered some of the questions on the questionnaire we gave you yesterday leads me to conclude that most of the important people in your life have let you down. Have I overstated your feeling or could this possibly be true?" The athlete must feel totally free to contest your interpretation. Typically there is an initial response of dismay, followed quickly by a sense of relief that long repressed feelings are now out.

It will be at this point where you will be put on trial as to the type of human being you are and the degree of integrity you possess. It is almost impossible to express the responsibility you assume as a professional, when you begin to open the doors of trust again in the life of your athletes. It may seem an overstatement but the actual truth is that within your hands is a precious and fragile burden from which most, if not all, adults in the athlete's life have simply backed away. If you are willing to face this challenge, you must be aware that these emotionally blocked individuals will have a need to put you on a pedestal. The best protection against this unrealistic idealization will be to keep the athlete constantly aware of your fallibility both as a professional and as a person. Remind him frequently that he is also responsible for keeping communication open and clear. These reminders will lessen the probability of his making negative projections upon you. Remember that he possesses an unconscious expectation that like all other important persons in his life, you too will fail him.

There will be those cases where "the damaged child of the past" may seek to reestablish emotional ties identical to those with the once loved and trusted parent. This is the phenomenon of transference which is a part of the professional reality of teachers, coaches, and others in the helping arts. The capacity and inclination to use this delicate emotional attachment for unselfish constructive means seems poorly distributed within the various professional groups. There will be those who choose not to become involved with the reestablishment or growth of trust for a variety of personal reasons, and they perhaps could direct the athlete to someone better equipped to form a helping relationship.

It has been my experience that the opportunity for the recreation of trust offered within the sports environment is superior to that of any other single social institution. The sensitive and intelligent utilization of such insight by those of us responsible for the development of our youth cannot be overstated. The rewards for those of you who choose to meet this challenge will be a level of allegiance and devotion on the part of the athlete greater than anything you have ever experienced.

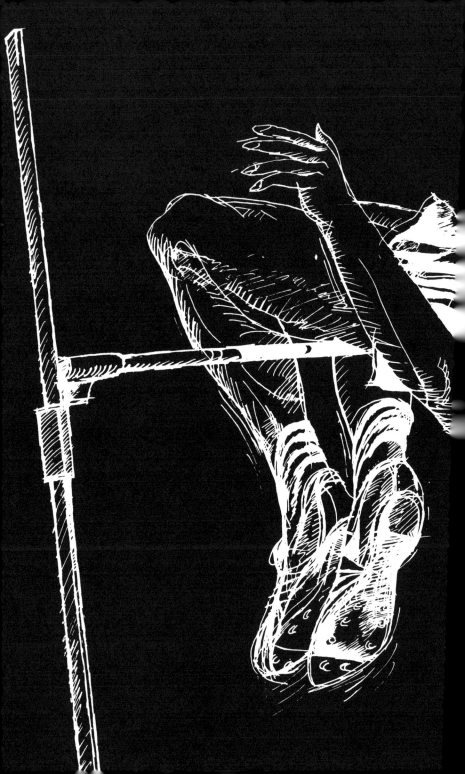

part 3

the psychology of peak performance

INTRODUCTION

Authors in Part Three probe into ways which will allow the athlete to function near the top of his potential. Although the approaches presented vary considerably, they all have tremendous implications for the athlete both in training and in competition. Nideffer in "The Role of Attention in Optimal Performance" examines the characteristics of attention demands in athletics and the capacity of athletes to shift attention rapidly, a capacity which is critical to performance. He proposes a test which assesses the attentional characteristics of athletes and discusses its usefulness in athletics. By following his own question and answer format throughout the chapter, he covers a lot of ground and provides answers to many relevant questions concerning anxiety problems, the capacity for self-control, and so on.

Hickman's chapter is an excellent exposition of psychophysical sport training which integrates the resources of mind and body. Such techniques as meditation, visualization, verbal formulas, and psychical self-regulation, to mention only a few, are discussed in detail. These along with various exercises are designed to develop energy awareness and capabilities in athletes much greater than ordinarily imagined. These methods, if mastered, generate the capacity to expand the boundaries of physical performance when competing.

Pressman and Pulos have both had extensive experience with the application of hypnosis to superior athletes. They describe their approaches in detail and give numerous examples of their work. While Pressman worked mostly with figure skaters, Pulos' experiences have been with the women's national volleyball team and track and field athletes. Both authors believe that hypnosis, along with other mental programs, such as mental rehearsal, can develop positive and relaxed attitudes which in turn help the individual athlete or indeed the entire team achieve their true physical potential. Pulos also suggests the athletes should learn self-hypnosis which he terms think-training. This technique further aids the athlete's ability to concentrate.

Klavora discusses some of the relationships between customary arousal levels in athletes and their performance. Based on his extensive experience in this area, he suggests a simple method to measure arousal levels of athletes before competition. This information may be useful to coaches in their attempts to monitor the arousal levels of individual athletes or the team.

The last chapter summarizes an informal dialogue between a group of national coaches and a panel of psychologists on such questions as out-of-body psychic experiences, narrow versus broad focus of attention, and so on

the role of attention in optimal athletic performance

Robert M. Nideffer

In this chapter I intend to discuss attentional demands in athletics. I am interested in a series of questions about the role of attentional processes—how they might be measured, whether they are stable characteristics, whether there are individual differences, and so on. Although I don't have all the answers, I will try to cast some light on these problems, by following my own question and answer format.

There is a lot of talk about optimal
performance; what does that mean?
When I speak about optimal performance, I am talking about those times that people function at their own maximal level. This does not mean that they are capable of transcending their own mental and physical limits. For example, it does not mean that I, at 160 pounds, can play defensive tackle for a professional football team. Often it does mean athletes transcend what they believe they are capable of, and they can even experience what might be called an altered state of consciousness.

What is required for an athlete to perform
at his full potential, or optimal level?
He must be making full use of his physical skill, and this must be coordinated with his ability to control attention or concentration. It is the ability to direct attentional processes that provides the key to performing at optimal levels.

Don't be fooled by a word like concentrate. It is too simple to say that to function at top levels athletes must concentrate. That is a tired old cliche, and few of us doubt the relevance of concentration. It is not enough to say concentrate however; we must be able to describe how to concentrate. Concentration is not something we either do or don't do. We are always concentrating or attending to something. The issue for the athlete is to learn what to attend to, when to attend to it, and how to be able to maintain that attention at the critical time.

What are the attentional abilities required for optimal performance?

Research on highly effective people (for example, masters of the martial arts, high level decision makers, executives) and on individuals suffering from various psychological disturbances (for example, schizophrenia) indicates that there are at least two dimensions of concentration or attention that are critical for effective performance.

First, athletes need to be able to control the width of attention and the amount of information they let into consciousness. At times they need to be able to broaden attention to consider a large amount of information. This might happen if they have to assess a problem and then try to design a solution. For example, a coach may need to figure out how to change his team's offense to counter the other team's defense. There are also times when attention must be narrowed in order to take some specific action and to avoid being distracted by irrelevant information. The athlete's ability to shift rapidly from a broad focus of attention to a narrow one, in response to changing conditions, is critical to performance.

The second dimension of concentration has to do with the direction of focus. There are occasions, particularly when planning for or rethinking a game, that an internal focus of attention is required. Likewise, an internal focus would be necessary if an athlete hoped to be sensitive to his own bodily feelings in order to know when to make a move. It is an internal focus of attention that is used by long distance runners when they "associate" to pain. The internal focus of attention can be contrasted to an external one. Reggie Jackson cannot hit a home run if he can't attend to the ball. It's an external focus that is required to react to a changing athletic situation, to react to an opponent's move.

Athletic situations, coaching demands, change from moment to moment and you may have to shift rapidly from one type of attention to another. At any given time, however, the attentional demands can be described on the basis of both width and direction of focus required. This means at one time you may need to have a broad-external focus of attention (for example, to read defensive keys in a football game). At another time a broad-internal focus of attention becomes important to plan pre-game stragegy, develop a training program, and so on. A narrow-external focus becomes important when taking a shot on goal in hockey. Finally, a narrow-internal focus is used to read your own pain tolerance, psyching yourself up, changing your negative thoughts to positive ones, and so on. If you are in the right place at the right time, you perform at your optimal level and may even be a hero. If you are in the wrong place, and everyone is at one time or another, you can end up the goat.

A Reggie Jackson does not make many mistakes, yet even he has mental lapses. The fact that even superstars make mistakes raises a whole series of questions that are critical to athletes, coaches, and sport psychologists alike. Questions like, can we measure attentional abilities? Do attentional abilities differ from athlete to athlete? Are attentional abilities stable over time and across situations? To what extent can we modify a person's attentional abilities?

In the second game of the world series Jackson was the final out. There were two runners on base and he could have been the hero; instead, he struck out. In a post-game interview, Jackson described his attention as so concentrated on the ball that he felt he could get a piece of any pitch thrown. The count went to three and two and with two outs, the runners were going to be taking off as soon as the pitcher began his delivery. Jackson forgot to "program" that fact, and it was his downfall. His narrow concentration was broken at the wrong time by the runners leaving the base. He was startled, and his attention became focused inward for a brief second. By the time he regained his control, the ball was by him. Had he developed that internal focus moments earlier and reminded himself of the situation, he might not have missed the ball.

A Reggie Jackson does not make many mistakes, yet even he has mental lapses. The fact that even superstars make mistakes raises a whole series of questions that are critical to athletes, coaches, and sport psychologists alike. Questions like, can we measure attentional abilities? Do attentional abilities differ from athlete to athlete? Are attentional abilities stable over time and across situations? To what extent can we modify a person's attentional abilities?

How can an athlete's attentional abilities be measured?

I cannot think of any direct, neurological way to measure the ability to concentrate. A number of psychophysiological techniques appear interesting, but we are a very long way from any usable objective measures. Instead, we must infer good or bad attentional control on the basis of an athlete's performance on those tasks we believe require certain abilities. To estimate these abilities we may observe the behavior ourselves, we may rely on past history, or we may use self-report techniques.

As a coach or consultant, you can observe an athlete consistently hit a baseball when it is pitched under a variety of circumstances, and with the potential for many distractions. On the basis of that performance, you could infer that the individual was capable of developing and maintaining a narrow-external focus of attention. Given enough time, and the knowledge concerning what to look for, it is possible to identify an athlete's attentional strengths and weaknesses on the basis of observations alone. Unfortunately, this approach requires a certain amount of theoretical knowledge, observational skill, and a great amount of time. It also requires that observations be made under a variety of conditions with different levels of stress. In an attempt to speed up this process, we developed the Test of Attentional and Interpersonal Style (TAIS). This is a paper and pencil self-report measure. The average athlete can respond to the 144 test items in about 25 minutes. On the basis of responses to the behaviorally oriented items, inferences are made about attentional strengths and weaknesses.

Those interested in more specific information about the test's validity, reliability, and utility should read Nideffer (1976a; 1976b; 1976c; 1977), DePalma and Nideffer (1977), and Nideffer and Sharpe (1978a; 1978b).

How stable are the attentional characteristics measured by the TAIS?

Unless the ability to control attention is a stable personality characteristic, information about presumed abilities can have little predictive validity. This point can be emphasized by reviewing the problems we have had with earlier psychological measures. Psychologists have identified a large number of interpersonal and personal factors that they have attempted to treat as stable traits. Tests have been developed to measure these traits, but they have lacked the predictive utility we would like. One of the major problems has been that the traits were not stable across situations. For example, honesty and aggressiveness varied tremendously, depending upon the environmental situation. In addition, traits often reflected an athlete's attitudes rather than abilities. We made the mistake of assuming that a salesman needed to be extroverted or a defensive lineman needed to be hostile. In fact, it was possible to function in either of these jobs without scoring high on measures of extroversion or hostility. The hope in developing measures of attentional abilities was that these would prove to be more stable across situations, and that they would be found to be performance relevant. Research on the TAIS would indicate that we may be moving in the right direction. I would emphasize, however, that there is a long way to go. What we have is proving useful in many instances, but it is far from perfect.

1. Test-retest correlations for the TAIS subscales average .83 (2 week), and .78 (one year). Correlations this high provide fairly strong evidence of the stability of test scores and provide some support for the concept of stable attentional traits.

2. Testing large numbers of subjects and comparing various groups of individuals (for example, comparing police to executives or athletes) appears to support the notion that there are individual differences in attentional abilities.

Furthermore, these differences make sense from a theoretical perspective. Thus, police are more capable of developing a broad-external focus of attention than a broad-internal one. In contrast, executives are more capable of developing a broad-internal focus.

What are the implications of individual differences in attentional abilities?

To the extent that the attentional characteristics that we measure are reliable and have good construct and predictive validity, there are a tremendous number of implications for athletics. Potential uses that become immediately obvious include selection and screening of athletes, and the development of training programs. My own bias is that test information should be used to help individuals function more effectively, for counseling and training purposes. The reality is that athletics is big business, and so selection and screening become highly valued activities. I would like to take a moment to highlight some of the cautions that must be taken when tests are used for selection and screening.

How is test information used in selection and screening?

The goal behind a testing program is to use the information gained from the tests to select the best possible person for a particular job or position. To do this, the test must be valid; it should measure characteristics that are related to performance. We know that if we test large enough groups of subjects, we can show that test information is significantly (statistically) related to performance. The problem is that in spite of being statistically significant, the relationship with any test (physical or psychological) is far from perfect; this means we cannot always rank people accurately in terms of ability. We can win with large numbers, but lose out with individual decisions.

When we use test information, or interview data for selection and screening, we must make between-subject comparisons. I must look at subject A's scores and see if they are higher or lower than subject B's. The difficulty in relying on these between-subject comparisons in individual cases is that various cultural and response style characteristics become important and can invalidate the results. For example, one person's need to appear modest, socially desirable, to be seen in the best or worst possible light, will dramatically influence his scores in comparison to another person who may not differ at all in terms of performance ability.

Test information can be used to improve the decisions that must be made in sports. In truth, coaches, managers, and owners will make decisions with or without the test data. It would be a mistake not to use information that could improve decision making abilities. It would also be a mistake to rely too strongly on one type of data, and not take steps to avoid making errors due to response style characteristics, cultural factors, and so on. These types of mistakes can be minimized by consensually validating test findings through interviews, other tests, observations, and the examination of past history.

How is attentional information used
in counseling and training?
As it becomes possible to identify and measure an athlete's attentional abilities, it also becomes possible to design training programs to maximize strengths and/or offset weaknesses. A major difference between this use of test data and selection and screening is that we are much less concerned with the absolute elevation of an individual's scores. We are not comparing athletes to each other, we are comparing them to themselves. The advantage to making these within-subject comparisons is that response style characteristics become far less important. As I mentioned at the start of the paper, you could be a superstar, but you will still make some mistakes. By looking at the relative position of your test scores, it becomes possible to anticipate where these mistakes are most likely to occur. Thus, the assessment can be useful at all levels of ability.

How do you use information on attentional
processes to anticipate strengths?
There are certain abilities associated with each of the four types of attention that I have described. By looking at the relative position of an athlete's scores on those attentional scales, measuring the different types of attention, it is easy to see areas of strength. For example, a coach who scores highest on the broad-internal focus of attention will be better at such things as analyzing situations, developing game plans, or figuring out who to draft. A coach who is high on broad-external focus will be able to read what is happening as the game progresses and able to adjust quickly; he will probably be good at recruiting, because he reads athletes well and is able to tell them what they want to hear. He has the type of attention associated with "street sense." A coach who has the highest attentional score on the scale measuring the ability to narrow will be very thorough. His strength will be his dedication and discipline.

What is the relationship between anxiety and
the ability to control attentional processes?

There is a large body of research that indicates that as anxiety and arousal increase, they interfere with the ability to shift attention from one type of focus to another. This knowledge allows us to use information about a person's attentional abilities to anticipate the problems that will develop under pressure. As pressure increases the ability to shift decreases, because we have a tendency to "play to our strength." In the past that attentional ability we obtained the highest score on has served us well. As pressure increases there is a tendency to rely on it, whether it is appropriate or not. The athlete who has a high score on the scale indicating an internal-analytical type of attention will tend to try and analyze under pressure. Often, the situation they are in requires just the opposite, a quick reaction. The mistake they make involves tuning out the environment.

When the person's greatest ability involves reading and reacting to the environment (broad-external attention), the tendency under pressure is to react without adequate thought or preparation. A coach with this type of attention may, for instance, abandon a game plan too soon, substitute without thinking. Those athletes with a very narrow focus of attention become even more locked in under pressure. They can become rigid, making the same mistakes over and over.

The changes mentioned so far occur before we are ever aware of increasing tension. As pressure increases further, additional changes occur that lead to the behavior which coaches refer to as choking.

With increasing levels of arousal, attention begins to narrow involuntarily. This means that the amount of information an athlete can attend to and organize at any one time decreases. This reduction in processing ability, when the information is still there to be dealt with, results in a feeling of being rushed. The athlete jumps quickly from one thought to another, trying to keep up but instead adding to his feeling of confusion. The next thing that happens is attention becomes more internally focused. This occurs because increasing arousal and worry cause mental and physical changes that demand attention. The person becomes distracted by his own bodily feelings (beating heart, muscle tension, and so on) and his thoughts (why did the runners leave the base, what's the matter with me, I might choke, and so on). As attention is directed internally, the ability to concentrate on the game deteriorates. As Reggie Jackson put it, by the time he regained control the ball was by him. Mistakes that are made then make us even more anxious, and things go from bad to worse; we have choked.

On the occasions just mentioned, the passage of time speeds up. Perceptually, things seem to be happening at a faster than normal speed. Our internal distractions cut frames out of the movie we are watching, giving us that 1920s effect. By gaining control, by relaxing and by knowing a skill well enough that we can perform it reflexively, it becomes possible to alter perception in the opposite direction. We can slow things down and develop those "peak experiences."

Who will choke?

Those people who choke and fall apart under pressure are unable to break the spiral I mentioned earlier. They are distracted and upset by their own thoughts and feelings. To calm down they need some external event or person to help get them out of their head.

I should make an important point here. Given enough pressure, everyone will choke at one time or another. There are those athletes, however, who have a low tolerance for stress and who have difficulty much more often. These people tend to have a narrower focus of attention than others, even in nonstressful situations. In addition, they indicate that they have a tendency to become caught in their thoughts. They cannot shift attention in order to break the internal focus. As a result they become overloaded by their own thoughts and feelings.

Can we predict when the average
person or the superstar is likely to choke?

To predict when the average athlete will become negatively affected by pressure, we must be able to identify those situations that are most likely to be stressful for a given individual.

Interpersonal characteristics or traits as well as attentional ones can provide clues useful for predicting the types of situations that an athlete may find stressful. Some of the characteristics that we have found important include: (1) the athlete's impulse control; (2) the need for control in interpersonal situations; (3) the level of self-esteem; and (4) the level of intellectual expressiveness.

How much change can occur in
a person's attentional ability?

As an individual working with others, the question of how much that individual can change becomes a critical one. As you might guess, there are tremendous individual differences. One of the jobs (if not the most critical one) of a consultant or trainer is to figure out the most cost-effective way to accomplish a desired goal. To do this it is necessary to estimate the athlete's ability to change, the coach's ability to change, and the organization's ability to change. There are some specific procedures for determining how flexible a person and/or organization will be, and test scores can go a long way towards making these judgments.

What can be done for the individual who has little
capacity for increasing self-control over attentional processes?

Notice that I emphasized here those individuals who cannot control attention on their own. The individual who chokes easily is often one of those who cannot regain control over attention without outside help.

For people who lack flexibility in terms of attention, change means finding ways to compensate for their weaknesses. Taking an athlete out of situations in which he does not do well is one way. This is a sensitive point and I would like to discuss it in a bit more detail. Coaches at lower levels of performance, working with younger kids, are much more likely to encounter those individuals who lack attentional flexibility. The reason for this is simple. In the present system, individuals who are not typically flexible don't survive to reach the upper levels of competition. One of the main reasons for the lack of survival is that early on those around the athlete, such as coaches and parents, expect him to be able to exert the self-control that other participants do. Both the athlete and those around him are unwilling to accept limitations and maintain unreasonable expectations. When these expectations cannot be met, the individual drops out, often feeling like a failure and so compounding his problem. By being more selective about what he asks athletes to do, a coach could keep them involved, help develop their strengths, and allow them to feel successful.

An athlete's experience and good coaching can provide another means of externally compensating for an attentional deficit. As an athlete becomes more experienced with a situation, he learns to attend to a smaller number of cues; in effect he becomes more efficient by learning what not to attend to. By helping the athlete with an overly narrow focus of attention to be more efficient, we can get him to compensate for his inability to broaden attention.

Another problem that some athletes have involves learning to be more analytical, to develop that broad-internal focus of attention. It is here that the concept of team building becomes important. A coach or teammate who is reflective can compensate for an athlete by reminding him of what he should do at critical times. Likewise, teammates can be used to get someone who is overly analytical out of his head. Testing can provide the basis for this type of team building. Telling us who should help who, and when.

What things can be done for those athletes
who have the capacity for self-control?

Fortunately, most athletes do have the capacity for change. When stress is not reducing attentional flexibility, and when there is the capacity for developing the desired type of attention, several procedures can be used to help improve concentration. Many times the insight provided by testing is all that is needed to anticipate and prevent problems.

To illustrate this, coaches or consultants might not be aware that they often confuse people with whom they are working by overloading them with information. The coach has a broad-internal focus of attention and forgets that others don't. There is a tendency, particularly when under pressure, for the coach to give too much information to an already overloaded athlete. The awareness of this tendency is often enough to control it, particularly if the coach can tell others to stop him when he gets carried away.

I cannot emphasize enough the importance of taking the time to analyze the attentional demands of athletic situations and to identify the "discriminate cues" (what should be attended to). As this is accomplished, the athlete can mentally rehearse those attentional skills that are so critical to optimal performance. This process is to attention control what physical practice is to skill development.

As pressure and anxiety become more of a destructive factor, special techniques are required to reduce distraction and disturbances in concentration. Because of the relationship between increasing arousal levels and attention control, there are a variety of stress reduction techniques that can be used to improve concentration. The choice of a particular technique should depend on several factors, including the situation, the severity and chronicity of the problem, and the level of confidence and experience of the athlete.

For the vast majority of athletes and problem situations, difficulties are not serious enough to justify extensive training in progressive relaxation, meditation, biofeedback, autogenic training, and so on. Procedures like these can be helpful in reducing chronic stress and maintaining attentional flexibility in an anxious athlete, prior to the start of a contest and during prolonged periods of inactivity. Unfortunately, these techniques are difficult to use during the actual competition. Appropriate application of many of these techniques can best be illustrated through actual

Lasse Viren

The experienced, world-class distance runners use associative strategies to cope with pain from running. They are open to the painful cues and objectively read them and react to them. In "associating" to the pain in an objective, rational way, they are "dissociating" from it emotionally. They are observing themselves as though they were specimens under a microscope. The emotional distance gives them an advantage, because they can learn from their bodies. In a very rational way they can test themselves to see what happens—"can I go faster?" for instance.

case examples. Unfortunately, space prevents that here. I would rather refer you to *The Inner Athlete* (Nideffer, 1976a), and *How to Put Anxiety Behind You* (Nideffer and Sharpe, 1978b).

Independent of the specific technique used to reduce stress, the goal of treatment is to reinstate attentional and physiological control through a redirection of attention and a reduction in arousal. As attention becomes more focused on nonstressful cues, the body relaxes and disturbances are reduced. As this occurs, the athlete can voluntarily redirect his attention to task relevant cues. It is at this point that rehearsal procedures can be used with some athletes to get them to modify their negative attitudes or to help them prepare for an anticipated event, to remind them of what they should attend to during competition.

I would like to make a point about different individuals' abilities to use positive imagery and mental rehearsal procedures. Some of the recent reports on "associative and dissociative" strategies in distance running relate to this.

Who can use associative and dissociative strategies?

Recent articles have supported the notion that experienced, world class distance runners use associative strategies to cope with pain from running. In contrast, less experienced runners tend to dissociate to the pain. They use little tricks to distract themselves, such as attempting to focus on a tune, or an object.

What I would suggest here is that both runners are dissociating to the pain of running. The difference is that the experienced runners' confidence and past successes allow them to be open to the painful cues and to objectively read and react to them. In "associating" to the pain in an objective, rational way, they are "dissociating" from it emotionally. They are observing themselves as though they were specimens under a microscope. The emotional distance gives them an advantage, because they can learn from their bodies. In a very rational way they can test themselves to see what happens—"can I go faster?" for instance. Less experienced runners cannot attend to the physical cues and maintain the same emotional distance. They lack the experience to know that they can survive. When these runners attend to the cues, they become frightened, and as a result their performance becomes impaired.

In working with athletes, one goal would be to teach them to be able to use associative cues, to read and react to their own feelings. In doing this however, it is imperative that we be sensitive to the limits that experience (or lack of it) places upon an individual's ability to comply. For the beginner, associative strategies are best attempted in practice.

Are there techniques that can be used to control attention and stress during an event?

As I mentioned, for most athletes traditional stress reduction techniques are not required. These people function very well the vast majority of the time. What they need more than anything else is increased sensitivity to their bodies and the ability to take the top off of their anxiety and arousal in a few key situations.

The goal is not to rid them of anxiety; some anxiety is a useful motivator and we never get rid of it all anyway. Instead the idea is to remove only a small portion, just enough to keep them from starting that downward spiral associated with choking.

Research on the physiological changes associated with simple breathing exercises indicates that normal individuals can learn to lower their arousal levels within the space of one to three breaths. This means that in a very short period of time athletes can learn to regain attentional control in key situations. At the University of Rochester we found that within four 45-minute sessions we could usually identify the type of attention an individual needed for a particular task. We could help them identify the discriminative cues within that situation. That is, we could show them what they needed to attend to in order to be successful. Finally, we could give them enough control over their own physiology so that they could attend in the desired way.

CONCLUSION

I believe that we are on the threshold of identifying and refining abilities in ways which will allow athletes to function near the top of their potential. I don't believe that many of us have any idea of what that potential is. Efforts made thus far are only small steps, but I would like to believe that they are pointing us in the right direction. We have a lot to learn and the future looks exciting. I hope that I have been able to communicate some of my excitement to you.

how to elicit supernormal capabilities in athletes

James L. Hickman

The Esalen Sports Center was established in 1972 within Esalen Institute. Its primary purpose is the development of new approaches to physical education, health, sports, and recreation, and the application of these approaches to schools, industry, professional and amateur athletics, medicine, and other fields. We have worked to accomplish these objectives through workshops, conferences, research programs, and long-term internships. Emphasis is placed on the integration of body, mind, emotion, and spirit in athletic activity to cultivate a positive state of health and an increase in overall performance capacity through competitive and non-competitive sports.

PSYCHIC SIDE OF SPORTS

A related research effort within Esalen Institute began in 1976. Named The Transformation Project, it is a systematic study of supernormal human functioning and the mental and physical strategies that accompany it. One area of investigation is extraordinary psychic events which occur in sport; events such as moments of illumination, out-of-body experiences, altered perceptions of time and space, exceptional feats of strength and endurance, states of ecstasy. Over the past six years, Michael Murphy, co-founder of Esalen Institute, and Rhea White, America's foremost archivist of parapsychology, have collected more than 4500 reports of such events. Their analysis of this research is presented in *The Psychic Side of Sports* (Murphy and White, 1978), and it lends insight into the subjective side of peak performance.

In hundreds of reports from athletes, we have found that the sport experience produces transcendent feelings similar to those described by artists, lovers, and mystics. Athletes report feelings of great calm and stillness, of control that results in total freedom, of weightlessness, and of total immersion in the present moment,

Athletes report feelings of great calm and stillness, of control that results in total freedom, of weightlessness, and of total immersion in the present moment, and these feelings occurred during times of great athletic achievement.

and these feelings occurred during times of great athletic achievement. Murphy and White also document that altered perceptions of space and time are common in sport and that the range of these altered perceptions resembles that reported in the literature of yoga and mysticism. Some athletes report instances of out-of-body experiences in the course of athletic endeavor.

There are numerous examples of outstanding performances by sportspeople, and Murphy and White suggest that athletes can sometimes "tap levels of ability that go far beyond what we have come to expect as the normal range of human accomplishment" (p. 77). Western athletes frequently experience spontaneous bursts of energy which contribute to exceptional performances. The eastern martial arts, however, teach techniques to develop reserves of energy—called *ki* in Japan, *chi* in China, and *prana* in India—unavailable to the ordinary person, by practicing methods of concentration, breath control, and mind-body unification. The energy produced is " . . . far more encompassing and comprehensive . . . than the common type of energy" (p. 79). Through mental and physical conditioning feats of extraordinary strength, speed, and endurance are possible.

The exceptional capacities to expand sensitivities, to perceive alternate realities, and to tap unusual reservoirs of energy often contribute to superior sport performance. By examining the environmental conditions, physiological and personality character-istics, and mental frameworks which accompany such experiences and then comparing them to supernormal capacities which arise throughout human life, we are beginning to isolate the factors that facilitate these abilities and to develop training routines that incorporate them. I will now turn to how we can gain access to these abilities and utilize them consciously in our training regimens.

A PSYCHOPHYSICAL TRAINING PROGRAM

In addition to sport, we are exploring other realms of human experience in which supernormal capacities appear. For example, the lives of contemplatives suggest that similar mystical or psychic experiences often accompany extended meditation practice (Thurston, 1952). Hypnosis research clearly demonstrates that through suggestion many people can win significant freedom from pain and disease (Schneck, 1966), change the structure of their bodies (Johnson and Barber, 1976), and increase certain skills and capacities (Weitzenhoffer, 1963). Research on the placebo effect shows that people can deliberately lower the amount of fat and protein in their blood, change their white cell count, relieve certain arthritic symptoms, and eliminate withdrawal effects from morphine; this ability shows how specific and effective human self-regenerative powers can be (Cousins, 1977). Biofeedback investigations suggest that any aspect of a person's chemistry or physiology that can be brought to awareness directly or through instruments can become accessible to conscious control (Green and Green, 1977). Visualization and meditation therapies have become increasingly successful in treating life-threatening diseases such as cancer (Simonton *et al.,* 1978). This kind of research dramatizes the fact that certain mental strategies exert tremendous influence on the human body. At the Esalen Sports Center, we are exploring the degree to which the mind can participate in the body's functions. We believe that the capacities which might emerge from a sophisticated mind-body synthesis would bring a new dimension to sport and contribute to a general revision of human possibilities.

Psychical Self-Regulation

Elements of the psychophysical approach to sport training have been applied for some time. Coaches and athletes all over the world are already using methods from yoga, the martial arts, hypnosis, meditation, and other disciplines to enrich their training programs. Some of these methods are described in this book. One of the most sophisticated programs exploring the application of these techniques has been developed in the USSR. During the 1960s a field of applied psychology called psychical self-regulation (PSR) was developed to explore the human capacity to regulate mentally physiological functioning. The Soviet researchers combined techniques from meditation, yoga, hypnosis, autogenic training, and the martial arts to form a PSR training system. Then, through extensive laboratory research, they learned that most people, without physiological feedback, could quickly learn to control their heart rates, blood circulation, pain threshold, and muscle tension through a combination of internal processes (Romen *et al.,* 1974). PSR techniques have been used with athletes for quick recovery from strenuous competitions, to provide brief rests during competition, to prevent psychosomatic problems during training, to train for specific movements, to increase speed of perception and reaction time, to increase strength and flexibility, and to overcome a variety of psychological problems. Most coaches and sport psychologists in the USSR are familiar with basic PSR exercises and all national teams include at least one psychologist who is thoroughly trained in PSR strategies (Lewis, 1976).

The purpose of PSR training is to develop a person's natural ability to influence their own physiological functions by purposefully directed mental processes. Soviet researchers maintain that this mental self-influence occurs through normal physiological pathways, such as the central nervous system, and at the micromolecular level, down to the most fundamental structures within living organisms (Lewis, 1977). Their studies indicate that all people exert some degree of mental influence on their own physiology, usually in an unconscious manner. Through a systematic training program, individuals learn to participate more consciously in this psychophysical process and to use this ability in many aspects of life. The initial training period varies from ten days to five weeks depending on each individual's progress. Participants learn the following basic exercises during this period: the practice of observing thoughts; achievement of muscular relaxation; mastery of breathing rhythms; cultivation of warmth and coolness

Udo Beyer of East Germany concentrates before his most successful shotput in his life. It earned him the gold medal at the Montreal Olympics.

in separate body parts; mastery of heart rhythms; the simultaneous achievement of temperature differentials in different body parts. Three primary elements comprise the exercises: an informational component which includes detailed explanations of the physiological responses to the exercises; a verbal formula or short phrase which affects bodily functions when repeated silently; a visualization technique which heightens kinesthetic contact with the assigned body part. For example, the initial exercise for achieving warmth in the right arm might go as follows: a description of the physiological processes involved; the silent repetition of the phrase, "my right arm is warm;"and the visualization of the right arm immersed in hot water. Regular practice of this and similar exercises develops the ability for psychophysiological control. With athletes, PSR exercises are then developed for specific application to individual sports. The Soviet research in this area has had a substantial influence on our training routines at the Esalen Sports Center.

Over the past few years we have experimented with various combinations of mental exercises and long-distance running. Specific routines have evolved to enrich our training programs and to assist the psychophysical development of other athletes. Mike Spino, the Sports Center's director, has developed effective mind-body training techniques for athletes at all levels of fitness and is teaching these techniques through his books and seminars (Spino, 1977). Through these research efforts we have formulated a preliminary approach to overall conditioning which will assist the development of athletic prowess and character. I will describe this approach by explaining the elements of the discipline and presenting specific exercises to enhance mind-body communication.

Meditation

Success in sport depends largely upon the steadiness and clarity of a participant's concentration. The nature of sport develops a certain capacity for concentration in a player, but additional meditation practice will refine the skill. Occasionally, a sportsperson will enter a deep state of concentration during a game, a state that some athletes call a "playing trance." The descriptions of such an experience are remarkably similar to advanced meditative states in which contemplatives win access to profound reservoirs of strength, peace, and joy. Since this "trance" state often accompanies superior performance, a meditation practice could facilitate such experience and help sustain it. Well-known athletes like Bill Walton, Joe Namath, and Billie Jean King have endorsed meditation as a valuable tool in their training. Regular meditation can improve both performance and enjoyment in sport, I believe, because it sustains contact with a more effective level of personal functioning.

Methods of meditation can be very simple. Certain Buddhist sitting practices involve the simple observation of breath or the contents of consciousness. In Buddhist walking meditation attention is focused on the sensations that arise from movement. Other practices stress concentration on a single point, either on an internal light or sound, or on an external point. Such methods stimulate the emergence of a deeper consciousness which brings forth more unified and harmonious action.

Patience and regularity are the most important elements of meditation practice. The insight and depth of meditation are maintained and amplified by practicing at regular intervals. Choose the specific method most appropriate for yourself and sit for 15 or

20 minutes twice a day. Lengthen the sessions when you feel comfortable doing so.

In our training we practice carrying the stillness of sitting meditation into the experience of walking and running. An example of a guided introduction to this practice follows:

> With everyone seated in a circle of chairs, let us begin by closing our eyes and allowing the thoughts that present themselves to flow through our minds. As each thought arises, observe it and let it go. Be the witness rather than the possessor of your thoughts. Each time you get caught in a chain of thoughts, acknowledge it and return to the witness position. Develop your capacity to observe. . . . As each thought arises, observe it and let it go. . . . Observe whatever thoughts may arise and allow them to flow through your mind. . . . The task is merely to quiet the mind and observe.
>
> (Fifteen minutes later) When it feels comfortable, slowly open your eyes and, without losing this state of consciousness, rise and stand behind your chair, facing to the left. Make a fist with your left hand, place it over your navel and cup your right palm over your fist.
>
> We will begin to carry the meditation into action with a slow walk around the circle. The goal is simply to move and witness. Place the left foot forward, making ground contact with the heel and slowly rock forward to the toes. . . . Hold. . . . Allow the right leg to slowly swing forward, making contact with the heel and slowly bringing the sole of the foot to the ground. Continue this motion around the circle, maintaining a state of observation within yourself. When you return to your chair, stop and face the center of the circle.
>
> (Five minutes later) Now allow your eyes to focus softly on the space directly in front of them. Observe your thoughts with eyes open in a soft focus. As each thought arises, observe it and allow it to disappear. Deepen your contact with your "witness" through "soft eyes." . . . Let us carry this experience with us for a short run. We will stay together as a group, the running tempo emerging as the most comfortable pace for the slowest runner among us. Let us maintain the sense of unity and witness which has developed during the meditation. (Hickman *et al.,* 1977, pp. 53-54.)

Visualization and Mental Rehearsal

Imagination is probably the most widely applied mental tool in modern sports. Extensive research has shown that appropriate visual images can affect physiological processes and improve motor skills. Studies by the American physiologist, Dr Edmund Jacobson (1942), show that when a person imagines running, small contractions can be measured in the muscles associated with running.

Other studies show that mentally rehearsing such tasks as basketball shooting, dart throwing, and ring tossing can improve scoring. And when this imagery is combined with physical training, performance exceeds that attained when either method is used alone. Related research is described in other chapters of this book.

Many top athletes have naturally incorporated visualization processes into their training routines. Fran Tarkenton, statistically the all-time leading passer in the National Football League, visualizes most aspects of an upcoming game. He studies each defensive opponent in his mind, mentally analyzes defensive weaknesses, rehearses his response to specific defensive calls, "trying to visualize every game situation, every defense they're going to throw at me" (Asinof, 1968). Bruce Jenner, while training for his 1976 Olympic decathlon victory, used visual imagery to rehearse every event. He kept a hurdle in his living room and mentally trained his hurdling form each evening after dinner. His inner training became so intense that he continued this mental conditioning during sleep. His wife Christie could identify which event he was practicing by observing his body movements while he was dreaming (Jenner and Finch, 1977). In his book, *Golf My Way*, Jack Nicklaus (1974, p. 79) says that his good shots are 10 per cent swing, 40 per cent setup and stance, and 50 per cent mental picture. He describes this visualization process:

> I never hit a shot, not even in practice, without having a very sharp, in-focus picture of it in my head. It's like a color movie. First I "see" the ball where I want it to finish, nice and white and sitting up high on the bright green grass. Then the scene quickly changes and I "see" the ball going there: its path, trajectory, and shape, even its behavior on landing. Then there is sort of a fade-out and the next scene shows me making the kind of swing that will turn the previous images into reality.

People who have difficulty creating an internal visual image can develop this capacity fairly quickly with a few minutes of daily practice. An effective training method could follow this sequence:

1. choose a time and place in which you will be undisturbed for 15 minutes and assume a comfortable posture;
2. close your eyes, breathe deeply into the chest and abdomen, and relax completely for two or three minutes;
3. create a blank white screen in your mind, focusing on it very clearly;
4. imagine a circle which fills the screen and slowly make the circle blue;
5. develop as rich and deep a blue as possible, then slowly

change to another color, repeating this process through four or five colors;

6. allow the images to disappear, relax, and observe the spontaneous imagery which arises;

7. on your blank screen, create the image of a glass (a simple object), develop it clearly in three dimensions, fill it with a colorful liquid (like coffee or kool-aid), add some ice cubes, insert a straw, and write a descriptive caption underneath;

8. allow the image to fade and repeat the process with other objects (choose items associated with your sport);

9. relax and observe the spontaneous imagery which arises;

10. select a variety of scenes and develop richly detailed images of them (practice with sport related environments such as a swimming pool, a track, etc.);

11. relax and observe;

12. practice visualizing people, including strangers, close friends, and yourself;

13. to end each session, breathe deeply three times, slowly open your eyes, and adjust to the external environment.

At this stage, it is important to begin each session with a relaxation process, to keep the sessions short and interesting, and to progress from the simpler to the more complex exercises at a comfortable pace. Whenever possible, include additional sensory stimulation such as smell and taste to your imagery experiences.

Applying visualization to sport is simple: just develop a very clear picture of yourself performing optimally and then imagine how that feels. When the experience is real for you, take the image and feeling into physical practice. A word of caution: do not hold too tightly to the image you have created. Sometimes the mind-body will make unconscious adjustments in your created image to correct a flaw in your consciously imagined form. With practice, you learn when to yield to this deeper self which integrates your mental preparation, your physical training, and your intuition. The following exercise combines spontaneous and created visual imagery to assist running form. After a short relaxation process, this idea is suggested:

Within your being exists a place of stillness, an eternal quiet. With each breath you take, your awareness of this center grows. Each inhalation deepens the contact and each exhalation steadies the witness. A sense of peace pervades this stillness. . . . Your personal sense of perfect form and beauty resides here. . . . Feel the stillness and the peace. . . . From this place create a grassy meadow in your mind. The sun is shining, the air is clean and fragrant. In the distance you see a human form beginning to emerge. This

> form emanates from that stillness where you dwell. It is the moving aspect of your "perfect being." The form is your "perfect runner" which carries "perfect knowledge" of yourself. Your "perfect runner" is your true guide to running excellence. . . . He or she is coming into greater definition now, running across the meadow with effortless strides of joy. . . . Observe the running form and surrender to its lead. . . . As the runner continues through your mind, picture yourself alongside, running stride for stride. . . . Effortlessly the two of you continue. . . . Now, with this image clearly in your mind, slowly rise and begin to walk around the field. Run *only* while you see the image clearly. Allow this messenger from your center to lead you to your natural running style. (Hickman *et al.,* 1977, p. 56.)

This kind of process can be adapted to many other sports.

Inner seeing. Through our studies of extraordinary human performance, we have identified a type of spontaneous visual imagery which goes beyond imagination or visualization. This mental ability, which we call "inner seeing," involves a *direct perception* of bodily structures or processes that are usually invisible to us. For example:

> A woman reported to us that during an acute psychotic episode she hallucinated her internal organs on the outside of her body, as if she "were turned inside out." After her psychosis had passed she was convinced that in some way she had directly perceived her body's insides. We have since discovered that many schizophrenic patients have similar experiences. . . . Many people say that they have seen internal body structures during the course of gestalt therapy, encounter groups or in other psychotherapeutic contexts. Such glimpses often come during exercises in which they are imagining what the inside of their bodies looks like. (Murphy and White, 1978, pp. 162-163.)

Various athletes have described similar experiences which occur spontaneously during sporting events. Some distance runners, for example, have told us that they occasionally catch glimpses of their own organs, muscles, and blood vessels. A few of these people believe they have even "seen" their cells. In one instance, a runner had lain down to recover after a hard workout when he was flooded with images of bursting capillaries. "In his mind's eye he suddenly saw red cells spurting from broken vessels with startling rapidity . . . [followed by] a sensation of healing in his chest and a pervasive sense of well-being" (Murphy and White, p. 162). In a dream a few nights later, identical imagery appeared to him; he now believes that such experiences indicate a deepening of one's rapport with physiological processes, in this case, the breakdown and buildup cycle in his training. Often, when we describe the "inner seeing" process during our public presentations, about one-fourth of the audience claims to have experienced it.

Although a consistency is evident in these anecdotes, we have no certain proof that such perceptions are of actual body structures. So what role can these experiences play in training programs? Since our understanding of this process is limited, we believe that it is best not to strain for it. Be aware of the possibility and, when it comes, let it happen. See what message the experience brings and where it wants to take you.

Sensory and Kinesthetic Awareness

In most modern cultures humans begin early in life to lose contact with various parts of their bodies in response to survival needs. Social and environmental pressures selectively stimulate or inhibit the development of certain physical and mental capabilities. Unconscious muscle tension patterns form as the body grows, impairing breathing, sensing, movement, and structural alignment. As body awareness diminishes, physical action becomes unconscious, introducing patterns of diminution and rigidity in the body's movement repertoire. Such unconscious functioning distorts the kinesthetic sense, reinforces muscular tension, and requires excessive force and energy for all physical activity (Masters and Houston, 1978).

A simple test of your kinesthetic sensitivity is to close your eyes and create an image of your whole body. Observe closely all the body parts and note which areas are incomplete. This internally perceived "body image" regulates to a large extent the ways we use our body. Recent research suggests that the "body image" may reflect subtle sensory connections between the brain and other body parts. The degree of clarity of the "body image" is one indicator of overall body awareness.

Athletics often contribute to unbalanced development, a further inhibition to proper bodily functioning. In almost every sport certain body parts are used and strengthened more than others, resulting in deformities of the physical structure and imbalances throughout the physiological system. Bertherat and Bernstein (1977), for example, point out that in a typical swimmer's physique the imbalance between overdevelopment of the back and underdevelopment of the front of the body often results in skeleton contraction and displacement. They attribute the digestive problems which are common among professional cyclists to the constant stomach compression and loss of tonicity in the abdominal muscles resulting from the demands of their racing form. "Practically without exception, athletes deform their bodies, sometimes monstrously, because they have only partial awareness of them" (p. 59).

A systematic program to expand bodily awareness will help remove accumulated muscular tensions, activate undeveloped and underdeveloped muscles, improve coordination, and sharpen reflexes. Choosing an appropriate system, however, is not a simple task. There is a vast literature describing various methods of sensory and kinesthetic training (Liepmann, 1973; Brooks, 1974; Masters and Houston, 1978). Growth centres such as Esalen Institute* offer a variety of workshops to explore these techniques, but a thorough exposure to all the approaches involves a substantial time commitment. Furthermore, it is difficult to describe such processes because they depend much more on the insights and talents of their practitioners than they do on automatically repeatable formulas.

As a supplement to most athletic training regimens, I recommend two systems which are available on audio tapes: the functional integration exercises of Moshe Feldenkreis** and the psychophysical re-education techniques of Masters and Houston.*** Both of these approaches have been refined through many years of research. They emphasize the release of structural and emotional blocks to efficient movement, the neural reprogramming of effective body awareness and function, and the use of kinesthetic awareness in this re-education process. Numerous sportspeople have found these systems to be valuable in enhancing their skills and expanding their range of athletic prowess.

Verbal Formulas

Human history is rich with stories that describe the use of words to alter deliberately the condition of one's own body or to influence the body of another person. Prayer, magical evocation,

---

* Esalen Institute catalog available from: Esalen Institute, Big Sur, California 93920.

** *Awareness Through Movement: The Feldenkreis Method:* 6 cassettes and 12 lesson experiences available from workshop cassettes, c/o Hot Springs Lodge, Big Sur, California 93920.

*** Masters and Houston tape catalog available from: Educational Frontiers Associates, 226 Remsen Avenue, Avenel, New Jersey 07001.

chants, and a multitude of healing rituals are examples of this usage. Language can communicate wishes to the brain and, since the brain controls the body, appropriately structured language can effect dramatic bodily changes. Recent brain research has demonstrated that, in most people, the right hemisphere is better at visual than verbal tasks and the left hemisphere is more verbal than visual (Ornstein, 1975). Therefore, to utilize the brain's capacity most effectively an integrated psychophysical training program must employ visual *and* verbal instructive techniques. This section will describe two methods of establishing verbal control over bodily responses.

The first system uses carefully constructed phrases to elicit predetermined physical changes. These mental exercises, called the Standard Formulae of Autogenic Training, are designed to "support those brain-directed self-regulatory (autogenic) mechanisms which normally participate in homeostatic, recuperative and self-normalizing processes" (Schultz and Luthe, 1969, p. 1). The system developed from extensive study of the physiological correlates to deep relaxation states, such as hypnosis, sleep, and yoga. Initial training involves the silent repetition of verbal formulas oriented towards six aspects of physiology: heaviness in the extremities, warmth in the extremities, regulation of cardiac activity, regulation of breathing, abdominal warmth, and cooling of the forehead. Two examples of the six standard phrases are, "my arms are very heavy" and "my arms are very warm." Concentration on these stimuli relieves internal stress and normalizes the body's metabolism. Eventually the body is trained to respond to almost any verbal suggestion. Other sensations are sometimes combined with the verbal commands to achieve particular bodily, emotional, or mental changes, but the primary emphasis is placed on the proper formulation of *verbal* instructions for psychophysical control.

The second system, the Alexander technique, was created by F. Matthias Alexander (1969) as a means to develop and maintain a reliable "sensory appreciation" throughout the human body. He believed that this sensitivity could be brought about by reliance on the individual's conscious guidance and control. According to Alexander, all persons develop defects in the use of their bodies as a result of life's stresses. These imperfections, which are reflected in their kinesthetic awareness, cause breakdowns in psychophysical functioning. Not until new correct experiences in "sensory appreciation" are established can the whole body function effectively. By a careful analysis of the factors which contribute to effective use of the body, Alexander discovered instructive techniques which enabled him to teach other people how to function more efficiently.

> The "pure" Alexander technique employs only explicit verbal instruction, carefully and repeatedly linked to particular sensations through the joint efforts of student and instructor. . . . A teacher, working with his (or her) hands, provides the sensations and organization of the body while the student translates the sensations he is experiencing into verbal commands. For example, the teacher might place his hands on the student's neck and raise him from a sitting position to a standing position, releasing and lengthening the neck while also positioning the head. The student articulates the accompanying sensations as "neck releasing and lengthening, head forward and up," or something of the sort. In time the neck and head will respond to the verbal commands alone. This allows the student to work on himself, until the "good use" becomes habitual. (Masters and Houston, 1978, p. 58.)

Autogenic training utilizes *standardized* phrases to release accumulated stress and to strengthen neural mechanisms which maintain the body's homeostasis. In the Alexander technique verbal commands are *particular to each individual* and reflect his immediate experience of the bodily sensations which accompany optimal psychophysical performance. Both systems are useful in athletic training. For example, I use autogenic phrases to assist my recovery from a workout: the phrases for regulation of cardiac activity and respiration, "my heart beats calmly and regularly" and "my breathing is calm and regular," reinforce the normalization of those processes. To prevent neck and shoulder tension during the Hawaiian marathon, I repeated an appropriate phrase for my optimal running form, as in the Alexander technique, at 15-minute intervals. The pain which was always present after 15 miles in my training runs did not develop through the entire race. Appropriate language is a powerful influence on physiological functioning.

Biofeedback

A variety of mental exercises have been combined with biofeedback training to teach a person selective control of heart rate, muscle tension, lymph flow, blood flow, blood pressure, gastrointestinal functions, air flow in bronchial tubes, and electrical characteristics of the skin and brain (Green and Green, 1977). In this procedure an instrument attached to a person's body generates auditory or visual signals (feedback) which reflect one or

There are numerous examples of outstanding performances by sportspeople, and Murphy and White (1978) suggest that athletes can sometimes "tap levels of ability that go far beyond what we have come to expect as the normal range of human accomplishment." Western athletes frequently experience spontaneous bursts of energy which contribute to exceptional performances. Through mental and physical conditioning feats of extraordinary strength, speed, and endurance are possible.

more of the person's physiological processes. As these processes change, corresponding fluctuations in the feedback are observed by the person. He gradually learns to associate various images, feelings, thoughts, and other factors with feedback changes and, by developing appropriate mental strategies to regulate the signals, gains control of the associated physiological process. With biofeedback some people have gained voluntary control of single nerve fibres (Basmajian, 1962).

Biofeedback can be very useful in athletic training. Learning to regulate pulse, blood pressure, level of arousal, muscular tension, or a variety of biochemical indices would contribute to any athlete's performance capability. The success with which biofeedback has been applied to the treatment of such health disorders as Raynaud's disease, Parkinson's disease, hypertension, neuromuscular problems, epilepsy, and cerebral palsy (Green and Green, 1977) illustrates its power to restructure human physiology. In my opinion, if creatively applied to high level fitness training, biofeedback techniques could facilitate optimal performance.

The Energy Body

There is an extensive tradition in both the east and west describing various energetic aspects of the human body. Some of these components are well defined. For instance, instruments can measure electrostatic, magnetic, thermal, and other radiant fields which surround the physical body and reflect its physiological state (Brenner *et al.,* 1978; Krippner and Rubin, 1975). However these are only a few rudimentary features of the "energy body," an as yet unquantifiable source of energy that is, in a sense, both separate from and intimately connected with our physical frame. Occasional glimpses of this energy have arisen spontaneously during athletic contests. David Meggyesey, former linebacker for the St Louis Cardinals, was hit on his head during a practice game against the Minnesota Vikings. Seated on the bench he felt: " 'an eerie calm and beauty' . . . [and] began to see 'auras around some of the players.' . . . In another game he found himself playing in 'a kind of trance where I could sense the movements of the running backs a split second before they happened'." (Murphy and White, 1978, p. 137.) Denise McCluggage (1977, pp. 20-21), while watching a basketball game, saw: "Bright cords of varying width connected the Golden State Warriors at their middle. The lines all emanated from Rick Barry . . . Rick was glowingly, obviously, the hub of the team that night. The changing thicknesses of the cords extending from him indicated where his next pass was going, even when he was looking in another direction. The ball followed a remarkably predictable path down shining corridors of energy."

Students of the martial arts sometimes develop a keen sensitivity to this *ki,* or subtle energy, and use it to accomplish exceptional physical feats. Training your awareness in this manner can provide an energy source that increases overall competence in sport.

In California Robert Nadeau and George Leonard (1975), two black-belt Aikido instructors, have developed unique energy awareness exercises to assist non-Aikido students in cultivating their *ki.* Most important for this kind of mastery is acceptance of the energy body's existence and permission to sense forms of energy not generally experienced in ordinary life. Over 25,000 people have attended energy awareness workshops that Leonard has conducted throughout the world during the last five years.

After two or three days of practice, participants are "frequently able to sense the location of other people in the room with their eyes closed, create an 'energy flow' by which they can resist force with considerable ease, transmute pain and shock into positive feelings of being energized, resist being lifted or become effectively lighter at will" (Murphy and White, 1978, p. 168).

Basic exercises for sensing and directing this subtle energy are described in Leonard's book *The Silent Pulse* (1978). The following practice is included here to offer the reader a simple technique for experiencing the power and strength contained in this energetic system:

> First have someone try to bend your extended arm at the elbow.
>
> Then stretch and shake your hand with wrist limp. Breathe deeply, allowing the abdomen to swell. Relax. Now stand with your right foot slightly in front of the left, weight evenly distributed on both feet, knees neither locked or bent. Let your right arm rise to a horizontal position in front of you, hand open, thumb up. Elbows should not be locked.
>
> Now imagine your arm is part of a beam of pure, smooth, unbendable energy. Your arm is in the center of this beam which extends a few inches all around it. With eyes soft (that is, not sharply focused on any specific object), imagine the beam of which your arm is a part extending through any object in front of you—the wall or whatever—across the horizon to the ends of the universe. Your arm is part of the beam. The beam is like a laser. It cannot be bent but it takes no effort on your part ot keep it from being bent. All you have to do is concentrate on its extension.
>
> Now have the same person try to bend your arm at the elbow, using the same amount of force as he used before. Have him use more force. Note the difference. (Murphy and White, 1978, p. 168.)

COMBINING THE ELEMENTS

Most of the systems described in the previous sections combine various psychophysical techniques in their training procedures. I have separated them to illustrate the essential elements of a mind-body conditioning program; there is considerable overlap among the categories. For example, effective mental rehearsal requires some degree of kinesthetic awareness; advanced autogenic training uses imagery with verbal formulas; and successful biofeedback strategies often employ verbal, visual, and kinesthetic modalities simultaneously. Athletic training regimens should integrate the elements I have described, using various combinations to achieve optimal results. Of course the most important aspect of conditioning is rigorous physical practice, but I believe that appropriate utilization of mental skills will enhance the sporting enterprise for all participants.

In the following paragraphs I outline a fitness program for overall psychophysical conditioning. It emphasizes running to develop cardiopulmonary and muscular endurance, stretching to increase flexibility and skeletal suppleness, and inner sensing to support physiological change. The techniques can be applied to any sport.

A running program should begin by creating a strong foundation of aerobic fitness. There are several good books that present effective approaches to this development (Cooper, 1977; Fixx, 1977). As fitness improves, the running experience will be enhanced by introducing various gaits and tempos, by exploring a variety of breathing patterns, by using specific styles of body movement, and by training anaerobic and speed development. Utilize mental skills to support these physical capacities. During a run imagine a stream flowing along with you, the momentum carrying you easily forward; or, imagine and feel a giant hand against your back pressing and lifting you along (this is especially helpful during interval and fartlek workouts). It is important to work with deliberate imagery that sustains your bodily awareness—*but pay close attention as well to all other internal sensations.* In a recent study of distance runners the non-world-class marathoners (men slower than 2:30) reported using dissociative mental strategies to distract their attention from painful sensations during hard runs. During a treadmill test they were unable to determine accurately their level of fatigue from internal cues. In contrast, champion marathoners were highly skilled at reading their body's fatigue level and reported the necessity for constant monitoring of physiological signals throughout a race in order to maximize performance. ''Rather than distract themselves, the best runners learn to listen'' (Moore, 1976, p. 90). If a pain develops, breathe into that part of the body and imagine a soothing, relaxing light flooding the area and relieving the stress. Combine the imagery with an appropriate phrase such as ''my knees are strong and relaxed.'' Be sensitive to your body's messages by observing your spontaneous imagery and inner voices. Learn from the sensations.

Bertherat and Bernstein (1977), Shelton (1971), and others have detailed the unbalanced development that often results from athletics. Running, for example, may stiffen muscles and contract them. Increasing flexibility throughout the body can prevent such imbalances. Stretching muscles lengthens them, counteracting the constrictions from running, and it helps prevent stress fractures, ligament problems, and other physiological breakdowns. Flexibility exercises can provide insurance against injury, if they are done right. One 15-minute session each day and a brief stretching routine before and after every workout is sufficient. Consistency will provide long-term benefits.

Specific techniques should be designed to meet individual needs. Feldenkreis exercises, the Alexander technique, and yoga asanas are especially helpful in breaking fixed patterns of movement to increase the range of physical flexibility. During stretching sessions stay aware of the sensations in each body part. Familiarize yourself with the structures being worked, picture them clearly in your mind and imagine the tension releasing while you repeat an appropriate phrase such as "my ankles are strong and flexible." Combine creative visualizations with free form stretches to enhance mind-body development.

Learning to influence your physiology mentally is an important missing ingredient in most western training systems. Everyone has some capacity to do this. Daily practice of such exercises as the basic autogenic training sequences will make this skill more accessible. The mastery of six tasks is fundamental to voluntary self-regulation. They are: achievement of self-suggested calm and muscular relaxation; control of breathing; control of heart rate; achievement of warmth in separate body parts; achievement of coolness in separate body parts; and achievement of temperature differentials in separate body parts simultaneously. Each session should begin with participants quietly observing their thoughts for five or ten minutes. At the end of every session the trainees should suggest to themselves greater achievement of their tasks next time. After sufficient training in these fundamental self-regulatory skills, athletes can begin to cause more specific physical changes. The East Germans, for instance, refer to one of their recovery exercises as "cellular rejuvenation," an experience apparently designed to stimulate their mental influence on cellular metabolism.

Mental techniques are especially effective during the recovery cycle of physical conditioning. Visualizations such as an energizing shower or a cool rubdown should always follow a training period or a competition. An example of one recovery routine is to "observe" oxygen molecules flowing into the lungs; "see" the oxygen absorbed into the millions of tiny alveoli within the lungs; "watch" the oxygen and carbon dioxide exchange between red blood cells and air sacs; follow the oxygenated cells' path through the heart and other tissue; imagine an increase in the ease with which your cellular recovery processes progress; and self-suggest the body's swift return to homeostasis. Develop individual processes which utilize similar combinations of inner sensing, deliberate and supportive imaging, and verbal suggestion.

CONCLUSION

Sport dramatizes the human ability to surpass physical limits in a way that is unique in human experience. Records are constantly broken. The supposed edges of physical performance expand with each world championship meet. Our interest in studying sport's supernormal experiences is to dramatize a vision of human possibilities which far exceeds the currently held image of human behavior and potential. For, as I have shown, such capacities seem to develop throughout the realms of human life.

There is compelling evidence to show that the natural resources which arise through an integrated mind-body discipline can carry us into territories of performance and ability far beyond what most of us generally imagine. The extraordinary experiences described in this chapter are probably only a small part of what we can achieve. If the increasing interest in psychophysical development can be harnessed and directed forward, who knows what discoveries we might make. The sport communities of many east European countries have begun such work in earnest; let us join in the enterprise. I believe that psychophysical sport training will open new vistas in mind-body potential for all humanity.

psychological techniques for the advancement of sport potential

Maurie D. Pressman

Our universe operates on but a few basic principles. The rules which govern the biology, psychology, and sociology of human beings also follow a few basic and universal tenets and are relevant to all human endeavor, including the pursuit of sport excellence. Psychology has been regarded in the sport world for too long as a *simple* affair, and a deep, scientific approach has been thought to be for eggheads, or for inferior competitors immersed in intellectual and irrelevant pursuits. This repression of the importance of the human psyche has been so effective that a huge chasm has appeared between what is practiced and what is available in sport psychology.

In this paper I will discuss the assistance that sport psychology can provide by examining in brief the role of the psychiatrist, the management of tension and the development of "refined aggression," and the relationship between personality and communication. I will then go on to examine the remarkable promise hypnotism offers for the advancement of sport by discussing my initial experience with it, the theoretical basis for its effectiveness, and the difficulties with and limitations to its use.

THE ROLE OF THE PSYCHIATRIST

One usually turns to a psychiatrist to seek information about *problems* in the athlete. But the responsibility of medicine, including psychiatry, is not to cure problems so much as to prevent illness and to improve health and enhance human potential. Thus in sport psychology, it is *not* that we wish to cure problems, but rather that we want to use our knowledge of how human beings function to release and increase potential. By using the discoveries of psychological sciences in recent years, we *can* do so, and in what follows I will relate some applications of these

133

advances to the release of potential and to advancing the athlete towards achievement.

There are certain principles of mental functioning that are relevant to this discussion. First, we all operate with essentially two minds—a conscious mind, and an unconscious mind. Those motivations that we *think* drive us are not our only motivations, and may not be the most important ones. The unconscious mind is a repository of buried, but active, sensitivities, hopes, wishes, fears, and impulses. The task of the sport psychologist and sport psychiatrist is to help bring unconscious motivations into the conscious mind and thus increase the athlete's energy and potential. The unconscious is active and ever present. As well as causing us to misinterpret our own actions, it causes us to misinterpret the actions of others. The sport psychologist and psychiatrist can help sort out communication problems that occur between athlete and coach, making more effective cooperation possible.

MANAGEMENT OF TENSION AND DEVELOPMENT OF "REFINED AGGRESSION"

There is a middle band of psychic tension at which an athlete achieves his best performance: too little tension leaves the athlete lethargic rather than energized toward competitive excellence; too much tension can create muscle binding, which blunts the edge of excellence of performance. We would like, therefore, to teach our athletes methods for desensitizing themselves to tension so that they may achieve that middle band, that kind of "refined indifference," which will enable their energies to flow smoothly toward a goal. We would also like to teach our athletes a kind of "refined aggression." We do not mean by this an aggression in which the rules would be subverted, or the niceties of human contact ignored; we mean an aggression through which we overcome the indoctrination that causes most, if not all, of us to feel guilty over the use of our aggressive and competitive energies. We have been inculcated with the idea that it is wrong to compete too much, that it is "bad" to vanquish the enemy. Competition is a refined version of war, and the successful overcoming of a competitor is equal to what was in more primitive times the vanquishing of an enemy. In these more refined times we have been taught that we should compete but not too hard; that we should try to win but not by too much; that we should feel sorry for our competitor if he is indeed vanquished. This kind of guilt has ruined many a performance and destroyed many a career. It is the individual who has the "killer instinct," who tends to win.

PERSONALITY AND COMMUNICATION

One's own personality is inescapable. One need not be, nor should one try to be someone else in the practice of a sport. In the case of figure skaters, we long ago noted that the personality seems to flow through the blade, so to speak. When an athlete is released to become himself and to skate his own performance, he achieves the most beautiful and effective performance. On the other hand, when he tries to perform as someone else would (either the coach or an idealized figure) the performance is inhibited, artificial, and ineffective. Therefore, the more we can help the particular athlete to be himself the more we can advance him toward his potential.

One's own personality is inescapable. One need not be, nor should one try to be someone else in the practice of a sport. In the case of figure skaters, we long ago noted that the personality seems to flow through the blade, so to speak.

The principles of communication are profoundly important in athletic endeavor. Even in solitary performance such as in figure skating there are essentially two types of individuals: the one who skates for the crowd and the one who skates for himself. Each skater must discover his own predilections and develop them. Some have a greater need to communicate with the audience, and receive a greater stimulus from the audience's response. Other skaters communicate more with themselves in their performance than with the outside. They too may be excellent as long as there is *communication* between athlete and performance; if the athlete is successful, the result of that communication reaches and fascinates the audience. Again, communication serves the principle of becoming oneself in order to achieve one's best.

INITIAL EXPERIENCE WITH HYPNOSIS

In the past five years the Association for the Advancement of Sports Potential*, composed of a group of physicians and coaches in Delaware Valley, U.S.A., has been working to improve figure skating and other sports. Initially the association tried to solve any problems brought to them and these related to many topics including: most favorable times for warm-up, how to minimize injuries; planning diets for those in a particular sport; ideal ages for a sport; and psychological factors which impair or improve performance. In the course of time, interest was increasingly focused on psychological factors. We were able to improve communication between coach and athlete, for instance, and we discovered that any sustained communication problem could destroy the effectiveness of the pair.

As we searched for psychological aids to help meet the stress of competition, we came to lean more and more upon a combination of relaxation and a visualized rehearsal of performance. We turned increasingly to hypnosis as the best method for relaxation and visual rehearsal, and we did so for several reasons. First, hypnosis was dramatic, and it was therefore quickly accepted by many athletes and parents. Undoubtedly too, much of the early accept-

---

* The Association for the Advancement of Sports Potential is a group of psychiatrists, neurologists, and orthopedists who banded together to support the sport of figure skating. We have expanded our efforts to include biomechanics, physiological, and psychological analyses of the athlete, working with the University of Delaware and the Temple University departments of physical education. We are now servicing the U.S. Equestrian Team.

ance resulted from the endorsement of prestigious coaches, but even greater acceptance was probably achieved through the rapid spread by word of mouth of its effectiveness. Hypnosis seemed to have a quick and at times startlingly positive effect on our athletes.

Our procedure was to put the athlete into a state of trance and to suggest that he visualize his performance. The athlete was advised to practice self-hypnosis several times a day. Those athletes who practiced self-hypnosis benefitted greatly, and because of their experience others then wished to follow suit.

Later, at the North Atlantic Training Center*, the effort was much enlarged. The author was invited as a psychiatrist to develop psychological aids for improving performance. The value of hypnosis and visual rehearsal was quickly validated and its reputation spread rapidly. Individual athletes were taught self-hypnosis; their performances benefitted almost immediately, and almost universally. This quick and heady success came as quite a surprise to several of us who had been sceptical because of our scientific training. Yet the overwhelming evidence seemed to indicate that the use of this instrument was causing the success. With the help of other well-known authorities we were able to evolve tentative answers to the question of how and why hypnosis is effective in helping the athlete achieve his potential and reach a level of excellence.

THEORETICAL BASIS FOR THE USE OF HYPNOSIS

The presence of a basic even biologic principle at work behind the effectiveness of hypnosis is suggested by the following points:
1. The ability to be hypnotized seems to be present in a number of species of the animal kingdom.
2. Hypnotic states seem to occur during such focused attention as highway driving, and in meditative states.
3. Recent studies indicate that the phenomenon of hypnosis may relate to the split nature of the brain.
4. Surprisingly uniform and widespread improvement has been experienced by hundreds of athletes following the use of hypnosis and visualization exercises.

* The North Atlantic Training Center at Lake Placid, New York, was founded by Ron Ludington, a U.S. Olympic coach. He was joined by such national and Olympic coaches as Mr Leitch of Canada, and Carlo Fassi. The training center trains figure skaters of Olympic calibre.

There is reason to believe that part of the success of hypnosis lies in the fact that one can achieve peak effort when in a state of relaxed energy. Dr Arnold Gessell, psychiatrist at the University of Pennsylvania who specializes in the function of the skeletal muscular system, pointed out that all thinking is, in fact, accompanied by motor movements, albeit movements at subliminal levels. (In this he follows the work of Jacobson dating back as far as 1932.) Dr Gessell indicated that hypnosis and visual rehearsal would therefore have a training effect upon the musculature and furthermore would improve coordination of the muscles insofar as antagonist muscles would learn to release at a more nearly optimal moment.

The practicing of positive attitudes is also likely significant and is related to behavior modification and learning theories as outlined in the work of Wolpe, Lazarus, Brady, Feather, and Birk. The recent split brain studies are fascinating and are well summarized (as they pertain to the functioning of the non-dominant side of the brain) by a man prominent in the field of communications theory, Paul Watzlawick. Of late, we have come to understand much more about the difference in the functioning of the two sides of the brain. Recent detailed studies have found that the two hemispheres function very differently. The dominant side of the brain (the left side in right-handed people) is given to logical thinking, to language, to details, and to building small efforts and details into a larger picture. The non-dominant side of the brain (the right side of the brain in right-handed people) is given to the perception of whole movements or whole ideas; it is given to pictures rather than words, and to music rather than ideas. Therefore, inhibiting or suspending the function of the left side of the brain, the dominant side, frees the right side to take over. There is reason to believe that hypnosis appeals directly to, and releases, the functioning of the non-dominant brain, which is one reason for its effectiveness. In a hypnotic state imagery is more vivid, rehearsal of programs is more effective, and the cultivation of positive attitudes is also much more assured. Therefore, we believe we have stumbled upon a mechanism that relates to the basic structure of the brain. In addition, by diminishing tension through hypnosis and the rehearsal of relaxed attitudes, we relax the muscles, allowing the performance to proceed more freely. We believe that insofar as we suspend the functions of the left side of the brain, we release the personality to flow into the sport activity unselfconsciously.

DIFFICULTIES IN THE USE OF HYPNOSIS

Individual personality factors must never be overlooked in the use of hypnosis. These personal factors show their influence in several ways. First, although hypnosis is a universal human phenomenon, there are nevertheless impediments to its use, usually arising from some form of personal anxiety. For example, a well-known skier wished to be hypnotized but couldn't achieve trance. Every time he allowed himself to relax and fall inward, he developed a sensation of dangerous falling. He associated this sensation with several experiences in which he had sustained severe injuries in skiing accidents. An even greater deterrent however, arose from his fear of being under the control of anyone who reminded him of his severe and dominant father. Once he realized what was behind his anxiety, he began to get into a deeper state although the result was never fully satisfactory.

The principle that is being described is that hypnosis does not stand alone but always combines with personality factors. The more one is at peace with one's personality, the more successful the hypnotic trance, and the more one can improve performance.

Much of our experience indicates that the visually rehearsed performance reproduces not only the performance itself but also the mistakes that result from personality factors. For example, a figure skater who has a predilection for failure will find the mistakes in his skating repeating in his visualized performance. In visualizing his mistakes, the athlete may rationalize that he is trying to overcome them, but in fact by trying to overcome them visually, he repeats, grooves, and nourishes them. By advising him to repeat his performance visually in an increasingly positive way, we achieve a more positive effect.

Although psychoanalysis teaches that negative attitudes and their origins must be uncovered in order to be corrected, there seems to be growing evidence that the teachings of Emile Coué on the value of auto-suggestion (popular at the beginning of this century) are being validated by experiences in positive thinking. This evidence certainly parallels our experience with skaters, skiers, bowlers, and others, including professional musicians.

It is clear, however, that some personality factors (emanating from unconscious sources) *will not* yield to hypnosis. It should be noted too that hypnosis is not magically lasting but must be reinforced periodically by the athlete as well as by the hypnotist. Incidentally, I believe it is possible for a coach to invoke rehearsal of performance and rehearsal of positive attitudes through the use of progressive relaxation, focused consciousness and image rehears-

There is reason to believe that hypnosis appeals directly to, and releases, the functioning of the non-dominant brain, which is one reason for its effectiveness. In a hypnotic state imagery is more vivid, rehearsal of programs is more effective, and the cultivation of positive attitudes is also much more assured. Therefore, we believe we have stumbled upon a mechanism that relates to the basic structure of the brain.

al, without necessarily waiting for the assistance of the psychologist or psychiatrist. It is my belief that the advanced athlete is a person with a strong ego who therefore is not susceptible to the dangers of hypnosis. Furthermore, I believe that the dangers of hypnosis are overstated, and although real enough for patients who are either paranoid psychotics or borderline psychotics, are not a factor for athletes who have advanced to any state of competitive achievement.

LIMITATIONS TO THE USE OF HYPNOSIS

There are examples in which hypnosis cannot be effective in managing major personality disorders, which often lie behind failure to achieve excellence or one's potential. When an athlete is having trouble with his performance, when he is not achieving his potential and the rehearsal techniques of hypnosis are not helping, there is reason to call for a psychiatric consultation. Similarly, when the members of an athletic pair or team are having grave difficulty working together, and the difficulty will not yield to the usual techniques of hypnosis and rehearsal, the psychological specialist should be called in. And especially when there are difficulties between coach and athlete, one should consult a specialist to ease the strain and to correct the communication problems. I would like to outline a few examples in which the special skills of the psychiatrist were necessary to deal with personality disorders.

An 18-year-old skater, a world level competitor, consistently prejudiced his career by clowning exhibitionistically and crudely. He arrived at the North Atlantic Training Center preceded by a bad reputation and continued his disruptive behavior; therefore I had the opportunity to learn quite a bit about him. He is a phenomenally talented athlete, who achieved prominence on a national level at age 12. He felt, however, that his success deprived him of his childhood. In addition his parents separated when he was 12; thereafter he missed his father terribly. He combated his anguish, loneliness and insecurity by becoming a clown—to convince the world as well as himself that he didn't really care. He seemed unaware of the fact that his clowning got him into trouble with his peers, with his coach, and with important people in the judging world. At the Center we were able to work through his clowning compulsion quickly, and to make him aware of his attitudes, and their impact, and the reasons for his behavior. To try to correct the misunderstanding between him and his coach we arranged for a joint interview. I acted as a mediator and interpreter of sorts. The skater was first made aware of the fact that he was acting obnoxiously, secondly, of the fact that his behavior was a threat to his career; thirdly, of the fact that he was hurting his coach. I knew that this skater was very fond of his coach; therefore, when the conversation revealed that by his clowning behavior he was threatening to destroy the camp and in this way hurting his coach, a great deal of insight and guilt was provoked and purposely maintained. The skater became eager to take himself in hand both for his own sake and for the sake of the teacher. He changed quickly, much to the satisfaction of all.

Another illustrative case has to do with a famous dance pair. They are extraordinarily artistic, have skated on Olympic and world levels, but had been confronted with the following problem. At a crucial moment, an argument would often erupt between them, destroying their ability to perform and lowering them in the opinion of the skating world. I had the opportunity to work intensively with the man, and learned that he felt that if he let his control slip, he would deteriorate completely, and that if he admitted to his partner his admiration for her, he would be lowered in her eyes. If he admitted that he thought that she was a better skater than he, he would be destroyed. His misconceptions were related to the fact that his father was very critical and autocratic and gave him the idea that he must be tough and disciplined at all times. After he became aware of the problem, this idea was corrected; he was able to tell his partner in my presence of his admiration for her. A great deal of the strain was relieved. He was also able to notice that every time he felt inferior or threatened in any way, he would become angry and begin to strike out. As time went on, we were able to see other hidden mechanisms at work. The woman, for example, was afraid of closeness and would try to evoke anger and criticism, and thus end any uncomfortable intimacy. When these problems were straightened out, the skating pair were able to perform quite smoothly, and achieved national prominence. This kind of insight could only be produced by someone who was trained and able to search out the hidden factors at work in the individuals and in the pair. It should also be noted that this work did not take long, and that it was not only effective but, in the sense of a sport career, also life saving.

Another illustrative case has to do with a famous dance pair. At a crucial moment, an argument would often erupt between them, destroying their ability to perform and lowering them in the opinion of the skating world. I had the opportunity to work intensively with the man and learned . . .

CONCLUSION

In what has been described, we are applying fundamental psycho-analytic and psychodynamic principles to a view of personality and of all human endeavor, including athletic endeavor. We expand the concept of athletic endeavor to embrace not only the athlete, but also the coach, the parents, and the judges. We believe we can increase the athlete's performance by improving the communication between the athlete and those around him as well as his own communication with himself. By the use of hypnosis (either in individual or group effort) along with rehearsal of programs, we can develop positive and relaxed attitudes, and free the person more and more to give himself over to the activity controlled by the right side of the brain. We have reason to believe that the smoothest, most coordinated and effective athletic effort results from activity dominated by the right side of the brain.

Much remains to be done but by combining psychological and psychiatric science with the efforts of the athlete, coach, and the supporting sports world, the athlete can be helped toward the achievement of his potential.

athletes
and self-hypnosis

Lee Pulos

INTRODUCTION

Psychological techniques for enhancing athletic performance vary widely from behavior modification and mental rehearsal to Zen meditation and the psychic self-regulation approach of the Soviet Union. An all too common method has been for psychologists to administer self-response personality inventories and look for special traits or profiles that distinguish the champion from the lesser athlete. Implicit in all these techniques is the question of whether one can learn how to extend human capacities and to repeat championship performances consistently. Another facet of the problem is what causes an athlete to excel on one occasion and perform poorly on the next. This writer has worked with a number of world-class athletes and sports teams since 1967, addressing himself to such questions. Although the primary technique in working with athletes has been self-hypnosis, variations have been incorporated which will be described later in the chapter.

The value of hypnosis to the athletic world has been the subject of considerable debate over the years. One carefully controlled study of the effect of psychological and pharmacological interventions on human strength (Ikai and Steinhaus, 1961) demonstrated that the greatest and most consistent extension of performance took place during the hypnotic trance state and that post-hypnotic suggestion was the next most effective. The authors concluded that psychological rather than physiological factors determine the limits of performance. A recent survey of U.S. high schools, junior colleges, and universities (Mitchell, 1972) indicated that 18 per cent of those responding used hypnosis to varying degrees with their athletes. A number of athletic stars have had success with hypnosis (Bell, 1974; Marliana, 1977), and I myself have worked with a number of professional athletes (including hockey players, football players, and racing car drivers), as have others.* Perhaps the most comprehensive approach encouraging athletes to influence and direct their own psychophysical processes has come from the work of A. S. Romen, a Soviet physician and sport psychologist, and is known as psychic self-regulation. The training methods include hypnosis and meditation but place particular stress on active self-suggestion.**

DEVELOPMENT OF TECHNIQUES

My work with athletes began with the Canadian Women's National Volleyball team when I tried to determine if hypnosis could be used to improve overall functioning. Hypnosis was used to facilitate athletic performance in the following ways: motivation for practice, mental practice under hypnosis, facilitation of relaxation and sleep, time regression under hypnosis to "review" a game, playing under hypnosis, and time distortions to improve reflexes. The coach coined the phrase "think training" for the hypnotic sessions and the girls seemed to prefer this reference rather than hypnosis. In the first year (of a total of four spent with the team), I met the team twice weekly for a group hypnotic induction. The team was given the post-hypnotic suggestion that during a practice or game, their concentration would be heightened and focused on the opposing players, the ball, and their teammates. It was added that outside noises, sounds, distractions, intruding throughts, and so on would fade into the background and not interfere with this concentration on the game.

Each girl was taught auto-hypnosis; most reportedly used self-hypnosis four to five times a week to reinforce various features of the team practice. A side benefit was that most of the girls were students and they used auto-hypnosis to improve their concentration for reading and studying. It was found they could put more into volleyball by realizing they were improving their study habits through hypnosis and not having to worry about the time given to practices each week.

* Charles Brumfield, five-time national racquetball champion, working with a clinical psychologist who employs hypnosis, has made a hypnotic training tape for his students.

** A.J. Lewis has summarized these methods in an unpublished monograph (1976); they are outlined by J.L. Hickman in chapter 12.

Hypnotic Time Regression

Of particular interest to me in this work was reviewing peak performances with athletes while they were under hypnosis. I was curious to learn if the subconscious learning that had taken place could be used for achievement of maximum effort. A world-class athlete, who had unofficially broken the world's 100-meter dash record in practice at the Olympic Games in Mexico City and who was losing races to lesser athletes, was concerned about not being able to regain the form that she had had. The experiment took place at the Physical Endurance Laboratory, Simon Fraser University, in the presence of her coach and trainer. Lying on a training table, she was attached to an electrocardiograph and spirometer measuring respiratory rate and tidal volume. Hypnosis was induced and she was taken through a mental "workout" including several practice starts and the "sprinting" of 220- and 330-yard dashes. Aside from the visible tension (movement in her legs, muscle twitching, and increased breathing rate), the connected apparatus registered remarkable changes. Respiration rate and volume increased to peak running conditions and her heart rate increased by 112 per cent. She was regressed hypnotically to that day in Mexico City when she ran the best race of her life. She then reran the race but was able to "run the movie in slow-motion" so that she could both "see" and experience physically what she was doing and how she was striding, pumping her arms, and so on. Upon being alerted, she was immediately aware of why she had performed so well and excitedly related all the details to her coach. In subsequent meets, she regained her old form and was undefeated for the remainder of the season. She did not achieve the Mexico City standard again; however, in this instance hypnosis was a useful technique for approaching a specific training problem.

CURRENT TRAINING PROCEDURES

Over the years I have revised the "think training" techniques and hypnotic procedures and the revisions have primarily been based on suggestions from athletes and their coaches. The following outline summarizes both the approach and the sequence in which information and experiences are presented to the athlete. Wherever possible, the coach is invited to participate in the first session and to help define the goals.

My work with athletes began with the Canadian Women's National Volleyball Team when I tried to determine if hypnosis could be used to improve overall functioning.

De-mystifying Hypnosis

The level of understanding of hypnosis varies widely among athletes and ranges from "giving up the will," "someone taking over your mind," and "losing consciousness" to "focused attention," "increased awareness," and—with more sophisticated subjects—the realization that you practice and perform in trance on many occasions. The terms hypnosis, trance, deep relaxation, deeper level of mind are used interchangeably. Although there is no agreement among psychologists on a theoretical definition of hypnosis let alone an operational definition, most textbooks emphasize that hypnosis is a process for making the subconscious conscious. It involves shifting from cortical to subcortical levels of mind and opening up the flow between conscious and subconscious levels of awareness. Most important is that hypnosis is a natural state of consciousness and that we slip into dozens of mini-trances daily. This turning inward and focusing on one's "inner reality" can happen during day-dreaming, listening to music, reading, or driving down a highway.

The purpose of learning hypnosis is to increase concentration and gain more control of body and mind. Through self-hypnosis it is possible to control voluntarily many events of the autonomic nervous system such as respiration, heart rate, and lactic acid levels, among others. In the hypnotic mode, the conscious, critical mind interferes less and the powerful forces of the subconscious can be mobilized much more easily so that a more natural flow of the desired physical skill can take place. Thus, overcoming the limitations of the conscious mind is a recurring theme of this approach in introducing the hypnotic mode to the athlete.

Importance of the Subconscious

To emphasize how much control resides in the subcortical areas of the brain, I frequently take time to discuss the "placebo effect." A placebo is an inert substance such as colored water that has no physiological effect of its own. If the placebo is identified as a useful drug, thus raising a subject's expectations, powerful and dramatic changes can occur. Norman Cousins (1977) summarized the placebo research following his own recovery from an illness diagnosed fatal in which placebo therapy was used. This information about the placebo effect is part of the initial education of the athlete, and discussion of how the subconscious can be mobilized for supernormal tasks frequently ensues.

Linking the Conscious and
Subconscious for Learning

A number of athletes have emphasized that superior performances seem to happen when there is less conscious effort or involvement. As one athlete stated, "when I allow things to flow without thinking of what I should be doing, then I can really get with it and nothing stands in my way." In other words, there seems to be a much greater range of abilities available when a person can shift from conscious to the more natural or subconscious linking of mind and body.

There is now considerable evidence that it is possible to harmonize altered states of consciousness with recitation or rehearsal and thereby enhance subconscious learning. Lozonov, a Bulgarian psychiatrist, has used light hypnosis, rhythmic breathing, classical Baroque music with a special beat of 3/4 or 4/4 time to teach foreign languages (Ostrander et al., 1979). His technique involves teaching the student how to go into light hypnosis; the student is then asked to focus all his conscious awareness on the music. The teacher synchronizes the presentation of the language material to a special rhythmic breathing that the student maintains while in light trance. There is frequent testing and after being taught in this mode for a month, four hours a day and five days a week, the average student has learned the grammar, vocabulary, and syntax equivalent to a grade ten student of that language.

I review Lozonov's work with the athlete to emphasize the importance of subconscious learning. The more one is able to create a link between the conscious and the subconscious, the easier it will become to create a learning style and to control and select the perceptions most useful for extending one's capacities. I am currently developing specific learning tapes for athletes in different sports, and I hope they will provide further impetus for athletes to try to expand the dimensions of awareness and create an easier flow between conscious and subconscious levels of mind.

Communicating with the Subconscious

A number of years in a clinical practice have convinced me that there is often a discrepancy between conscious goals and sub-conscious motivation. This is true of patients with personal problems and high performance persons, such as athletes or corporation executives. There are a number of so-called uncovering methods which can be used to communicate with the "inner mind." The one I have most frequently used is ideo-motor signaling which involves receiving signals from the unconscious through the fingers indicating yes or no responses. Ideo-motor signaling can occur as effectively while the person is awake as in hypnosis. Before hypnosis training is undertaken, ideo-motor signals are established by having the person sit calmly with hands relaxed and then thinking "yes" over and over. In response, the subconscious will select and levitate or twitch a finger, thumb, or sometimes several fingers. A "no" finger is established in the same manner. This technique usually impresses the subjects—the movements are involuntary and invariably bring exclamations of surprise. Thus, while in a conscious, alert state the first step in establishing communication with the subconscious is accomplished. To demonstrate how the technique works, questions are then asked of the "fingers" to determine if there is any resistance to learning hypnosis. In most instances, the athletes have been in favor of proceeding but this step ensures that any misconceptions or other interferences to utilizing self-hypnosis can be dealt with at this time.

Ideo-motor questioning has proved invaluable in uncovering and putting into perspective such issues as goal-setting, confidence levels, motivation for competing, and even such things as ideal training schedules for a particular athlete. For example, a young middle-distance runner wanted to find out why she had suddenly lost her rhythm and was not competing as expected in track meets. On a conscious level, she was not aware of anything that would have precipitated the setback. During ideo-motor questioning whe was surprised to discover that changes in training tactics and particularly a shift from longer to shorter sprints were what her "inner mind" indicated was the source of the problem. She discussed the findings with her coach, returned to her old schedule, and within a short time regained her old form.

The important feature of this technique is that after the first session, athletes can use it on their own. As with self-hypnosis, it underscores the importance of taking personal responsibility for making changes, and it shows that it is possible and exciting to discover how the different levels of the self can work with or against each other.

Lee Pulos in a teaching session with Nancy McCarthy, a middle-distance runner from Vancouver.

Mental Rehearsal and Visualization Training

The techniques and importance of visualizing and mentally re-hearsing desired performance have been described in a number of sources (Gallwey, 1976; Harrison and Reilly, 1975). These approaches are discussed with the athletes and reference is usually made to some of the studies where different groups of subjects were allotted a certain time (a) to practice a skill physically, (b) to rehearse only mentally, and (c) to have no practice at all. After a certain period tests of skills usually indicated that mental rehearsal was almost as effective as physical practice. Robert Foster, a former national rifle champion, was called to Viet Nam in a non-combat capacity and mentally rehearsed rifle shooting ten minutes a day for the year that he was away. Upon return to the United States, and with practically no actual practice with his competition rifle, he entered a national meet and broke his own world record.

I also review with athletes the work of Dr Carl Simonton, a radiologist specializing in the treatment of cancer (Simonton *et al.,* 1978). Simonton believes that the course of cancer can be influenced by the emotional and psychological factors that affect the immunological system. He teaches all his patients self-hypnosis, acquaints them with the interaction of chemotherapy and radiation with the immunological system, and wherever possible shows them photographs of their particular cancer cells and asks them to go into light hypnosis and visualize in their mind's eye the cancer cells or tumors being destroyed. In a number of instances there was a remarkable degree of adjustment and physical improvement in relation to the technique of visualization.

The energy that is attached to thought, be it conscious or subconscious, is stressed repeatedly; this energy can be positive or negative depending on the intention behind it. The background material discussed thus far usually takes 20 or 30 minutes to cover along with questions and discussion.

Teaching Self-Hypnosis

All hypnosis is self-hypnosis. Unless a person is willing to partici-pate he cannot be hypnotized. It is only by cooperating with the suggestions that a person can learn to enter selective states of consciousness. There is no loss of awareness, and in most instances there is greater acuity in hypnosis because of the focused concentration. There is however a narrowing of awareness or a kind of "tunnel vision" so that extraneous sounds are usually ignored.

Hypnosis is learned like any other skill and with practice it is easier to enter that state of mind. The ability to be hypnotized is distributed randomly in the population. Some persons are naturals and can learn in the first session while others must practice and try different approaches before achieving a hypnotic state.

Generally, the first induction is a simple form of progressive relaxation and then at least two or three different fantasy inductions are taught. Once the person feels comfortable entering a "deeper level of mind" shorter forms of self-hypnosis are demonstrated along with two different deepening techniques. It should be noted that particular attention is paid to which sensory channel the subject is partial to. This will determine whether kinesthetic, auditory, visual, or tactile induction is used. Side remarks, such as "I see what you mean," "I hear you," or "That feels good," usually provide clues as to how the subject prefers to integrate learning. Wherever possible, this information is translated into specific approaches that are applicable to the particular sport and its training processes.

A distinction is made between learning hypnosis and utilizing hypnosis. During the first three or four hypnotic training inductions, post-hypnotic suggestions are given, reinforcing the person's ability to enter trance on his own. The athlete then selects the induction he feels most comfortable with and practices self-hypnosis. Once this is achieved—and most subjects can master it in the first session—we begin examining and defining the specific suggestions and program to be utilized by the athlete. Books such as Le Cron (1964) and Morris (1974), which detail further hypnotic techniques and specific wording of inductions, are also generally recommended.

Utilizing Self-Hypnosis

Athletes spend the remainder of the first session and subsequent sessions in "deep relaxation" or "trance" mentally rehearsing and visualizing themselves executing specific skills and general events or subconsciously reviewing problem areas in their sport. They are taught to suggest post-hypnotically that what they have executed ideally in their mind's eye they will be able to translate into action during practice or competition. The suggestion is also made that their body is learning at a physiological and neurological level while they are rehearsing mentally; they are "laying the proper neurological tracks" through their hypnotic mental imagery. It is generally recognized that this method will facilitate action currents in the muscles involved in the actual movements which in turn reinforces neuromuscular coordination.

Self-hypnosis is also used to motivate the athlete to practice, to improve relaxation and sleep, to reduce the interfering aspects of stress upon concentration, and in time regressions to review hypnotically both peak days and notable lapses in performance.

HYPNOTIC IMAGERY FOR SELF-HEALING AND REJUVENATION

Based on the work of Simonton (1978) and my own experiences with cross-cultural healing practices, I emphasize to the athlete that hypnotic imagery should be used as an adjunct to conventional medical treatment. For example, one athlete suffered from acute tendonitis in both knees following practice and competition. She was not responding to friction massage, ice packs, or ultra-sound. It was decided that she would combine her treatment with hypnotically induced imagery, and she "saw" special whirlpools in her knees that were working with the ultra-sonic treatment. She visualized a reduction of the inflammation, the toxins being pushed out, and the tendons returning to a normal, whitish, glistening outer texture. The response was almost immediate; she was able to finish the competition from which she had previously considered withdrawing.

Many of the athletes at the 1978 Commonwealth Games in Edmonton complained of fatigue and low energy levels following sustained competition. I have devised a cleansing and rejuvenation fantasy that is hypnotically induced and can be done either individually or in groups. Once having learned and experienced the process, the athletes utilize it on their own when needed and frequently go through the experience at the end of the day or just before going to sleep.

GOAL-SETTING

When the techniques and approaches described above have been mastered, the athletes' goals are examined in the context of how they wish to program themselves. On several occasions athletes, particularly the younger ones, have aimed just to get to the Commonwealth or Pan American Games—but not necessarily to win. Louis Tice described to me his work with a major U.S. college football team incorporating deep relaxation and goal-setting principles. The team had been expected to have an 8 to 3 win-loss record. In their sessions with Tice, they set a goal of being invited to one of the major post-season bowls; they won all their games, went to the bowl, but were beaten badly. Again they were prepared to get to the bowl, but not to win. In interviewing athletes in depth, particularly when using ideo-motor questioning, important information is elicited that is related to expectations, motivation, confidence levels, goals, and whether there is a subconscious cross-current that might be interfering with achievement of the stated goals.

CONCLUSION

A large number of the athletes I have worked with have felt that hypnotic training has improved their concentration and sport skills significantly. The fact that this training is an integral part of the athletes' preparation reinforces the idea that it is not a frill or gimmick but that physical skills and mental preparation are vitally important for world-class athletes. Implicit in this approach is that the athletes are expected to take more responsibility for their mental preparation in addition to increasing their sensitivity to subconscious motivations and attitudes. It should be pointed out that when the volleyball team lost in the semi-finals, they approached the coach to ask for extra practice sessions and drills during the week to improve their game. In other words, there was no suggestion of a dependency on hypnosis, they were able to keep this training in perspective as an adjunct to general training strategy. Self-hypnosis thus was, as it should be, but one dimension in the preparation of an athlete.

customary arousal for peak athletic performance

Peter Klavora

Several chapters in Parts Three and Five are devoted to various psychological techniques designed to control emotional arousal of athletes prior to competition. However, the ability to adjust the athlete's pre-competitive arousal level, either to elevate it or to reduce it, is but one side of the matter. The other side the athlete must deal with is the problem of "to what level of arousal should I adjust myself?" This question is related to the athlete's customary competitive level of arousal which elicits his best performance. Other related questions important to the athlete and the coach are: How do I go about measuring my arousal levels? How does the coach know that the athlete or the team is "up" for the game or at their customary competitive level of arousal? Are there any differences among players in their arousal levels prior to competition? Is the athletes' pre-game behavior related to their pre-game arousal? In this chapter I intend to provide some of the answers to these questions. They are based on my investigations with athletes competing in various sports and at different levels of skill. The reader is warned that at this stage much of the discussion is still considered to be speculative since this kind of research is only beginning in sport practice. I will start with two theoretical models cited most often. Next, I will lead you through my work with athletes testing these models. The chapter will conclude with the implications of this work for sport practice.

COMPETITIVE AROUSAL* AND
PERFORMANCE: TWO MODELS

Most coaches, particularly in team sports, are of the opinion that their teams' performances improve in direct relationship with in-

---

*Arousal in this chapter refers to heightened emotions of athletes prior to competition, self-assessed by athletes using a pencil-and-paper psychological inventory.

(a) Drive Theory Model

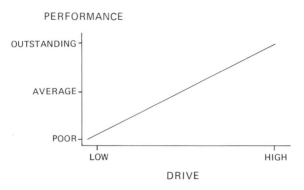

(b) Inverted-U Theory Model

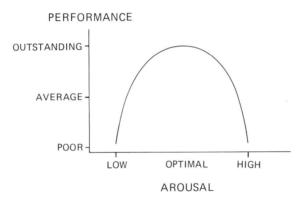

Figure 1. Two psychological models showing the relationship between arousal and performance in sport.

creased arousal of the players. The idea is, in other words, the more the players are "psyched up" or "high," the better will be the expected performance. This belief is the very reason why coaches consider their pre-game or mid-game motivational talks, also known as pep talks, as the ultimate extension of their coaching ability. The higher they can bring their teams' emotions, the better they will feel. This is exemplified by excerpts of an emotional pre-game rally of the head coach of a professional football team before the Grey Cup game of a few years ago that went like this: "I want you up, I want you ready, you've got to go all out; this has got to be your greatest performance . . . ."

Supporters of this view agree with the notion that the level of arousal is open-ended and that there is no limit to how high a competitor can become. The higher his pre-game emotions, the better he will play, seems to be the general rule. The psychological principle behind this view is the *drive theory* which states that performance on a well-learned task increases as the drive, in many respects synonymous with arousal, becomes stronger. This relationship is shown in Figure 1a.

Another concept known to coaches is the relationship between arousal and performance that resembles a bell. This is shown in Figure 1b. The psychological principle behind this view is the inverted-U theory model. According to this theory, the pre-game arousal can be both facilitative or detrimental in the following way: The performance of a competitor becomes better as his arousal level rises—but only to a point. Beyond this point, often termed as the optimal level of arousal, performance decreases as the competitor's arousal increases further.

From their experience coaches know that when, before or during a game, athletes become too "psyched up" or too "high," their performance suffers. Interestingly, the professional football coach quoted above was also aware of this phenomenon operating in the game of football. In the same pep talk he was heard saying: " . . . relax, don't be nervous, you are too high; take it easy on yourself so that you can perform well." Obviously, the coach in point was very much confused as to the kind of motivational speech he should deliver to his team before a championship game. On one hand he was psyching the athletes up to the highest pitch and seconds later he brought them down to the optimal level at which he thought they would perform well.

Coaches are generally confused concerning the emotional levels of athletes before or during competition. Their confusion is most likely a reflection of the uncertainty by psychologists themselves who still have not provided correct answers to the questions related to the arousal-performance relationship in sport practice. The reasons for this are many, but one of the most salient ones is the fact that psychologists have not as yet gone out to the competitive field and directly researched the problem. The vast body of research available in this area has been carried out in laboratories. At best there has been only a faint resemblance between laboratory tasks and laboratory-induced arousal levels in experimental subjects (in most cases non-athletes) and what is going on at a stadium filled with thousands of spectators.

I have been concerned with this topic since 1973. All my studies were conducted in competitive athletic environment with athletes competing in various sports and at various levels of competition. Some of this work is presented below.

TESTING THE MODELS
WITH BASKETBALL PLAYERS

Basketball activity was chosen for testing the two models in Figure 1. In basketball, the team membership is small and the competitive schedule offers enough games spaced equally throughout the competitive season. The study (Klavora, 1978) involved 145 senior high school basketball players competing in the 1973/74 City of Edmonton and Province of Alberta championships. All players' pre-game arousal levels were measured by the state anxiety scale from the State-Trait Anxiety Inventory (STAI) of Spielberger *et al.* (1970). This scale asks the player to indicate how he feels at a particular moment in time, for example, immediately prior to the game. The performance of each player was then evaluated by his coach after the game on a three-point scale that includes the following ratings of individual performance: poor or below his performance ability, average or close to his performance ability, and outstanding performance.

The data, the players' pre-game arousal levels and their subsequent performance ratings, were collected beginning in the middle of the regular season, with eight games remaining. Collection of data continued throughout the city playoffs for all qualifying teams, who played one to three additional games. The first two finishers qualified for the provincial championship tournament where three more games were played. Data from these games were also collected for 24 players (12 on each team) who were members of the two top Edmonton teams participating in the finals of the Alberta basketball tournament.

Thus the number of pairings (pre-game arousal-game performance scores) of most of the players ranged between a minimum of eight and a maximum of fourteen depending on the quality of the team.

The results of this investigation were interesting. Figure 2 presents the raw score profiles of two players belonging to the team that went all the way to the provincial finals. The pairings of pre-game arousal and game performance for both players cluster typically between the two coordinates. If the pre-game arousal scores of the clusters are averaged and if these averages are connected by a curve, bell-shaped curves for both players emerge. Player 1, for example, played poorly three times, played as expected nine times, and played outstandingly two times. Player 2, on the other hand, had two poor and two outstanding performances, and

(a) Player 1 Profile

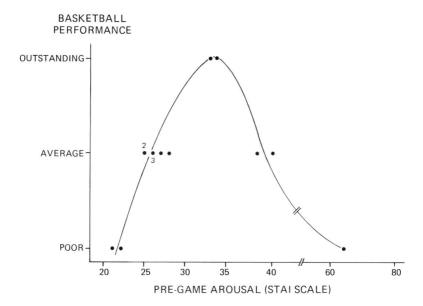

(b) Player 2 Profile

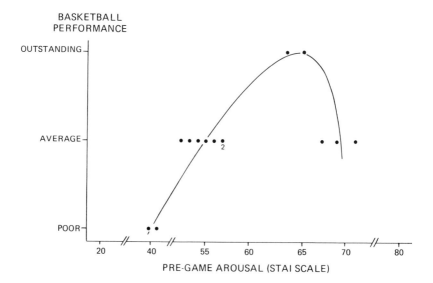

Figure 2. Raw score profile of two basketball players showing pre-game arousal-game performance relationship.

played as expected ten times.

The most important finding of this investigation is the fact that the two curves confirm the inverted-U model and not the drive theory model of Figure 1. Various clusters of pre-game arousal scores on both, poor and average levels of performance indicate that indeed a basketball player may be performing poorly (or only at an average level) because of two quite different reasons: either he is psychologically not ready for the upcoming competition, or he is too excited about it (Player 1's pre-game arousal scores of 21 and 22, and 62). The same argument can be used when examining the pre-game arousal scores associated with their average or as expected performances for both players.

Another significant observation when comparing the two curves is that although both curves show similarity in shape, they are positioned at different levels in the STAI scale continuum which has minimum and maximum boundaries at 20 and 80, respectively. Player 1's curve is located in the low range score, whereas Player 2's curve is located in the high range score of the scale. What does this difference mean? The differences in pre-game arousal levels between the two players indicate that Player 2 is generally a more excitable person than is Player 1. By inspection of Figure 2, the pre-game arousal scores associated with average and outstanding performances range between 25 and 40 for Player 1. In comparison, this range for Player 2 is 53 to 71.

The implications of the above observation are significant for basketball coaches. It tells the coach that both types of players have to be aroused if they are to perform according to his expectations. Player 1's arousal level has to climb from a low level (around 20 on the STAI scale) by about 12 points to reach the level which is conducive to an outstanding performance. Player 2's arousal level, on the other hand, is relatively high (in comparison to Player 1's) to begin with, but it must nevertheless increase by at least 20 points if he is to perform brilliantly in the game. Thus, although there is initially a remarkable difference in the arousal levels of the players, they both need a motivational boost (regardless of what form it takes) prior to the game playing time.

CUSTOMARY LEVEL OF AROUSAL
FOR CUSTOMARY LEVEL OF PERFORMANCE

From experience we know that even though a poor performance is not desirable, a basketball player occasionally does play poorly. However, this kind of performance must be rare during the overall season if the player is to stay on the team. This, of course, is determined by the winning emphasis in athletic competition.

Most often, however, the basketball player selected for the team is playing up to his potential as is expected of him by the coach. Thus, his performance during most games is consistently above the poor level on either side of the inverted-U curve. Most often (this was the case with Player 1 and Player 2 in Figure 2) it is in the average range and on occasion it is outstanding. I termed these types of performance *the customary level of performance* of a player. According to the inverted-U model, a player's *customary level of performance* is associated with his *customary level of arousal* which is a *range* on an arousal continuum. In our example from Figure 2 this range for Player 1 spans between 25 to 40 and for Player 2 between 53 and 71 on the STAI scale.

Based on these preliminary results it is reasonable to assume that there is a characteristic customary level of arousal for every athlete on a basketball team. It is also reasonable to assume that the width of the range as well as where this range is found on an arousal continuum varies from player to player. That this is so will become more apparent below when trait anxiety variable is introduced.

LOW TRAIT AND HIGH
TRAIT ANXIETY ATHLETES

At this point it should be noted that similar inverted-U curves, based on pre-game arousal-game performance pairings, could be plotted for other players involved in the study. Many, but not all, curves were as well defined as the two presented in Figure 2. Again, some of these curves were clustered more at the lower end of the STAI scale, whereas others were found to be at the higher end of the scale. Subsequent analysis revealed that generally players scoring low on the trait anxiety inventory of the STAI had typically demonstrated a low customary level of arousal, whereas players scoring high on the trait anxiety inventory typically demonstrated a high customary level of arousal. Player 1's trait anxiety score, for example, was 27, whereas Player 2's trait anxiety score was 52. When inverted-U curves were plotted for very low and very high trait anxiety players, two completely separate bell-shaped curves placed at the lower and the higher end of the STAI scale continuum were found (Klavora, 1974).

Trait anxiety, according to Spielberger *et al.,* (1970), refers to relatively stable individual differences in anxiety proneness. It is the uneasy feeling derived from some stressor (a comprehensive list of competitive stressors has been compiled by Kroll in Table 1, p. 217) that differentially affects the pre-game arousal levels of athletes.

The research reported here confirms what coaches have already known from their experience; namely, that there are basically two kinds of athletes: the first kind are the calm, low strung, relaxed, composed players. The other kind are the nervous, high strung, excitable, anxious players. However, this research also denies the quite common belief that each group of athletes has to be treated differently regarding pre-game motivational preparations. It has been generally believed that high trait anxiety athletes are usually overaroused in competition, whereas the opposite is true for low trait anxiety athletes. Therefore, high trait anxiety players have to be calmed down and low trait anxiety players have to be activated to achieve optimal performnace. On the contrary, the findings of the reported research suggest that both the low and the high trait anxiety athletes have to be approached in the same way. They all have to be activated before competition if they are to reach their *customary level of performance.*

In our investigations in basketball, football, hockey, rowing, gymnastics, wrestling, fending, and volleyball (Klavora, 1979a; 1979b; 1975a; 1975b) we have found that high trait anxiety athletes exhibit consistently higher levels of customary arousal than low trait anxiety athletes, both during the regular season games and the playoffs. Similar differences were also found in the "practice" or "basal" arousal level of tested athletes.

Thus it appears that the trait anxiety personality variable seems to be the most important factor affecting the arousal levels of athletes prior to competition and in training.

CONTROL AND ASSESSMENT
OF AROUSAL LEVELS IN ATHLETES

Earlier it was stated that before competition *all* the athletes on a basketball team must be activated to their customary level of arousal. This is not to say, however, that this does not imply that an overexcited athlete, or the whole team for that matter, performing very poorly is not a possibility. Player 1 in Figure 2, for example, completely bombed out in the final game of the provincial championships. Although he was by far the tallest athlete in both teams, measuring in height 197 cm, he did not score a single point as a center until two minutes before the end of the game. Based on his pre-game arousal (62 points on the STAI scale) which was significantly higher than his previous scores during the regular season and playoffs, I predicted the disastrous performance of this player. I passed this information to the coach, but there was nothing he could do since, this being his first appearance in the provincial finals, his arousal was noticeably just as high as the players'.

It is important that the coach should know the heights of pre-game emotions of his players. An astute coach will sense these levels by observation of the players' behavior before the contest. In order to determine athletes' pre-game arousal more accurately, a simple test like the Spielberger STAI State Anxiety Inventory can be administered. The test takes only seconds to do and hand scoring of the responses can be done in a few minutes for the entire team. Based on the overall pre-game arousal level of the team or individual players, the coach could, on one hand, employ various techniques for motivating the players to a higher level if desired, or, on the other hand, administer relaxing techniques (discussed in this book by several writers) if the arousal of the team or individual players has already passed the customary levels which are conducive to optimal performance.

By administering a trait anxiety inventory to the team, the coach could learn more about the pre-game arousal characteristics of his players very early in the season. This would further help him in psychological guidance of the team. The Spielberger STAI Trait Anxiety Inventory could be used for this purpose. It is a short test and easy to score. Another test is Martens' Sport Competitive Anxiety Test (1977) which has similar properties.

CONCLUSION

Based on our research on several hundred athletes, particularly the basketball players, we believe that the customary level of arousal of each player can be determined by using appropriate instruments coupled with astute observation of players' pre-game and training behavior. Based on these assessments, various motivational techniques can then be employed to bring the individual athlete (or the entire team) to within his customary level of arousal. The customary level of arousal was in this chapter defined as the pre-game arousal level which facilitates an acceptable performance by an athlete. We also believe that the methods used on basketball players as described here could be employed in other sport environments with equal success. The key to this work is, however, a geniune interest on the part of the coach to get to know his players as much as he can. Only then will he be able to use his coaching techniques to full advantage.

discussion with the sport psychologist

Edited by
Cameron J.R. Blimkie

Editor's Introduction

This section summarizes the proceedings of an informal discussion session entitled "Dialogue with the Sport Psychologist," which was part of the Applied Sciences Symposium of the 1978 Congress of the Canadian Society for Psychomotor Learning and Sport Psychology. The panel members included Dr R. Nideffer, Mr J. Hickman, Dr V. Wilson, and Dr M.D. Pressman, who responded to questions posed by the audience on the practical application of psychological principles and techniques in the sport world. Dr T. Tutko chaired this session and fielded questions on a variety of topics including coping with out-of-body psychic experiences, narrow versus broad focus of attention, and sport psychology credibility.

Question: *How is it possible for an athlete to process or attend to changing cues during performance, when in an altered state of consciousness?*

Hickman: I would like to point out that consciousness is continually being altered and when I talk of an altered state of consciousness I refer to a somewhat more intense state than that in which the athlete normally finds himself. It is important to realize that there are ways of processing information other than those normally used. For example, we learn to use some of these other cognitive modes culturally in the expression of artistic creativity. I feel that we might become a bit more comfortable with these techniques after further exploration of these alternatives and begin to utilize them better in application to sport.

Pressman: I do not totally agree with what Mr Hickman has just said. I do not think that the types of processing we use in an altered state are basically the same but only slightly more intense than those we normally use. We use hypnosis with figure skaters in lieu of other techniques of relaxation to attain an altered state of consciousness. While under hypnosis, certain mental functions apparently become much more accessible compared to

164

normal thinking processes, and the results in terms of training the skater for performance are really quite surprising and very positive.

Not only is this technique successful, but its application appears justified based on recent brain function studies. Through fairly valid split brain studies, we have discovered that our two cerebral hemispheres really function quite differently. It appears that by using hypnosis or other psychological techniques we can suspend the activities of the dominant side of the brain which normally interfere with the imagery, coordination, and gestalt that are functions of the non-dominant cerebral hemisphere. As a result, we become much more spontaneous and coordinated in movement.

I think that it is possible to train this capacity and to develop and utilize this kind of mental processing in sport. We are just on the edge of validating these processes in terms of hard scientific study.

Nideffer: I would like to comment on the altered state or peak experience phenomenon. I will base my comments on personal peak experiences during diving. Often there will be a point in time just when I am taking the hurdle step when everything feels right in terms of performing this action. Somehow, I feel released and become a passive observer of the dive not really thinking or worrying about the detail of its execution. I agree, though, with the suggestion in your question that one must concentrate in an active way during new skill acquisition because this passive approach or passive focus of attention is not part of the learning process at that stage.

Pressman: I am afraid that I do not totally agree with Dr Nideffer's comment. I agree that certain sports require broad attention and others more focused or narrow attention. But, within this framework I feel that we can train athletes to improve and incorporate both types of attention for the betterment of performance.

We as psychiatrists, for instance, train our attention to spread in order to absorb the maximum amount of information. However, we try at the same time to concentrate on specifics while attempting to maintain a relaxed and spread focus of attention. I believe that athletes will trip up if they use other psychological techniques such as muscle-binding tension which are based on narrow focus of attention. They would be far better off to use relaxed or spread attention techniques, in my opinion.

With hypnosis, we rehearse those positive experiences that one has when everything is flowing together. Excessive attention to the detail of the activity will spoil the gestalt and result in tripping up the performance. There are some athletes who, while in an altered state of consciousness, think about failure "in the interest of overcoming failure." We feel that these individuals actually rehearse failure rather than the positive aspects of the experience and that this type of rehearsal could be detrimental to performance. So, in summary I feel that the use of hypnosis or other ordered processes to attain an altered state of consciousness wherein one rehearses and remembers positive experiences will undoubtedly enhance attitudes and effect better performances from athletes.

Question: *Much of what has been discussed centres on individual sports. How does an athlete in team competition cope with that situation's factors that are beyond his control while in an altered state of consciousness?*

Nideffer: I think that many of the responses or reactions in team sports can be reflexive. For example, in basketball there comes a time when the athlete must decide whether to take a shot or pass to another player. That decision can be reflexive, based on the feeling the athlete has about his opponent's position and how he perceives the situation strategically. This decision can be made reflexively without much conscious thinking, again depending upon the athlete's level of development and sport experience. If the decision is made reflexively, then the athlete will be freed up to the experience of that kind of altered state. But if the athlete does not have the necessary level of skill development, he will not be able to respond in this manner.

Hickman: I agree with Dr Nideffer and I think that an athlete has the capacity to perform incredible, unrehearsed reactions on the spur of the moment, once he has learned the basic fundamental lessons. I do not think that it is necessary to concentrate on every little detail of the performance because we have this amazing amount of coping ability integrated in our minds. I think that the athlete has access to these capacities provided he has the fundamental level of skill development required in his sport.

Question: *I am concerned about what happens to high level athletes after the sport experience, at the point in their lives when they are underproductive and on the way out. Have you worked with athletes in this situation and what role do you see the psychologist/coach playing to assist the athlete in making this adjustment in his life?*

Wilson: I think that this is one of the worst jobs that we as coaches do. We do not prepare athletes to leave the sport. In my own work we have had the opportunity over the past few years of assisting ten or twelve athletes to depart from competitive sport, or to prepare for re-entry into normal life. We are currently assisting in re-entry programs for athletes ranging from the very young up to the professional ranks. It seems that in the past all of our efforts as coaches and teachers were spent on focusing the athletes' attention and energies on his sport. Most of the athletes' positive reinforcement in life centred on sport. Suddenly all of these aspects, the practices, the competitions, the positive experiences which gave purpose and meaning to life are for some reason or another lost to the athlete.

I feel that we must somehow try to facilitate this process of re-entry, perhaps by taking advantage of the athletes' special skills and using them as demonstrators or assistant coaches in sport programs. There is a great deal yet to be learned about this problem and much work to be done in providing these athletes with alternative and meaningful avenues in life.

Hickman: The Esalen Sports Center in California was founded by two ex-athletes exactly for that reason—to do something with sport at a level outside competition. We have designed and implemented a number of community development programs in the San Francisco Bay area over the last couple of years wherein we introduced the participants to alternate ways of mind and body development. We feel that these techniques and the benefits derived from them will carry over into everyday life and open up a whole new way of experiencing life. We are also finding that as more and more people open up to daily life experiences through these techniques, they become more and more disinterested in the types of experiences that competitive sport provided in the past.

Wilson: We have had several reports of extreme depression upon withdrawal from competitive sport. Some of the athletes say that they will never train again, that they are sick of exercise. Yet we find that it is the lack of physical activity that underlies the depression. I think that the depression may be due to a classical case of exercise addiction while in the competitive state. We find that this depression soon disappears if the athletes take up physical activity in a sport other than that in which they were competitive.

Question: *How credible is the field of sport psychology in the general sport world? Do you encounter much hostility or resistance in the field?*

Hickman: There are a number of controversial areas in sport psychology which elicit scepticism even among psychologists. For example, the Russians have a whole area of research called psychic self-regulation wherein the human capacity to control psychically physiologic functions once thought to be completely under the control of the autonomic nervous system is investigated. This type of research is viewed with scepticism in the western world. So I feel that there is a credibility gap even within our own field and that there is still a great deal of resistance in traditional science to spread its boundaries to include these types of phenomena.

Nideffer: As clinical psychologists, we have reputations as shrinks, as people who find and treat severe pathology. Unfortunately, this stigma remains with us even when we work with essentially normal individuals such as athletes. I cannot help but think that our poor interpersonal communication skills have also made it even more difficult for us to sell ourselves and our services. We have been hiding behind technical jargon for too long. Furthermore, sport psychologists do not have an identity. We do not have a curriculum and we have not clarified what we can do for sport. I think that with further exposure and success with ongoing programs we will gradually gain more acceptance in the sport world.

Tutko: There was a time when it was considered weird for a psychologist to be working with an athlete let alone the athlete reporting or writing about psychic experiences. We are just beginning to break the barriers, to shed the stigma that you are a weirdo if you have these psychic experiences and can benefit from psychological assistance. So in answer to your question, we are just coming out of the closet and becoming free enough to discuss these phenomena openly. We must be conscious, though, of the bandwagon effect, that is, athletes might feel that they must have psychic or altered experiences to be successful. In the future, we must guard against unsavory exploitation of these phenomena by commercial interests.

Pressman: I would like to emphasize that treatment of pathological behavior or psychic experiences is not the total essence of psychological assistance. It is important to realize that psychological programs including the use of imagery, visual rehearsal, and relaxation training can and have been used systematically to improve performance in athletes who never have or may never have "peak psychic experiences."

General Comments

Wilson: I would like to comment on the use of relaxation training techniques with athletes. I think that if you use relaxation training or other techniques to attain altered states of consciousness that you had better be prepared for unusual experiences. One of my gymnasts had an "out-of-body experience" while doing relaxation training. Never having experienced this situation before, my first reaction was: "Oh my God, what happens if she decides to stay up there?" These types of experiences can and do happen to ordinary people and I think that it is important for the psychological well-being of the athlete that coaches respond to these situations with understanding and sensitivity.

Hickman: I would like to react to Dr Wilson's comment. We have found in our work that there is no cultural context within which to hold this kind of "out-of-body experience." Consequently, these experiences are usually repressed. Dr Wilson's story was in a sense atypical. Usually coaches, or whoever, do not want to hear about this type of phenomenon and athletes are sometimes more than reluctant to report them. I think, therefore, that it is extremely important to educate ourselves about this extraordinary range of capacities so that experiences such as these are not frightening and can be held in a useful context when they do occur.

Pressman: I do not feel that one requires any special preparation in dealing with athletes who have "out-of-body experiences." These people tend to have strong and substantial personality organization with very, very strong egos. So, in my opinion, we do not really have to worry about them not coming back to their bodies. The strength of their egos ensures that they will return.

the prediction & shaping of future behavior of athletes

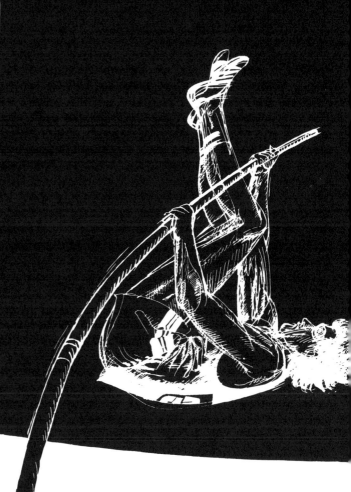

part 4

INTRODUCTION

Prediction abilities based on psychometrics and the shaping of future performances of athletes by various motivational and coaching techniques and programs are the essence of Part Four. The first chapter by Morgan deals with the usefulness of personology in sport practice. Morgan, however, warns the coach and the sport psychologist to keep their expectations about the predictive power based on psychological data realistic. The message Morgan is conveying is that coaches should be reasonable in the kinds of requests they make of sport psychologists, and the psychologists should consider promising less than they feel they can deliver. According to Morgan, the state of the art is at present far from perfect and does not justify selection of athletes based upon psychological data alone.

Halliwell, and McClements and Botterill present strategies for enhancing motivation in sport. Halliwell first introduces the incentive motivation model which he then applies to sport practice. Several useful motivation strategies based on the incentive motivation systems are presented and are further illustrated by numerous practical examples from coaching.

Goal-setting strategies for sport training are discussed by McClements and Botterill. The authors consider the commitment to well defined goals as one of the most important aspects of motivation for training. The correct selection of goals is crucial in this process. As an aid in optimal goal-setting the authors present a mathematical model which can be used for determining future performance based on past data.

Kroll in "The Stress of High Performance Athletics" examines the various causes of anxiety in athletic competition. He suggests that training and coaching practices be designed to reduce excessive anxiety by the elimination of the stimulus elements which generate the emotional response in athletes.

In the last chapter, Rothstein discusses some of the new developments concerning information feedback in coaching skilled athletes.

prediction of performance in athletics

William P. Morgan

Athletes in any given sport sometimes appear to lack the physiological prerequisites for success, but they are observed to perform at a very high level nevertheless. The explanation for success (or overachievement) in such a case usually centers around the psychological assets possessed by the athlete. That is, he or she is said to overcome acknowledged physiological inadequacies as a result of psychological assets such as drive, desire, persistence, determination, and so on. Conversely, athletes who appear to lack the psychological prerequisites for high level performance are sometimes quite successful, and it seems reasonable to suggest that success in such a case results from the athlete's superior physiological makeup. Hence, physiological or psychological data alone would never predict success in a highly reliable fashion. It is only when the athlete is viewed as a complex psychobiologic organism that one can hope to more closely approximate ideal levels of prediction. While there is often a tendency to dismiss such a view as merely philosophical, it has been supported empirically in research dealing with elite performers in various sports such as rowing, wrestling, swimming, and distance running (Morgan, 1973; Morgan and Pollock, 1977; Nagle *et al.,* 1975). In this chapter, however, I will limit my remarks to issues of a psychometric and perceptual nature. Furthermore, the focus will be directed toward the role of mental health in athletics.

THE CREDULOUS-SKEPTICAL ARGUMENT

There are basically two personology camps in contemporary sport psychology, and the members of these two camps espouse either a *credulous* or a *skeptical* viewpoint concerning prediction of athletic success from psychological data. The credulous psychologist would lead us to believe that psychological data is extremely useful in predicting success, whereas the skeptical would argue that psychological data is of little or no value whatsoever. An objective review of existing research, however, leads to the conclusion that neither the skeptical nor the credulous viewpoint can be supported in a consistent manner (Morgan, 1978). That is, success in athletics seems to be dependent in part on psychological states and traits, but the relationship between psychological structure and success is far from perfect. Since available prediction models are accurate in about 70 per cent of the predictions advanced, it is proposed that a more appropriate position would be one which is mid-way on the *credulous-skeptical* continuum. At any rate, it is quite clear that the present "state of the art" does not permit the selection of national teams on the basis of psychological data alone. On the other hand, use of an athlete's personality profile, in concert with input variables such as past experience, coaches' ratings, anatomic and physiologic characteristics, and so on, can clearly enhance the accuracy of prediction in sports such as rowing (Morgan and Johnson, 1978), distance running (Morgan and Pollock, 1977), and wrestling (Nagle *et al.*, 1975).

THE PSYCHOLOGICAL INVENTORY

The question of *which psychological inventory to employ* has been debated for some time, and I suspect that we will not see an end to this debate in the near future. Some psychologists argue for the use of inventories which have been designed to measure traits, others feel that assessment of states is more appropriate, some argue that state-trait models are best, while still others reject all existing psychometric tools in favor of "situation-specific" measures. However, it seems to me that the *best* inventory in any given situation is governed by the question being asked.

In our research involving Olympic athletes competing in the final selection camps the following psychological inventories have been employed:

1. State-Trait Anxiety Inventory (STAI), Spielberger *et al.*, 1970.
2. Somatic Perception Questionnaire, Landy and Stern, 1971.
3. Depression Adjective Checklist (DACL), Lubin, 1967.
4. Profile of Mood States (POMS), McNair *et al.*, 1971.
5. Eysenck Personality Inventory (EPI), Eysenck and Eysenck, 1968.

These inventories have been designed to measure various psychological states and traits, and the EPI also contains a conformity or lie scale. The use of psychological states and traits in concert has consistently accounted for more of the variance than either approach alone. This observation has also held in our research deal-ing with the psychometric correlates of pain perception (Morgan and Horstman, 1978), and perceived exertion (Morgan, 1973). Selected scales of the POMS and EPI, however, have been the most consistent predictors, and I will elaborate on these findings later.

U.S. NATIONAL ROWING TEAMS

The U.S. college eight-oared crews and independent club eights such as Vesper from Philadelphia dominated international regattas for many years. As a matter of fact, from 1920 to 1956, U.S. college eights won eight straight Olympiads. In 1960, however, for the first time in almost 50 years, none of the U.S. crews even made the Olympic finals. In retrospect it appeared as though European equipment and technique had outdistanced the more conservative U.S. models. At any rate, the European crews dom-inated the international regattas for the next four years, and it seemed unlikely that college crews from the U.S. could regain their former stature. One of the former independent clubs still active was the Vesper Club. They began to experiment with European methods, and they adopted the Italian racing shells which were lighter and sleeker. This strategy paid off, and the Vesper eight went on to win the 1964 Olympics. However, the Eastern European teams regained dominance of international crew, and by 1970 the U.S. found itself a distant third behind the German Democratic Republic and the Soviet Union.

Leaders in the U.S. crew movement decided that it would no longer be possible to perform well on the international circuit with intact crews from a single club or college. It was felt that a national eight should be formed in which the best rowers from all of the colleges and clubs would become members of a national eight. This resulted in the development of a *camp system* in which the best rowers in the U.S. were invited to a national camp. The idea was to evaluate all rowers in the camp, and then select the best for the national boat. I was contacted during the summer of 1974 by Allen Rosenberg, coach of the national heavyweight eight, and he requested that I join their group at the national camp for the purpose of assisting in the selection process. The following section outlines the results of this initial work.

1974 U.S. HEAVYWEIGHT EIGHT

The training camp was held at the Kent School in Connecticut. Allen Rosenberg served as head coach, and he was assisted by four college coaches and a team physician. Sixty rowers from around the U.S. had assembled at the training camp, and a final eight would be determined from this number. The national eight would then proceed to Lucerne for the international championships. I met with this group, and a summary of my dialogue with the coaching staff follows.

Allen Rosenberg, coach of the national heavyweight eight, asked me to join their group at the national camp for the purpose of assisting in the selection process.

Staff: *We understand that you were able to predict who nine of the ten wrestlers would be on the 1972 Olympic team prior to their final selection from a group of 40. We have a similar problem, and we would like you to help us select the top rowers from our group of 60 candidates. Also, we know that the East Germans rely a great deal on psychological test results in selection of their crews. Can you help us with this problem?*

Response: *Yes and no. Unfortunately, any help that I might be able to provide would be in subsequent years. We could evaluate your rowers psychologically at the beginning of the camp, characterize those you ultimately select and cut, and then proceed to evaluate whether or not the two groups differ from the outset. If there are differences, it might be possible to predict success and failure on later crews. Also, while we were rather successful in predicting who would make the 1972 Olympic Wrestling Team, there is no reason to think that the personality structure of rowers and wrestlers interacts with athletic performance in a similar fashion. Therefore, I would like to suggest that we enter the camp this year; test those rowers who consent to be tested; not use the data for selection purposes; evaluate the results of our testing; and then determine in a subsequent camp the extent to which prediction is possible.*

Staff: *OK, that is agreeable, but we have two additional problems of an applied nature that we are attempting to solve, and we would like your advice on these matters as well. First of all, is there any way we can alter our training program to ensure that we will perform well at the altitude in Switzerland. Second, we have always had some problems with jet lag effects on these trips. How many days do we need to be in Switzerland before competition in order to be confident that we will not have problems with jet lag?*

Response: *I do not have the immediate answer to either of those questions, but I will attempt to have some recommendations for you when we meet next week.*

In retrospect it appears that we were being asked to deliver far more than the present state of the art would permit us to deliver. We had previously administered the Minnesota Multiphasic Personality Inventory (MMPI) to 50 college oarsmen during the first week of their freshman year, and their athletic records were examined four years later in order to identify successful (N=13) and unsuccessful (N=37) rowers from the outset. The successful oarsmen possessed more favorable scores on each of the eight

clinical scales of the MMPI from the outset of their careers. However, we had no reason to believe that positive mental health
would covary with success in national camp (Morgan and Johnson,
1978). Therefore, the conservative approach we adopted seemed
to be appropriate. Also, the response of a well-known U.S. cox-
swain of the day to the question of what makes a good boat
follows, and the subjective, artistic tone of his response would
suggest that prediction with *soft* or *hard* data might be equally
inaccurate:

> When you're doing it right, you get this really beautiful thing
> called swing. It's the feeling of everybody doing precisely the
> right thing at precisely the right time. And you feel not only the
> people in the boat working as a team, but the people in the boat
> and the boat itself working as a team. It's this great interrelation
> of flesh, wood, and water. It is poetry in motion.

As we proceeded with the psychometric portion of this study
we became aware of the fact that selection, no matter how it was
approached, would be somewhat subjective. Indeed, it would be
extremely subjective in comparison with round-robin wrestle-offs
or running times recorded to a tenth of a second. At any rate, we
made the assumption that the coaching staff selected and cut the
correct rower in every case. In making this assumption we obviously reduced the likelihood of making correct predictions. In other
words, the resulting predictions would be conservative by definition.

Results. Fifty-seven of the 60 rowers signed informed consent
statements, and they agreed to participate in our study. All testing was carried out prior to the initiation of training or selection.
The rowers were assured that the psychological data would not be
used in selecting individuals for the team, and this agreement was,
in fact, strictly adhered to. No individual psychological profile was
evaluated until *after* selection of the top 16 oarsmen had taken
place. The 16 finalists for the lightweight eight were also evaluated
prior to their final cut. Again, however, individual profiles were
not examined until *after* the selections were actually made. Based
upon the findings from five successive freshman crews at the University of Wisconsin, we predicted that rowers with positive
mental health would be more likely to make the final cut than
those with poor mental health. The psychological inventories mentioned earlier yielded a series of measures which are illustrated in
Figure 1. It was predicted that a rower scoring low on state
anxiety, trait anxiety, tension, depression, anger, fatigue, confusion, neuroticism, and conformity, but high on vigor and extro-

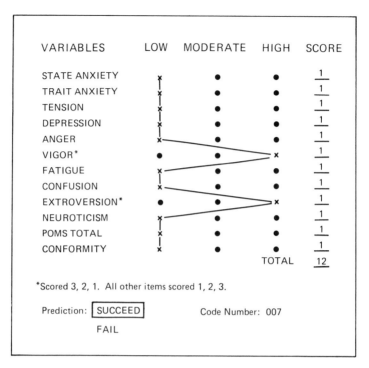

Figure 1. The psychological profile of a successful U.S. oarsman in 1974.

version, would be more likely to earn a berth on the boat than a rower with the mirror image of this profile. The rower illustrated in Figure 1 achieved the lowest possible score (12), and it was predicted that he would be one of the final 16. He actually made the final cut and represented the U.S. on the 1974 heavyweight eight. The rower depicted in Figure 2 had the reverse profile, and this resulted in a total raw score of 35. It was predicted that this anxious, depressed, fatigued, confused, withdrawn, neurotic individual would not earn a berth on the boat, and he was actually cut during the early part of the training camp. Needless to say, these extreme cases are presented for the sake of illustration, and most athletes do not manifest such clear-cut profiles. Ten of the 16 final selections were identified using this prediction model, and 31 of those who were rejected were correctly identified. In other words, 41 of the 57 predictions were correct. It should be kept in mind that these clinical predictions were made *a priori.* A *post hoc* analysis was carried out using a stepwise discriminant function analysis,

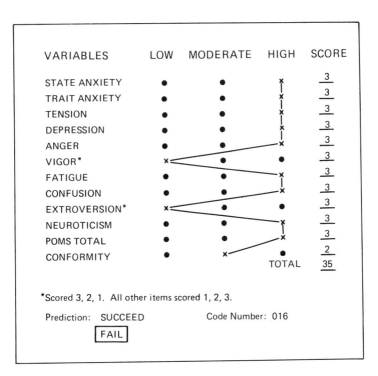

Figure 2. The psychological profile of an unsuccessful U.S. oarsman in 1974.

and this resulted in 40 of 57 correct predictions. In other words, the clinical (*a priori*) and statistical (*post hoc*) procedures were equally effective (70 per cent).

Nine of the 16 finalists for the lightweight eight possessed psychological profiles which were sufficiently unique to permit prediction, while seven of the group did not exhibit remarkable profiles. Predictions were not possible for this latter group. However, all of the predicted failures (five) and successes (four) were correct where prediction was possible. The results of this study have subsequently been replicated with candidates for the 1976 Olympic team. It seems reasonable to conclude that positive mental health plays a role in the performance of the elite rower. It would be a very serious mistake, however, to employ psychological data of the type described here to select national teams. The accuracy of such data is far from perfect, and it should only be used in concert with other information. For those exercise scientists and humanists who argue that data of any type, physiological, biomechanical, or psychological, should not be employed in the selection of athletes for national teams, the *flip of the coin* model will remain the method of choice!

The above data were of interest to the coach after the study was completed for several reasons. First, in most cases where uncertainty had existed relative to cuts, the psychological data offered corroboration. This served to reinforce the decision-making process he had adopted. Also, both the heavyweight and lightweight eights earned gold medals in Lucerne, and this served as further reinforcement.

The altitude problem raised in the first meeting turned out to be an easy one to solve. Upon returning to the lab and evaluating the altitude question we learned that Lucerne was not at high altitude! Therefore, we are quite confident that we addressed the *altitude training question* in the correct way. Elimination of pseudo problems, however, may oftentimes be just as important as resolving the real ones.

Inspection of the aviation medicine literature revealed that a rough rule to follow in order to avoid jet lag effects is to plan on arriving in the new country a number of days prior to competition. Existing physiological research indicated that approximately one day for every time zone traversed is needed to assure return to base line values. This formula would have required that the crew arrive 11 days prior to competition. This was regarded as undesirable because of (1) the cost factor and (2) the temporal nature of training, peaking, tapering, and arriving for competition too early. It was possible to evaluate 25 adult males on a transcontinental trip involving 12 time zones, and we tested these individuals before, during travel, and following their arrival in a new country (Morgan and Vogel, 1975). This revealed that rather substantial psychological changes took place across the 12 time zones, but the response only lasted for 48 hours. All of the measured mood states had returned to base line within 72 hours. Therefore, our recommendation to athletic teams has been that they allow approximately four days in the country prior to competition if possible.

THE ELITE WRESTLER

A related study involved an attempt to (1) psychologically characterize the elite wrestler, and (2) examine the role of mental health in success and failure for the sport of wrestling. Eighty-one University of Wisconsin wrestlers, representing five successive freshman classes, completed the MMPI during the first week of school and their varsity careers were evaluated four years later in order to psychologically characterize the successful and unsuccessful. A stepwise discriminant function analysis revealed that psychological differences existed from the outset, with the successful wrestler possessing more desirable mental health (Morgan and Johnson, 1977).

These findings were replicated with the 1972 and 1976 U.S. Olympic Wrestling Teams. Results of the 1972 study are summarized in Figure 3. It will be noted that successful candidates for

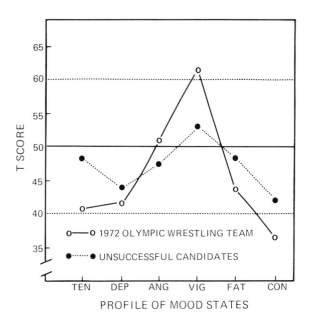

Figure 3. Psychological profiles of successful and unsuccessful U.S. wrestlers in 1972.

the 1972 team scored lower than the unsuccessful ones on tension, depression, anger, fatigue, and confusion, and they scored significantly higher on vigor. This successful profile has been dubbed the *iceberg* profile since the negative variables all fall below the 50th T score, and the one positive variable is above the 50 or *surface.* Nine members of the 1972 team completed the psychological testing prior to the final wrestle-off, and eight of these nine were predicted to make the team based upon their psychological *and* physiological profiles (Nagle *et al.,* 1975).

The results of this study were used in developing a prediction model which was then tested with candidates for the 1976 U.S. Olympic team. The results of this testing are presented in Figure 4. The major findings revealed that (1) all significant differences favored the successful candidates, with lower anxiety and higher psychic vigor being the most notable distinctions, and (2) the *iceberg* profile was observed in the successful candidates. These findings suggest that positive mental health, even within the homogeneous setting of an Olympic camp, plays an important

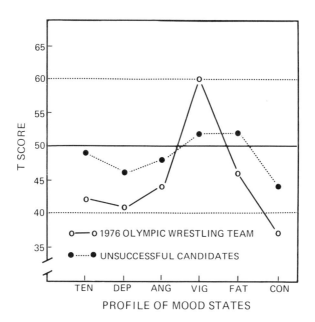

Figure 4. Psychological profiles of successful and unsuccessful U.S. wrestlers in 1976.

role in governing the candidate's likelihood of success.

It is often difficult to replicate psychological findings in the complex psychodynamic milieu which exists in sport. Therefore, the agreement between the data presented in Figures 3 and 4 is of particular importance in terms of prediction. For this reason the psychological profiles of the 1972 and 1976 U.S. Wrestling Teams are presented in Figure 5. The *iceberg* profile referred to earlier is clearly demonstrated in the following Figure. It should also be kept in mind that these wrestlers were tested at the beginning of a three day wrestle-off designed to identify the individuals who would perform on the U.S. Olympic team. Despite the stressful nature of such an event, the wrestlers are noted to be uniformly low on tension, depression, fatigue, and confusion, but well above average on vigor.

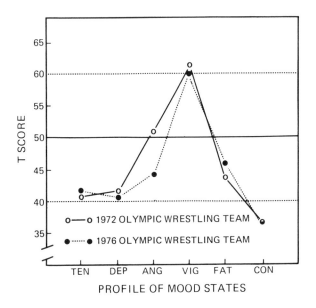

Figure 5. Psychological profiles of 1972 and 1976 U.S. Olympic Wrestling teams.

THE ELITE DISTANCE RUNNER

The same psychological tests administered to the rowers and wrestlers have also been given to distance runners of differing ability levels in an attempt to characterize the elite distance runner. Our observation has been that distance runners of various ability levels possess the *iceberg* profile referred to earlier. That is, running long distances either produces or requires positive mental health, but individuals of differing ability levels do not differ in this respect. However, there is a major difference in the manner in which elite runners process sensory input while competing in contrast with less capable runners. These differences have been elaborated upon in a recent paper by Morgan and Pollock (1977). The difference involves adoption of cognitive strategies which are governed by *association*, or paying attention to one's body, versus the converse which is known as *dissociating* or ignoring sensory input. The elite runners employ the associative strategy which is characterized by continuous monitoring of their bodies. This particular cognitive strategy has been shown to not only discriminate between the elite and less capable, but it also appears to play a role in the success of the elite performer.

It is of some interest that elite performers in sports such as wrestling, long distance running, and rowing are more alike from a personality standpoint than they are unalike. The results of psychological testing with such diverse groups appear in Figure 6. Significant differences are noted by an asterisk in this Figure.

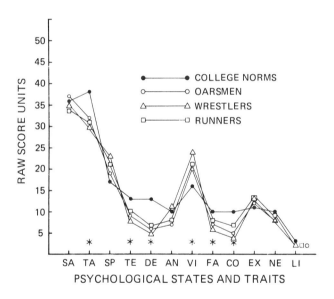

Figure 6. Psychological profiles of successful U.S. oarsmen, wrestlers, and runners.

Differences are noted for trait anxiety, tension, depression, vigor, fatigue, and confusion. All of these differences are between the elite athletes and the college norms or population mean, and in every case the difference favors the athlete samples. In other words, these elite athletes are remarkably similar, and they only differ from the general population in a positive way.

CONCLUSION

In this chapter I have attempted to summarize the results of our work with elite athletes in various sports such as rowing, wrestling, and long distance running. I have proposed that a variety of psychological states and traits have been useful in our attempt to discriminate between athletes of differing ability levels. The primary characteristic of the elite athlete from such diverse sports appears to be the presence of positive mental health, and wrestlers, rowers, and runners are more alike than they are dissimilar. Coaches should be reasonable in the kinds of requests they make of sport psychologists, and psychologists should avoid *overselling* their programs. As a general rule psychologists might consider promising less than they actually feel they can deliver. In terms of prediction it appears that psychological data can be used to identify successful and unsuccessful candidates from the outset. However, the precision afforded by such prediction is far from perfect (about 70 per cent), and the present state of the art does not justify selection based upon psychological data alone. Psychological data, however, when employed in concert with other input variables, should serve to enhance prediction.

/trategie/ for enhancing motivation in /port

Wayne R. Halliwell

One of the most satisfying experiences for any coach is to coach a group of athletes who train hard during practice sessions and consistently play with a great deal of intensity during games. In this case, winning is merely a bonus as the real satisfaction comes from knowing that each athlete worked as hard as he possibly could. On the other hand, nothing can be more frustrating than coaching a talented athlete who does not play up to his potential because he is unwilling to give an honest effort in practice or game situations. In both examples, the source of the coach's satisfaction or frustration is an athlete's or a group of athletes' level of motivation.

Unfortunately, from a psychological perspective, there is no easy explanation for the varying levels of individual and team motivation which we observe in all sports at all levels of competition. However, the study of motivation can help us to get a handle on some of the psychological processes which underly human motivation and thereby obtain a further awareness of the factors which influence this important determinant of sport performance. In this chapter, we will examine sport motivation from a theoretical perspective and attempt to offer the coach some practical suggestions for enhancing motivation.

THE WHY OF SPORT MOTIVATION

When sport psychologists study motivation, they are essentially trying to answer a number of questions which begin with the word "why." In psychological terminology, these "why" questions deal with the direction, intensity, and persistence dimensions of an athlete's behavior. Typical of questions representing these three components of athletic behavior are:
1. Why do certain athletes choose to participate in certain sports?

187

2. Why do certain athletes work harder or play with greater intensity than other athletes?
3. Why do certain athletes continue to participate in sports while others drop out?

Of primary concern to most coaches is the second question which deals with the intensity of an athlete's behavior. In other words, they want to know what can be done to maximize each athlete's effort every time that he steps on the field, floor, or ice. To answer this question, it is necessary to backtrack for a moment and determine why the athlete is playing the sport in the first place. With this knowledge in hand, we can begin to create a sports environment that will satisfy his needs and expectations and thereby enhance his motivation.

INCENTIVE MOTIVATION

Based on a theoretical model of incentive motivation formulated by Birch and Veroff (1966), recent research by Alderman and Wood (1976) has shown that affiliation and excellence are the two strongest incentive conditions for young athletes (see figure). These findings indicate that participation in competitive sport is perceived to be important to athletes because it provides them with an opportunity to establish or maintain close personal relationships and be accepted as an important member of a group. In addition, the competitive sport experience provides an opportunity to do something very well for its own sake or to do it better than anyone else.

Although the Alderman and Wood (1976) findings were based on a study of young amateur athletes, it can be contended that affiliation and excellence are important incentives for athletes at all levels of competition. For example, when injury forced Bobby Orr to end prematurely an illustrious hockey career, he was quoted as saying that the thing he would miss the most about not playing was the camaraderie and fun that went along with being with "the guys." Also, when asked why he had decided to cut short his comeback attempt and retire from the game of hockey, Orr replied quite simply: "I worked hard and tried my best, but it wasn't good enough." In other words, his battered knees prevented him from achieving a level of excellence that he felt was necessary to continue playing. Quite clearly, for this extremely talented professional athlete, affiliation and excellence were important sources of satisfaction.

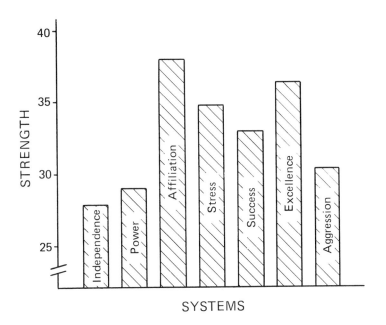

Figure 1.   Strength of incentive systems for young hockey players based on 425 subjects (Alderman and Wood, 1976).

Although Alderman and Wood found affiliation and excellence to be the two strongest incentive systems in sport, stress incentives were also reported to be important. These incentives are provided in sport by the opportunities for excitement, tension, and interesting experiences, with special emphasis on the aspects of novelty, uncertainty, and complexity. In psychological terminology, athletes appear to be "stress-seekers." I recently had confirmation of the importance of stress as an incentive for young hockey players when a 12-year-old boy came up to me during a try-out camp and asked when we were going to play a "real game." Obviously, he was looking forward to the competitive stress which accompanies regular season games.

From the figure given above, it can be seen that success is also a relatively strong incentive for young athletes. Success incentives in sport are those that are attached to the extrinsic rewards derived from the competitive sport experiences, such as opportunities for status, prestige, recognition, and social approval.

In sum, the results of the analysis of motivation in young athletes indicate quite clearly that affiliation, excellence, stress, and success are strong incentives. Based on these findings, strategies for enhancing motivation can be formulated by creating sports environments which provide the athletes with opportunities to satisfy these goals.

IMPLICATIONS OF INCENTIVE MOTIVATION RESEARCH

The seven major motive-incentive systems as shown in the figure cannot be considered as separate entities. Instead, they interact with one another in special ways and attempts to accomplish one goal may either help or hinder the accomplishment of another goal. With this note of caution in mind, we can explore various ways of building motivation by utilizing techniques which provide opportunities for affiliation, excellence, stress, and success.

1. Make sure that each athlete feels that his contribution to the team is important.

In team sports, most of the glory goes to players who possess great offensive talents and thereby score a lot of goals, baskets, touch downs, and so on. Little recognition is given to defensive players who make equally important contributions to a team's success. To enhance a defensive player's perception of the significance of his role on a team, coaches should provide positive reinforcement in the form of praise or individual statistics which point out the value of each player's contribution. Examples of individual statistics for defensive efforts that are often overlooked include: number of face-offs won in hockey, number of shots blocked in basketball, or the number of tackles executed in football. In all team sports, many defensive functions go unnoticed. Thus, coaches should analyze thoroughly the tasks demanded of each player's position and attempt to provide positive feedback for personal accomplishments.

Although certain offensive feats in team sports provide adequate recognition, there are other less spectacular offensive efforts that are rarely reinforced. Examples include: advancing a runner in baseball, executing a good block in football, or screening an opponent in basketball. Once again, a thorough analysis of each player's offensive functions will enable a coach to compile comprehensive personal statistics which can be used to provide feedback to a player concerning his contribution to the team.

In the same manner certain players should be recognized for their value to the team as "emotional leaders" in the dressing room or on the playing field. These players are not always the most talented athletes, but their leadership skills are extremely important to the team. Similarly, certain players are more disciplined than others and will seldom take a foolish retaliation penalty ofter a foul has been committed on them by an opposing player. Such examples of disciplined behavior should also be praised by a perceptive coach.

This list represents but a small sample of individual accomplishments that frequently go unrecognized by spectators at athletic contests. However, an astute coach can increase an athlete's motivation by providing social approval and statistics which indicate to the athlete that his efforts are indeed appreciated by the team.

2. Evaluation should be based on performance as opposed to performance outcome.

In almost all sports we observe instances in which a player performs a motor task with great skill but the result of his performance is unsuccessful. In baseball, for example, a batter may hit four consecutive line drives that are caught by members of the opposing team. In this case, the performance outcome is no base hits in four times at bat. However, the performance or execution of the player in question could not have been any better. Thus, the coach should provide the hitter with positive reinforcement and direct attention to the great contact he made with the ball rather than to the consequences of the ball being caught.

Similarly, if a team of average ability plays with great intensity but loses to a team of vastly superior ability, a coach should be quick to praise his players for their effort. In other words, the coach is basing his feedback on the team's performance rather than their performance outcome.

3. Encourage players to develop pride in performance through realistic goal-setting and task analysis.

The satisfaction that results from doing something well, as opposed to the satisfaction derived from rewards and status, is referred to in this recommendation. Coaches should encourage players to establish individual goals which they hope to accomplish throughout the season. These goals should be specific, measurable, and challenging but attainable. They form a type of "psychological contract" between coach and athlete which motivates the athlete to improve his own level of personal competence. Research findings on goal-setting in sports (Botterill, 1978) have shown that athletes are more highly motivated to accomplish goals which they had a hand in setting. The value of establishing personal goals is that the athlete has a criterion by which he can evaluate his own performance and it is this evaluation process that provides him with pride in his accomplishments.

It should be noted that personal goals should not be limited to the performance of certain motor skills. On the contrary, athletes should be encouraged to set other goals which lie within the cognitive, social, and affective domains of human behavior. An example of a cognitive goal would be an athlete's attempt to eliminate certain mental errors such as a flanker running the wrong pattern or a blocker missing his assignment in football. Typical of social and affective goals would be attempts to encourage teammates more often and efforts to control one's level of anxiety in important games. In all cases the goals help the athlete to become aware of what he can realistically ask of himself, and they serve as a source of personal pride if he is able to accomplish them.

Since many athletes tend to set unrealistically high goals which may lead to frustration, coaches are advised to help athletes establish realistic goals, especially during their initial attempts at goal-setting. The question of course arises: "How do a coach and athlete go about establishing realistic goals?" The answer lies in a thorough task analysis and an objective assessment of the athlete's present abilities.

If faced with a difficult task, the athlete should be encouraged to analyze it and determine where the difficulty lies. Once analyzed, steps can be taken to make the task less difficult by formulating strategies to overcome certain obstacles. Short-term goals can be established and the athlete's efforts in practice can be geared toward accomplishing these objectives. Thus, the link between personal effort and success will be strengthened, feelings of self-management will develop, and pride in performance will be heightened.

4. Encourage players to develop team pride.

In some sports, it is important that the desire for group success be stronger than the personal motive to achieve success. That is, if a team member is more interested in his own performance than the team's, his actions may be detrimental to the team. This is especially true in sports such as hockey, basketball, volleyball, soccer, and football.

Dr Alvin Zander, a prominent social psychologist, has recognized that the desire for success of the team can be a powerful motivating force on team members. A summary of his suggestions for generating a commitment to the team and developing team pride is given below (Zander, 1975).

1. Emphasize the importance of pride in the group, its sources, and its consequences for the team. One coach I know makes his seniors responsible for developing these ideas as well as building enthusiasm during practice and games.

2. Make sure that each member understands that his contribution to the team is valued.

3. Use various means to underscore how each teammate depends upon the work of each other for the success of their unit.

4. Emphasize the unity of the group, the score as a product of team effort, and the perception that all members are within the group's boundary.

5. Indicate to members separately how membership helps each individual, so that each will see the group as an attractive entity.

6. Take care in the selection of group goals so that they are realistic challenges and not unreasonably hard or easy. Set standards of excellence for all skills and activities.

7. Do not be afraid to change goals that are found to be unreasonably difficult. The warmest pride comes from living up to reasonable expectations for that group, not in failing impossibly difficult ends.

8. Once goals have been set, consider what obstacles might prevent their fulfillment and how the obstacles might be overcome by the team.

9. Encourage talk in the group about how performance can be improved and how the boring parts of athletics can be made more involving.

10. Avoid fear of failure and the tendency to evade challenges that is engendered thereby.

Although each of the recommendations has important implications for building pride in the group and subsequent group motivation, space limitations do not allow us to discuss each suggestion in detail. However, one of Zander's recommendations will be expanded upon to illustrate its application in specific situations. In this regard, suggestion number three will be discussed and an example provided to show what a coach can do to "underscore how each teammate depends upon the work of each other for the success of their unit."

If a certain player is loafing in practices and plays with little intensity in games, a coach could use recommendation number three to motivate him by pointing out that the success of the team is dependent upon each team member working hard for each other. By "dogging it" or "going through the motions" the player in question is in effect depriving the team of a chance to be successful. Instead of hurling insults at the player for being lazy, the coach should sit down with him and appeal to his commitment to the team. It should be emphasized that by not working hard, the player is not only disappointing his coaches, but he is letting down each and every one of his teammates. This group pressure and appeal to the player's pride can prove to be effective motivators.

From Zander's list of recommendations, we can see the value of affiliation and group cohesion as a determinant of pride in the group. In a recent inteview, Jim Corrigal, nine-year all-star defensive end for the Toronto Argonauts professional football team, corroborated the importance of cohesion as a source of team pride. Near the end of a particularly difficult season, Corrigal stated: "This has been my most frustrating year in football since I started playing the game. I don't mean just professionally, but right back to Scollard Hall in North Bay. It's been an unfun season, not because we're 4-10 but because of the environment here; with the continuous changes in personnel, there is just no camaraderie in the club. The players in the Argo clubhouse remind me of pieces of a puzzle—just fragments really—that no one can put together as a unit."

Although cohesion is an important determinant of pride in the group, the meaning of the term cohesion must be examined a bit further to obtain a complete understanding of the relationship between cohesion and group performance. In a recent review of the literature on group cohesion (Loy *et al.*, 1978), it has been pointed out that "task cohesion" is more important than "social cohesion" if a group wishes to be productive. In other words, if members of a team spend too much time working on establishing group harmony and positive interpersonal relations, the time and energy spent in this pursuit may prove to be counterproductive to accomplishing the task at hand. Thus a coach should be aware of the different components of cohesion and the possible negative effects on group performance if the team members rate the social goals of the group to be more important than the achievement of certain performance objectives. The solution it seems is to obtain an ideal blend of social cohesion and task cohesion so that pride in team success is supported by harmonious group relations.

5. Use innovative techniques to make training sessions interesting.

Since athletes perceive their sport experience to be a source of excitement and arousal, coaches should take steps to satisfy these needs by making practices as interesting as possible. The list of possible ways of developing interest and enthusiasm depends on the creativeness of the coach and his players.

A few examples from different levels of competition will, we hope, enable coaches to devise innovative techniques which are specific to their sports. At the professional level, Roger Neilson, coach of the Toronto Maple Leafs hockey team, has gained much recognition for the innovative measures he takes to increase interest during practice sessions. Last winter when the inevitable boredom of a long season began to take its toll, Neilson increased interest at a practice by running a scrimmage in which all right-hand shots were required to shoot left and vice versa for left-hand shots. The result was a spirited scrimmage accompanied by lots of boyish enthusiasm. By creating a situation which his players had never experienced before, coach Neilson effectively increased the players' level of motivation and the pace of the rest of the practice picked up considerably. Similar innovative techniques could easily be used to add variety and fun to basketball, baseball, volleyball, and other team sport practice sessions. Examples include scrimmages between the tallest players ("hulks") and the smallest players ("runts"), or between "righties" and "lefties."

Asking players to play different positions during practice can also be an effective means of heightening enthusiasm. This technique pays further dividends because it enables players to appreciate the demands of other positions on the team. It is nice to see that in certain areas little league administrators are using a rotational rule in which players are required to change positions after each inning. By offering youngsters new experiences, the little league baseball programs are heightening the intrinsic attractiveness of the game and thereby increasing the likelihood that youngsters will enjoy themselves and want to continue participating.

6. Encourage athletes to accept personal responsibility for their own actions.

This recommendation is derived from the work of Dr Richard deCharms (1968), a well-known psychologist, who has had a lot of success in raising the motivation levels of under-achieving students. He found that when students perceived that they were responsible for their own actions, they became more involved and motivated. On the other hand, students were less motivated if they felt that their actions were controlled by others.

In sport settings increased feelings of personal responsibility can be created by using a participant leadership approach. Tom Watt, successful coach of the University of Toronto hockey team and a strong advocate of this approach, asks each player to direct at least one practice session during the season. Besides being an effective motivational technique which enhances the players' feelings of perceived responsibility, this approach also enables the players to empathize with the daily problems that the coach may encounter in running practices.

At the University of British Columbia, coach Bert Halliwell challenges his players to suggest at least one new drill per week and this challenge has proven to be an effective motivational tool. He also requests players to direct certain segments of practice sessions and the players respond enthusiastically to this opportunity to put their teammates through their paces.

With younger athletes, leadership input in practices may consist of leading the stretching exercises in the warm-up session, or it may consist of suggesting "fun" games to be played during a designated portion of the practice. In determining the amount of par-

The best coaches demonstrate the desired behavior first ("like this"), quickly imitate the player's mistake ("not like this"), and then follow with another demonstration of the proper execution of the skill ("like this").

ticipant leadership that can be expected from a team, a coach must analyze the team's level of maturity and experience carefully. At the professional level, veteran players should be encouraged to voice their opinions on game strategies. Lamar Leachman, defensive line coach of the Montreal Alouettes professional football team, has apparently learned the value of participant leadership as a motivational technique. In a recent article, he commented: "I understand the way that they want to be coached. This is a smart group of players. They want to be *responsible for some input* too. I listen to them all the time. Most of the time they come up with super ideas. Heck, they're out on the field. What they have to offer can be very beneficial."

In contrast to Leachman's new democratic approach, Vern Rapp, ex-manager of the St Louis Cardinals baseball team, overlooked an excellent opportunity to utilize the knowledge of one of his veteran ball players at last year's spring training camp. Specifically, although Lou Brock holds the major league record for stolen bases, he was not asked to help in coaching the younger players; instead, he was asked to participate in all the base-stealing drills along with the other rookies. Highly upset about the incident, Brock was quoted as saying, "The man is robbing us of our self-dignity." Thus, instead of increasing an athlete's motivation by enhancing his feelings of self-worth, the manager alienated a key veteran ballplayer and started a chain of events which led to his own dismissal a couple of months later.

From the preceding discussion of individual and group motivation, it becomes evident that there is no simple formula for motivating athletes. Instead, several personal, situational, and task variables must be considered in the formulation of effective motivational strategies.

POSITIVE-NEGATIVE-POSITIVE
APPROACH IN COACHING

Since certain coaches seem to be very successful in motivating their players, valuable information can also be obtained by observing their coaching behavior and heeding their advice. To this end, John Wooden, the legendary basketball coach at U.C.L.A., warns: "You will never motivate an athlete by alienating him." (Wooden, 1972.) His actions support his words. Results of a recent behavioral analysis of Wooden's interaction with his players at practice sessions indicated that when he did scold a player, Wooden was quick to follow this negative remark with a positive reinstruction (Tharp and Gallimore, 1976).

In pointing out a mistake, Wooden used a positive-negative-positive approach in which he demonstrated the desired behavior ("like this"), quickly imitated the player's mistake ("not like this"), and then followed with another demonstration of the proper execution of the skill ("like this"). This sequence of demonstrations conveyed a maximum amount of information to the athlete and enabled him to understand what he was doing wrong. Too often, it seems that coaches criticize players without explaining what should be done to correct certain errors. In contrast, 75 per cent of Wooden's comments and actions contained information which helped his players improve their performance. Thus chances of alienating a player were minimized, and criticism was perceived to be constructive and informative.

The positive-negative-positive approach advocated by John Wooden is also used by Fred Shero, the successful coach and general manager of the New York Rangers professional hockey team (Shero, 1975). When he calls a player into his office to discuss a problem, he tries to start the conversation on a positive note; for example, reference might be made to games in which the player played extremely well. Having gained the player's attention and raised his feelings of self-worth, Shero will then point out certain deficiencies in the player's recent performance and offer solutions to improve his play. Having made his point, this perceptive coach will end the conversation in a positive manner by emphasizing how important the player's contribution is to the team's subsequent success.

The positive-negative-positive approach to social reinforcement is clearly an important motivational technique which has been used by two successful coaches. Sport psychologists and coaches alike can indeed learn a lot about motivating athletes by studying the interpersonal styles of master teacher-coaches such as Fred Shero and John Wooden.

CONCLUSION

The strategies for enhancing motivation discussed in this chapter have been extrapolated from a number of sources including the study of individual motivation, group motivation, and the behavioral analysis of successful coaching styles. These recommendations do not by any means represent an exhaustive list of motivational techniques. They are merely intended to provide a point of departure from which coaches can formulate the most effective motivational strategies for their coaching situations.

goal-setting in shaping of future performance of athletes

James D. McClements
Cal B. Botterill

The basic idea behind this chapter is that children and athletes are opting out of physical activity and sport, because they are not getting enough from their participation. That is to say, sport and physical activity are not rewarding or self-reinforcing enough to maintain involvement. If there is one concept that we know about in human behavior, it is that we participate in what we like (approach) and stay away from what we don't like (avoidance). For most of us who are committed to sport and physical activity it is difficult to accept the idea that kids don't get enough out of sport, especially when we believe that sport and competition have such positive values. It is too easy to rationalize that the athlete just wasn't *tough enough* or *wasn't a winner* or *didn't have enough jam* to *stay at it* or *be a winner* or *be aggressive*. The athlete may not have had the ability to achieve the goal of winning, but perhaps given his limits he was still a success.

GOAL-SETTING, PLANNING, AND EVALUATION

If sport and competition have social values, then *each individual has the right to be successful.* Proper setting of goals and evaluation of this attainment can facilitate this right. Each person involved with sport has the responsibility to promote the right to be successful. In order to ensure the opportunity for success, the planning process should include the goal-setting and evaluation as equal partners with the skill learning, physical training, and team work (Figure 1).

Certain factors interact to improve performance. (1) The program is planned so that the current level advances to the terminal level defined by the goal; therefore, the program is a product of the individual's own goal. (2) Evaluation is part of the planning

199

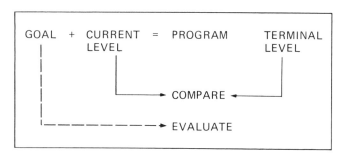

Figure 1. Interaction goal-setting, program development, and evaluation.

process in that each of the goals must be able to be evaluated. Evaluation is not something done as hindsight at the end of a season, but built into the entire season.

What Dimensions Should Be Considered in Goal-Setting?

The goals must be more than just a wish or a dream; they must be realistic. Specific factors must be considered in setting goals.

1. *Performance.* The basic factors used in setting performance goals are the individual's long-term goal, the individual's current level, and the number of seasons available to achieve the long-term goal. These are used to set a reasonable season or short-term goal as the intermediary step to achieving a long-term goal.

2. *Commitment of the Individual.* A less obvious but crucial factor in planning goals is the commitment of the individual. This relates to the amount of time and the degree of effort that the individual is willing to dedicate to achieving his goals.

3. *Opportunity.* It is also important to consider how effective the opportunity is for the individual to achieve his goals. The following types of opportunity should be considered: (a) practice time and facilities available; (b) the limits of coaches; (c) competitions available; (d) funds; and (e) climatic conditions.

4. *Potential.* The last factor—the individual's potential—is the most difficult to assess. Coaches sometimes think that they "know" their athlete's potential; however, the certainty of this subjective evaluation is at best suspect. One clue to an athlete's potential may come from a review of the individual's rate of improvement, allowing for opportunity and effort. This necessitates that progress, opportunity, and effort be regularly recorded and evaluated.

If the short-term goal appears to be unreasonable when the coach and athlete are planning the season, it is important to consider the feasibility of the long-term goal.

What Do You Evaluate First—Effort or Performance?

Basically, a program plan should be based on a seasonal goal which is set by considering the athlete's long-term goal, commitment, potential, and opportunity. It is assumed that the athlete uses the program plan to train, practice, and compete (Figure 2). There are

Figure 2. Programming degree of success and evaluation.

two major categories of success: *effort* and *performance*. Every coach is aware of athletes who have fallen short of their potential. Sometimes this occurs because of unreasonable goal-setting (athletes want too much too fast). Adequate planning of a series of goals and evaluations should offset this problem. Setting and achieving short-term or seasonal goals should be reinforcing, and this reinforcement should encourage effort. Coaches should not assume that athletes are capable of evaluating success on their own, because athletes often have inadequate reference-points and cannot be objective about themselves. Other times athletes fall short of their goals, because they either did not realize and generate the effort necessary to achieve their goal, or they were unwilling to do whatever was required to achieve it. Setting readily measurable goals for effort should help reduce this problem. Planning for commitment as a method of overcoming the lack of effort will be discussed later. The main point at this time is that *if the athlete makes the effort, he has achieved success.* The evaluation of performance is only meaningful, if the athlete has made the effort to complete the program. *It is crucial to evaluate effort before evaluating performance!*

Let us assume that an athlete has made the effort. Then and only then, the *degree of performance-success* can be considered. It is very important in performance evaluation to avoid the *either-or thinking* that leads to labeling success or failure. It is more important to determine the *the degree of success* and to identify the cause, that is, the program, commitment, opportunity, long-term goal, or individual potential. Again, it is vital that we as coaches assist the athletes with the evaluation, because they are usually too emotionally involved to be objective. Once the degree of success has been established and the causes have been identified, then these causes can be used to plan for the upcoming season or perhaps to reconsider long-term goals. It is important to note that this process does not evaluate the person *per se*, but rather evaluates the total program which includes the individual.

COMMITMENT AND GOALS

Perhaps the most frustrating problem for coaches concerned about athletes is the lack of commitment. How does commitment relate to performance? Commitment is the starting point for adequate preparation (Figure 3). The preparation includes physical training (strength, cardio-vascular, flexibility, etc.), the learning of basic skills, plays, and strategies, mental preparation for optimal arousal and concentration, and finally developing a life-style that complements rather than opposes the goal. This type of preparation cannot be legislated for by rules or supervised by coaches. This preparation is the individual athlete's responsibility. Adequate preparation is the key to developing the confidence which is crucial for optimal performance.

Figure 3. Products of commitment.

Can You Plan for Commitment?

Commitment sometimes comes prepackaged in the athlete; however, this is not always so. Commitment can also be developed through careful planning. It is not something that an athlete either does or does not have. There are three steps recommended to develop commitment.

1. *Setting Reasonable Goals.* These goals must relate to both performance and preparation. (These are discussed later.)

2. *Writing Contracts.* Commitment is defined by writing contracts. Research suggests that there is more goal acceptance and, therefore, more improvement, if the contracts are written using certain restrictions: (a) the goals and the contract must be determined by the athlete; (b) the contract must be clear and explicit; (c) the contract must make reasonably difficult and challenging demands; and (d) the contract must be public at least among the athlete's peers and others who are significant to him.

3. *Management by Objectives.* Commitment is maintained by a process labeled *management by objectives.* Chronological records should be maintained of training programs, health, and life-style. This requires that diaries refer to the athlete's goals of effort and performance. It is crucial that coaches check an athlete's diary regularly and assist the athletes to evaluate objectively their relative successes and failures.

What Are Goals? What Function Do They Have?

It is very important that goals be set that are both difficult enough to challenge, yet realistic enough to be achieved (Figure 4). Evaluation of these goals certainly becomes a form of *feedback.* This feedback serves the function of *reinforcement.* Success becomes the positive reinforcement which is the basic unit of all learning and behavior modification. If an athlete is successful, this should enhance the will to become even better. On the other hand, if the

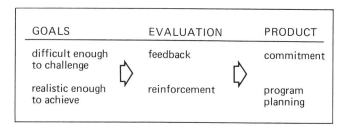

Figure 4. Goal evaluation.

athlete is not successful, the process of evaluation should pinpoint the cause of his falling short of the goal. The identification of the cause and effect should provide a basis for planning future success. In either case, the results should produce more effective program planning.

How Do You Set Goals That Are Difficult Yet Realistic?

Goals have been divided into three categories (Figure 5). The first two categories, general subjective and general objective, have some

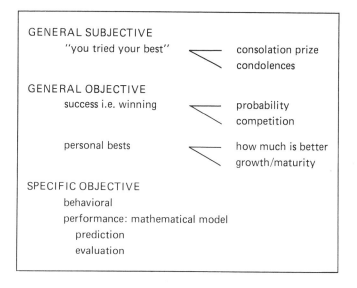

Figure 5. What types of goals?

basic evaluation problems. The general subjective analysis, even by coaches and others significant to the athlete, which says, "you tried your best," is usually used after the fact as a consolation prize or a form of condolence for athletes who did not win. These comments are always well meant; however, they are not always based on fact. Unfortunately, they actually convey the message "you were not good enough."

Better coaches have recognized the problem of subjective analysis and have also tried to avoid evaluating success on a win-loss basis. The issue of win-loss evaluation is linked to the dual problems of probability of success and the quality of competition. It is quite possible for two or more individuals to be progressing rapidly towards international-level performance and become discouraged, because they compete against each other with at best a 50 per cent chance of success. On the other hand, victories are often meaningless and hollow, if the competition is weak. Each athlete in a competition should have the potential for personal success. One popular way of avoiding this issue is the concept of personal bests. This technique is reasonably good; however, it does beg the question: how much is better? It is often difficult not to improve as one grows older and gains maturity. Is a teenage 800m runner who improves from 1:52.0 to 1:51.9 minutes over a season of training a success? He certainly improved, but was this enough improvement to be called success? How much improvment is necessary for it to be meaningful?

Research outside sport recommends that behavior is readily changed by setting *measurable objective goals* and evaluating these goals. In sport, these goals could be concerned with life-style, practice, physical training, and performance. Specific *life-style* goals could be food (including type, amount, and calories), rest patterns (specifically hours of sleep), work habits in sport, school, or work, and recreation patterns. *Practice goals* would be related to skill-learning and could include amount of time on each skill, and the degree of concentration while practicing as well as actual improvement of specific skills. Physical *training goals* could specify the amount of time and intensity for each component of a physical training program, for example, strength, flexibility, warm-up, warm-down, and cardiovascular. *Performance goals* should be specific, difficult yet achievable, and not merely wishful thinking. It appears that if these are stated, recorded, and checked using the model of *management by objectives,* athletes are more likely to behave (living and training) in a pattern that optimizes their probability of success. Ideally, the process becomes a self-fulfilling prophecy in that proper training and living patterns lead to changes in performance that reinforce the training and living patterns.

MATHEMATICAL MODEL AS AN AID IN GOAL-SETTING

The evaluation of success, of course, must include perfromance in a competitive environment. Setting demanding yet reasonable performance goals requires good predictors, not only for the individual athlete but also for the future competitions. In order to have good predictors for the timed and measured sports of speedskating, track and field, and swimming a mathematical model of improvement has been developed.* The basic concept in predicting future performance is the principle of diminishing returns. This states that it is more difficult to achieve a unit of performance improvement as this performance approaches its theoretical limits. Simply stated, it is easier to improve from 13.0 seconds in the 100m dash to 12.9 seconds (a 0.1 second improvement), than it is to improve from 10.0 seconds to 9.9 seconds (also a 0.1 second improvement). In the mathematical model, recent performance trends in individual events were used to represent the difficulty of improvement. The general form of the equation is:

$$Y = ae^{bx} + c$$

where
Y = predicted performance
b = rate of change
a = a constant
c = theoretical limit of man
x = number of years
e = exponential function.

A typical curve, men's 1500m speedskating, is presented in Figure 6.

Applications

There are essentially four applications of the mathematical model.
   1. *Prediction of Future Performance.* The model allows a pre-

* The method of developing this model can be found in McClements, J.D., and Laverty, W.M. "A Mathematical Model of Speedskating Performance Improvement for Goal-Setting and Program Evaluation," *Canadian Journal of Applied Sport Sciences,* accepted for publication in October, 1978.

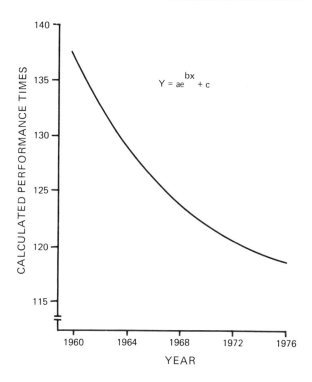

Figure 6. A men's 1500m speedskating curve.

diction of world class performance in each of the measured and timed events which can be used to set long-term goals.

2. *Individual Goal-Setting.* The curves were developed to facilitate the setting of objective short-term goals that are demanding yet reasonable. It is assumed that an athlete can state a long-term goal. In this example, an athlete has a long-term goal of competing internationally by 1984 in the men's 1500m speedskating (Figure 7). The index units associated with his long-term goal equal 28 (Y = 28 in Figure 7). His current level of performance is 2 minutes 35 seconds or 155 seconds. The index units associated with his current level equal 0 (x = 0 in Figure 7). In this example, it is assumed that the current year is 1976. In order to determine a one-year goal, one must calculate the index units from the goal,

$$\text{index units from goal} = Y - x$$
$$= 28 - 0 = 28 \text{ units};$$

and the number of years available,

$$\text{years available} = 1984 - 1976$$
$$= 8 \text{ years.}$$

$$\text{The one year goal} = \frac{Y - x}{\text{years available}}$$
$$= \frac{28}{8} = 3.5 \text{ units.}$$

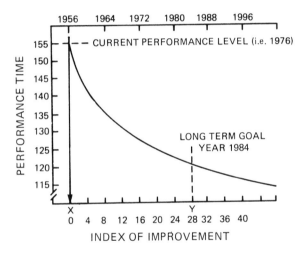

Figure 7. Individual goal-setting curve.

His next year's goal in index units is his current level in index units plus his one year goal in index units.

$$\text{Next year's goal} = x + \text{one year goal}$$
$$= 0 + 3.5 = 3.5 \text{ units.}$$

These index units are used to determine the performance goal for the upcoming season (Figure 8). In this example, the performance goal would be 141.5 seconds or a 13.4 second improvement.*

* While graphs have been used in this paper, it is recommended that for actual use, detailed tables or computer calculations be applied. The tables and the computer services for speedskating, swimming, and track and field are available at cost from Dr Jim McClements, College of Physical Education, University of Saskatchewan, Saskatoon, Saskatchewan, S7N 0W0.

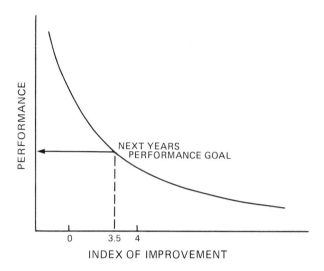

Figure 8. The performance goal for the upcoming season.

Assuming the athlete maintained a perfect critical path over the eight years, the *equal units of improvement* would yield progressively smaller absolute performance improvements for each successive year. In the above example, the absolute performance improvement required each year would be 13.4 seconds in the first year, 8.6 seconds in the second year, 5.9 seconds in the third year, and so forth up to 0.7 seconds in the eighth year. These performance goals would be reconsidered and revised, if necessary, for each season. However, if the one year goal is achieved, then the athlete is on target for this long-term goal. It is important to remember that this evaluation process is only part of the interaction between goal-setting, program-planning, and performance. The presented model has been developed to facilitate planning for international-level competition. It is possible to use the same model to plan for other long-term goals, such as national-level, inter-collegiate, club, etc. Application methods for these long-term goals are also available from the author.

3. *Evaluation of Training Programs.* The classical problems in evaluating programs which involve behavioral change are who to place in which training program, the effect of different coaches or the bias of a coach to the selected training program, and the specificity of the training program. The research design using the same coach and the same athletes in successive years has not been utilized because of the principle of diminishing returns.

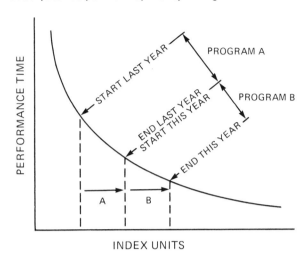

Figure 9. Index of improvement curve.

However, in real life, this is how training programs are conducted. In fact, most coaches evaluate the effect of training by using a subjective evaluation of performance or ranking.

The concept of the *index of improvement* is likely to make this evaluation more objective. This is illustrated in Figure 9. Quite simply, the performance change of programs A and B are converted into index units, and these units are placed in a ratio; if the ratio is less than one, the numerator program is more effective; if the ratio is greater than one, the denominator program is more effective. For this to be true, one must assume that there was the same amount of talent and interest in both programs or years. Perhaps it would be better to consider each individual on the two training programs and base the general decision on the trend of the individual change.

4. *Evaluation of Total Program.* Another possible application of the *index of improvement* concerns the evaluation of a total program such as a national program. Traditional political and press evaluation of programs is unfortunately based on medal counts. It is theoretically possible to be effecting dramatic national program changes without reaping any more medals. If a program curve was calculated and compared to international curves, one could estimate when a program would become internationally competitive. This same method of evaluation by using the *index of improvement* might be used to direct emphasis in funding, coaching, and/or promotion.

the stress of the performance athletics

Walter Kroll

The stress associated with athletic competition is significant not only for the sport psychologists who endeavor to study it, but also for the coaches and athletes who must often secretly and as a matter of routine survive the troublesome—and sometimes debilitating—symptoms of nervous panic. No one needs to be told that anxiety exists prior to competition; not because of the amount of research attesting to its presence, but simply because it is self-evident to even the most casual observer. The athlete, the coach, the official, the spectator, the usher, and even the sports fan viewing the contest thousands of miles away on television can sense the excitement and emotional tension.

Few of us, however, are fully aware of just how important anxiety really is in athletics. Naruse (1965), for example, interviewed 125 Japanese athletes returning from the Rome Olympics in 1960 and found that nearly all of the athletes reported being troubled by anxiety to the extent that it affected their competitive performance. The cumulative stress of athletic competition is also suggested in the finding that about 50 per cent of the nationally ranked swimmers in 1968 had quit swimming by 1978. As reported in *Swimming Technique,** eight out of ten times the reason cited for leaving competition was not the arduous physical training required in the sport, but the external pressures created by an inability to live up to the expectations of coaches and parents in performance.

It is also consistently reported that athletes have lower anxiety levels than non-athletes. Such a finding could indicate that athletes learn to control and reduce anxiety (Layman, 1974). But the result could also be interpreted as meaning that athletes with higher anxiety levels simply drop out of competition, either by their own decision based upon an inability to tolerate high anxiety situations in athletics or by being forced out because of deficien-

---

* Editorial. *Swimming Technique,* July, 1973.

,ies in performance caused by the high anxiety. The implication is that a low anxiety level is a prerequisite to success in athletics and an elevated anxiety level is detrimental to optimal performance.

Anxiety is not, of course, a significant phenomenon in athletics alone, since there is universal concern over its adverse effects upon emotional well-being. No major personality theory would be considered completely adequate, unless it incorporated anxiety in a nuclear context. Surprisingly, however, the first popular scale to measure anxiety was developed by a group of experimental psychologists intent upon studying Hullian learning theory (Taylor, 1953). Whether the appearance of the Taylor Manifest Anxiety Scale was the only catalyst or not, Sarason noted in 1960 that few areas in psychology had as much research output as that concerning scales to measure anxiety. Sarason also noted that literature reviews generally agreed in reporting unreplicability and inconsistency of results in studies using available anxiety scales.

ANXIETY INVENTORIES

At the present time considerable disagreement exists over the definition of anxiety, and several different theoretical approaches to the study of anxiety are competing for more widespread recognition and acceptance. Comparison of competing theories of anxiety is made difficult, since proponents of different theories tend to restrict experimental and theoretical work to their own theory and mostly ignore competing theories (Spielberger, 1972). Without becoming entangled in a debate about which is the best theory, one can reasonably adopt an operational system forwarded by Spielberger (1972) with which to consider the phenomenon of anxiety in the athletic context. As shown in Figure 1, the impending athletic competition represents the stress stimulus; individual athletes may perceive the stress stimulus elements in athletic competition differently, depending upon such factors as prior experiences, age, sex, intelligence, motivation, ability, and the like; and the effect of both the stress stimulus properties and the individual perception of the stress stimulus elements is presumed to be the cause of an emotional response which is typically designated as an anxiety state.

Now it is an important observation that most anxiety scales seek to monitor the intensity of anxiety signs and symptoms present in the emotional response stage. The causes of such an emotional response, which must surely lie within the stress stimulus itself or the perception of the stress stimulus elements by an

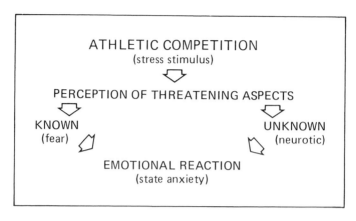

Figure 1. Athletic competition as a stimulus for anxiety re-actions.

individual, remain fairly well unstudied by contemporary sport psychologists. At best, the kind of stress presented in laboratory studies may be manipulated and the investigators predict what the variation in the stress stimulus means.

Whether the signs and symptoms be somatic complaints or behavioral aberrations, anxiety scales are primarily designed for the assessment of the consequences of the emotional response to stress stimuli. This observation applies equally well to both trait and state anxiety scales. Since most anxiety scales contain items pertaining to the end result of the stress stimulus and its percep-tion by subjects, the nature of the stress stimulus itself and the nature of the perception of the stress stimulus by subjects, escapes definition. In effect, little attempt is being made to identify the causative factors responsible for pre-competitive anxiety, and as a result we are faced with unconscious classification of athletic competition as an unknown fear composite.

SPECIFIC SITUATION ANXIETY INVENTORIES

Because of conflicting results with available inventories, many investigators have recommended the development of more specific anxiety scales. Sarason (1960), for example, stated that an anxiety scale containing items directly related to a specific stress situation would be a more useful measurement tool; Endler and Hunt (1962) made much the same statement. More recently, Martens

(1971) concluded that the Taylor Manifest Anxiety Scale should be abandoned, and further suggested beginning an "in-depth study of the competitive situation and its influence on motor behavior."

Of the available anxiety scales Martens recommended the Spielberger STAI which has separate scales for state and trait anxiety. Our analysis of the STAI suggests that the items assess the presence of anxiety, and not the causes. In fact, Spielberger (1971) states that "the essential qualities evaluated by the STAI A-state scale involve feelings of tension, worry, and apprehension." Feelings of tension, worry, and apprehension are, of course, the effects of stress, and a scale comprised of adjectives describing such feelings cannot be expected to convey much insight into the causes of such feelings. Martens has worked on the development of the Sport Competitive Anxiety Test (SCAT) which is reported as being a ". . . trait anxiety scale designed for measuring a predisposition to respond with varying levels of anxiety to competitive sport situations" (1977, p. 18). Several items in the SCAT come close to helping in the identifying of probable causes of anxiety in the athletic competition context. SCAT items which appear to relate to the causes of competitive anxiety would be:

1. Competing against others is fun.
3. Before I compete I worry about not performing well.
4. I am a good sportsman when I compete.
5. When I compete I worry about making mistakes.
7. Setting a goal is important when competing.
10. I like rough games.

Most of the remaining ten items in the SCAT, however, appear to be assessing the effects of competition as a stress stimulus:

2. Before I compete I feel uneasy.
6. Before I compete I am calm.
8. Before I compete I get a funny feeling in my stomach.
9. Just before competing I notice my heart beats faster than usual.
11. Before I compete I feel relaxed.
12. Before I compete I am nervous.
14. I get nervous wanting the game to start.
15. Before I compete I usually get up tight.

If one has a purpose understanding what causes pre-competitive anxiety, it does not appear that either the Spielberger STAI or the Martens SCAT promise much hope of defining the stress stimulus features inherent in athletic competition or in identifying the ways in which athletes may differentially perceive the stress stimulus features in athletic competition. Since neither the STAI nor the SCAT ever claimed to be measuring the causes of anxiety, the above comments are merely observations and not criticism. Both the STAI and the SCAT, of course, are well-constructed and highly respected measurement instruments, deserving of their fine reputation.

THE COMPETITIVE ATHLETIC STRESS SCALE

A few years ago we decided to start from square one. We began constructing a Competitive Athletic Stress Scale which *seeks to identify the causes of anxiety in athletic competition.* Our first efforts were thus aimed at identifying the specific factors which contribute to the athlete's heightened anxiety level prior to competition. In effect, we wanted to find out what caused the nausea, sweaty hands, pounding heart beat, trembling, and other somatic complaints. We wanted to find out what caused the feelings of uneasiness, irritability, general restlessness, being afraid, and other psychological manifestations. If manifest anxiety was caused by unknown fears, then we wanted to know what specific fear was causing the anxiety seen in athletes prior to competition.

We began our quest for identifying the specific causes responsible for athletic anxiety with a shrewd and scientifically sophisticated research strategy—a research strategy that understandably can only be utilized by highly trained investigators and even then only after years of specialized training: we decided to ask athletes what made them get uptight prior to competition. We asked athletes to imagine themselves in pre-competitive situations and to write essays describing what they were thinking about, concerned about, apprehensive about, worried about, or fearful about prior to competition. Following such field work a list of items was compiled which was then screened for duplication, similarity, and clarity. Eventually, we had a working list of about 125 items.

In the preliminary screening of items resulting from the essay and interview process, it was arbitrarily decided that an item had to have been suggested by at least five per cent of the athletes studied in order to be retained. Such a decision may or may not have been a sound basis for preliminary selection of items. It seems obvious, for example, that different items in an inventory may not have equivalent potential for eliciting an emotional response in any one individual, and that the same item might elicit different emotional responses in different individuals. It is quite possible that the construct represented in a single item may be sufficient to produce an intense effect in one individual and little or no effect in another individual. Some of the items deleted may have represented a construct which could be a key element, capable of eliciting an extreme emotional response in some one athlete. Such a state of affairs makes statistical purification and subsequent analysis a risky venture.

CAUSATIVE FACTORS OF COMPETITIVE STRESS

Why are athletes troubled by pre-competitive anxiety? By careful examination of individual items, certain items appeared to be related in terms of common causative factor. Subsequent analysis of item inter-correlation matrices, correlation of an item with its proposed sub-scale, and even early factor analysis results suggested some categories of causative factors. Even without the benefit of statistical analysis, some of the resulting item clusters hint at theoretically acceptable constructs, capable of qualifying as anxiety producing factors in athletic competition. The items, however, come from athletes and not from theory or computer printouts. The five major clusters with specific items are presented in Table 1.

Somatic Complaints

It is not surprising that athletes report being concerned about physical manifestations of anxiety, since somatic sensations are an inherent feature of the emotional response to stress stimuli. Most of the items appearing on a list of somatic complaints are familiar ones and appear in one form or another on many anxiety scales with the possible exception of the item, *yawning too much.* One physiological explanation for yawning is that it is a mechanism for increasing the supply of oxygen to the vital organs, particularly the brain. Since worry and apprehension are presumably capable of creating an oxygen deficiency, the appearance of yawning on an anxiety scale is not too surprising, even if it was unexpected.

Fear of Failure

Atkinson and Raynor (1974) theorized that the motivation set known as fear of failure constituted the *source of the conscious experience of anxiety,* and that the amount of anxiety induced in any situation would be proportionate to the intensity of the fear of failure present. Such a fear of failure construct seems to be

Table 1. The competitive athletic stress scale clusters showing specific anxiety producing factors.

SOMATIC COMPLAINTS ITEMS

tightness in neck	urge to urinate	throwing up
upset stomach	ringing in my ears	general body sweating
nervousness	yawning too much	sore muscles
awareness of heart beat	trembling	

FEAR OF FAILURE ITEMS

making a foolish mistake	poor workouts	improving upon my last performance
letting teammates down	mind going blank	value of athletics
performing up to my level of ability	making a critical mistake	psychological pre-paredness
losing	choking up	living up to coach's expectations
quitting the team	falling for a sucker play	presence of friends/ relatives among spectators
pressure to win	criticism by coach	

FEELINGS OF INADEQUACY ITEMS

getting tired	not enough rest	going stale
lack of desire	inability to psych up	general restlessness
feeling weak	running out of gas	biting my finger nails
my physical appearance	being afraid	unable to concentrate
poor fit of equipment	remembering instructions	feeling silly
coach ignoring me	fear	physical condition

LOSS OF CONTROL ITEMS

jinx	boisterous spectators	people asking questions
behavior of spectators	poor officials	being outcoached
equipment failure	bad luck	poor spectator turnout
conduct of opponents	temperature	condition of playing surface
unfair officials	weather	noisy locker room
		being injured

GUILT ITEMS

hurting an opponent	not being mean enough	losing my temper
making my opponent look foolish	swearing too much	my sex life
playing dirty	sportsmanship	spectator's booing

---

represented by the items of *letting teammates down, performing up to my level of ability, losing,* and *living up to coach's expectations.* One can also identify items with suggestive similarity to the construct of possible embarrassment which Sarason (1960) has shown to be linked to anxiety. Items such as *making a foolish mistake, falling for a sucker play,* and *choking* appear to align themselves with a possible embarrassment construct.

Feelings of Inadequacy

The feelings of inadequacy list contains items similar to those found on the fear of failure list which also suggest the Sarason construct of possible embarrassment. However, the items on the feelings of inadequacy list seem to describe a construct slightly different from one of possible embarrassment. The items on the feelings of inadequacy list characterize an attitude of "something is wrong with me," or as has sometimes been suggested, an attitude of self-depreciation and personal dissatisfaction (Sarason, 1960).

Loss of Control

The items on the loss of control list suggest a striking similarity to Rotter's (1966) concept of an external locus of control in which forces beyond one's own control are operative and the individual has no control over events taking place. The individual characterized by an external locus of control is more likely to feel that desirable outcomes are mostly determined by good luck rather than by hard work.

Guilt

The items appearing on the guilt list suggest problems of morality and aggression. As is known, of course, guilt can contribute to heightened anxiety, and it would appear that guilt is one of the causes of anxiety in the pre-competitive situation. (The item, *my sex life,* by the way, is actually a purified version of some of the terms suggested by the athletes studied.)

CONCLUSION

A tremendous amount of work is yet to be done before the Competitive Athletic Stress Scale can seek acceptance as a well-constructed and validated measurement instrument. Preliminary results, however, do support the contention that a research strategy which seeks to identify the causes of anxiety in athletic competition can offer considerable insight into what athletes actually perceive as anxiety producers. Looking ahead, the inventory may be a beginning toward achieving a diagnostic index of specific anxiety producing elements for individual athletes; that is, some athletes may exhibit a similar emotional response to different aspects of the athletic competition, and it would be more helpful to know what specific elements of athletic competition are causing the emotional response than it would be to know that they have the same level of emotional response. On away games, for example, a different configuration of items may be causing anxiety as compared to home games. Different sports or different coaches may elicit identifiable item configurations. A losing season may produce a configuration of items different from a winning season. In short, it may be possible to assess the causes of pre-competitive anxiety in different athletes in different situations, and suggest training and coaching practices designed to reduce undesirable levels of anxiety by the elimination of the stress stimulus elements which cause the emotional response.

information feedback in coaching of highly skilled athletes

Anne L. Rothstein

In my own attempts to integrate the several areas that bear upon the performance of highly skilled athletes, I have found the recent emphasis on a process-oriented approach most helpful. The shift toward a process-oriented approach reflects an emphasis on understanding the changes that occur within the individual and in the interaction between the individual and the environment during learning and performance. It allows us the luxury of integrating the individual and the environment and of looking upon the sport environment as a *holistic* enterprise with all its attendant complexity.

The process-oriented approach is also useful because it attempts to integrate the diverse areas which bear upon the achievement of excellence by asking questions such as the following: What effect does anxiety have on the functional visual field (peripheral vision)? What are the psychological, emotional, sociological, and environmental factors associated with the *home court advantage*? What is the relationship between the physical structure (morphology) and body composition of the athlete and motor performance? Behavior is viewed as the sum of all the factors impinging upon the individual. The gestalt I am trying to illustrate is an ideal toward which we need to move, if we hope to use research to enhance sport performance through the coaching process. It is within this framework that I would like to consider a crucial variable in motor learning and performance—information feedback.

USING FEEDBACK
TO ENHANCE PERFORMANCE

If I were asked to choose the single most powerful tool that teachers and coaches have available to them, it would be information feedback. It has been suggested, and rightly so, that information feedback is the single most important variable governing acquisition and performance of motor skills. The teacher and coach must assume primary responsibility for structuring the performance environment, so that feedback is available and must, in addition, decide what type of feedback to provide and how to assist performers in its use.

Regardless of the type of feedback provided, the performer must *learn* to use the information to change behavior. Miller (1953) has suggested that to use feedback effectively to modify performance, the performer must:

1. discriminate the feedback signal (involves knowing what to look for);
2. connect the motor response with the feedback signal (what did I do to cause the observed outcome?);
3. connect the response with the environmental conditions present at the time of response selection (particularly true in open skills*);
4. design a response which will reduce the perceived error in the outcome; and
5. practice the new motor response under the appropriate conditions.

The relationship which illustrates the points listed above is that of the angle of the racket face in tennis, and the resultant flight of the ball. If the flight path of the ball carried it six feet above the net and the ball landed beyond the baseline, the player might surmise that a probable cause of the error was the angle of the racket face at contact and that the racket face was open. The player must determine which movement error may have resulted in the racket face being open at contact. Was it the grip, the path of the racket head, the rotation of the wrist, the action of the whole body, or some other factor? Then the performer must attempt to correct the error or errors on the next trial. Perhaps most important, the performer must ascertain whether the error was related to a mismatch between the environmental conditions at the time of response selection, or to the inability to execute the response as planned. For this reason it is important that the performer connect the response with the environmental conditions present at the time of response selection. An example from golf should be sufficient to convey the message. In hitting a ball from an uphill or a downhill lie, the player must modify the address

---

* Hockey, basketball, and volleyball are considered open skills, whereas golf, shooting, and diving are closed skills. Open environments, characteristic for open skills, are highly unpredictable, unstable, and in constant flux, while closed environments, characteristic for closed skills, are highly predictable, stable, and unchanging over time.

position from that used in a normal situation. Once in the proper position the player executes the response. If the player fails to hit the ball toward the intended target (or in the intended direction), the error might be one of response selection, that is, the player recognized the lie situation in question, but failed to choose the appropriate address position to accommodate himself to it, or he did not recognize that the situation was different from the normal one and for that reason failed to accommodate himself to it. It is also possible that the error might be one of response execution, that is, the performer recognized the situation, planned to accommodate himself to it through an appropriate stance, but was unable to execute the stance or swing as planned. Both the performer and the teacher or coach must know which type of error has been made, so that the feedback will be specifically related to the locus of the difficulty.

The Videotape Replay

One very popular method of providing feedback is that of video-tape replay. (A similar method is available through Polaroid's Instant Movies, but the quality may not be very good.) Although there are few studies in which videotape replay has been used with advanced or world-class performers, the possibilities for its use are global in application. These possibilities involve all levels of performance as well as most types of feedback:

1. Cues to viewing the videotape replay or to using available feedback are important, particularly for beginners and novice performers, but they are also helpful for more advanced performers, especially when they are using specialized types of feedback.
2. Feedback techniques which focus on particular aspects of the performance, using a zoom lens in conjunction with videotape or using specific verbal cues, should be particularly helpful for highly skilled individuals.
3. Practice following the administration of feedback, after decisions are made regarding what should be modified and how, is crucial. (In open environments it is important that the important cues to response selection be recreated, if possible, in the post-feedback practice.) In addition, this practice should occur as soon as possible after feedback administration.
4. The videotape replay should be used at least five times, with multiple replays each time, for benefits to accrue. (It has been suggested that the replay system at the Montreal Olym-

pics may have operated to the advantage of those performers whose performances were constantly replayed).

5. The focus of the videotape replay or other feedback should be shifted to afford attention to other aspects or views of the same performance. (In the world series this point was reinforced through the replays from many different vantage points; each view afforded different information.)

6. The view provided via videotape, or the information provided via other types of feedback, should be consistent with the skill to be learned or improved.

7. Finally (a negative application), when fine discriminations are required, videotape replay is seldom useful because the action will be blurred and the necessary information will not be extractable. In these instances high speed motion pictures would be useful for the performer who has a consistent error or for general use if the film could be developed within several hours.

Knowledge of Results and Knowledge of Performance

The notion that the view provided via videotape or other feedback should be consistent with the skill to be learned or improved deserves additional consideration. It has been suggested that Knowledge of Results (KR) is the most appropriate feedback for skills which take place in open environments. In these situations the goal involves achieving a particular outcome, but the movements which are successful in achieving that outcome vary in accordance with the particular environmental conditions which will be in effect at the time of response execution. The emphasis for the performer in open environments is on prediction and anticipation of events and on the selection of a response which will match the environmental constraints. It has been suggested that Knowledge of Performance (KP) is the most appropriate feedback for skills which take place in closed environments. In these environments the goal is to achieve consistency of performance under relatively fixed and highly predictable conditions. As KR and KP have been defined, neither can be instrumental in aiding the performer in correction of errors in response selection, because neither of these modes emphasizes the *relationship between the environment and the response.* Traditional KR emphasizes the outcome, while traditional KP emphasizes the movement.

For the performer who consistently errs in response selection some notion of the relationship between the environment at the

The videotape replay should be used at least five times, with multiple replays each time, for benefits to accrue. It has been suggested that the replay system at the Montreal Olympics may have operated to the advantage of those performers whose performances were constantly replayed.

time of response selection or formulation and the response which was selected or formulated must be provided. The response selection error may result from a misinterpretation of the environmental events or may result from a mismatch between correctly interpreted events and response selection. (If time were available, we could identify factors related to the misinterpretation of the environment.)

In the first study, to my knowledge, to employ a type of videotape feedback that enabled the performer to view the relationship between environment and response selection and initiation in studying both open and closed skills, it was found that groundstrokes in tennis showed least improvement (the difference in performance with practice not being significant) under *performance information feedback* and made the greatest gains under a combination of performance and environmental feedback conditions. It is important that *neither performance nor environmental feedback alone* was as helpful in terms of performance gains as the combination of focusing on performance (the movement) alternately with focusing on performance in relation to the environment, and that performance feedback information was associated with the poorest performance. The serve also benefited from a combination of performance and environmental feedback conditions, but in contrast to groundstrokes, performers made little or no gains under *environmental feedback alone.* The contrast therefore is in relation to the feedback conditions that did not enhance performance effectively rather than in terms of those that did. More work needs to be done with the combinations used in this study, before we can be certain of the benefits. It appears, however, that KR alone or KP alone may not be the best of all possible means of enhancing performance.

For the performer who consistently errs in response execution KP would be appropriate (particularly in skills which take place in closed environments), but should be related to the specific response execution errors affecting performance, that is, spatial sequencing, timing (internal), and forced errors. In addition to using videotape replay to provide KP, researchers have used EMG recording, biofeedback, visual cues, auditory cues, and kinematics to good advantage.

EMG recording, biofeedback, visual cues and auditory cues are moderately complicated techniques requiring laboratory conditions not available to everyone. Kinematics or the use of high speed film cameras is of great value and is a readily available research method. I might give one example related to kinematics for both feedforward and feedback: the acceleration curves of weightlifting performance were used in one study to provide the performer with a picture of the "ideal" acceleration rate of the weight in the lift. Thus equipped, performers were then asked to duplicate these visual curves, and were provided feedback by the superimposition of their curves and the "ideal" curve. Something of this nature could be easily adapted in other types of skills and would provide intermediate and advanced performers with the specific information they need to optimize performance.

CONCLUSION

By viewing information feedback as a means through which the performer is able to assess the success of each aspect of performance, and by realizing that feedback is a specialized form of input and thus subject to all the factors that govern input (selective attention, orienting, encoding, overload, and so on), the teacher or coach should be able to provide information which is useful to performers and specifically related to the difficulties that may prevent them from achieving excellence.

psychological programs for athletes as practiced in various countries

part 5

ZANDER

INTRODUCTION

Part Five presents an overview of psychological practice in sport in five countries: Canada, U.S.A., Sweden, Norway, and the Soviet Union. It begins with an excellent explication of the status of contemporary Soviet sport psychology by Shneidman. In the Soviet Union, according to the author, a great number of sport psychologists who are normally employed at sport research institutes and colleges for physical culture are permanently attached to national teams. Their responsibility is to implement the findings of applied and experimental research to sport practice with the primary purpose to better prepare the Soviet athletes and teams for important international competition. Another important characteristic of the Soviet sport institutes is the highly coordinated effort in development of new knowledge in the field of sport psychology. And lastly, Shneidman confirms the well-known fact that important findings related to the preparation of Soviet teams are not published. The chapter concludes with an appendix containing samples of published research of practical nature.

Willi Railo of Norway and Lars-Eric Unestahl of Sweden present us with an insight into psychological work in high performance athletics as practiced in Scandinavia. Railo addressed the development of high performance sport psychology and reviews psychological training techniques most often applied to superior athletes. He goes on to point out techniques of mental training and the importance of dissemination of psychological knowledge and techniques to the coaches. He closes with showing that the trend in Scandinavia is to educate the coaches in psychology of sport as well as provide service to them by supervision from sport psychologists and cassette programs.

Unestahl describes further developments in Scandinavia, in particular a three-month psychic training program for athletes from different sports. He points out that mental training techniques are designed to stimulate the resources of the individual, no matter whether he be an athlete or a participant in some other kind of endeavor. Unestahl concludes the chapter by discussing the values and the procedures of application of mental and various forms of relaxation training to joggers and school children.

Canadian developments are exemplified in articles by Wilson and Minden who in partnership developed a unique psychological support program for the Canadian Gymnastic Federation. Wilson discusses her experience in constructing this program for the young women amateur athletes involved in a serious training regimen in training for international competition. She closes with several suggestions for sport psychologists who may become interested in embarking on a similar intensive psychological program with a group of athletes. Minden, her partner in this project, elaborates on this experience, emphasizing the need to deal with such diverse problems as parent pressure and emotional changes that take place in puberty. He furthermore observes that all agents of the coaching process need support service for it to be effective. He closes by alerting us to the conviction that from their experience, there is a definite role for the sport psychologist in an amateur sport setting as clinicians and as researchers.

Richard Suinn provides us with a look at one psychologist's work with world-class competitors. His approach, labeled Visuo-Motor Behavior Rehearsal, starts with behavioral assessment in order to identify a target pattern of behavior, the conditions inhibiting it and the cues that might promote it. On the evidence of this assessment, recommendations for psychological training are made. In the psychological training itself, he emphasizes techniques for the management of stress, and the need for the training to continue during the competition situation.

The psychological programs discussed in this part provide us with an interesting panorama of a relatively new phenomenon—that of practical support service of sport psychology to enhance personal growth of athletes and to reach for new levels of performance. It seems that the knowledge explosion and the application of this knowledge to a holistic approach in coaching are with us.

/oviet /port p/ychology in the 1970/ and the /uperior athlete

N. Norman Shneidman

INTRODUCTION

Athletic excellence and the ability to show the best possible results in the most important international competitions are usually the result of a long and arduous training process in which the physical capacity of an athlete is taxed to its limits. And yet, the realities of the last decades, in which sport competitions acquired a new, political, ideological, and often nationalistic coloring, prompt coaches and administrators, the media and the public at large, to encourage and to demand that athletes continue to improve their results and secure further victories in international competitions. The time when improving one's health was the dominant reason for sport training and competition, and when high athletic performance was synonymous with good health, has long since passed. Today most leading athletes have learned to cope with the excessive demands of training, but heavy workloads often are detrimental to the health of those concerned. Dembo (1972) points out that the number of athletes with pathological conditions and illness, in particular those with overstrained hearts, increased by 18 to 20 times since 1955; cardiac arhythmias are more common in athletes than among those who do not participate in sport activities.

Since there are limits to the physical strain that a human body can endure, athletes, coaches, and scholars must look for other, additional, means to stimulate the growth of athletic mastery and make possible victories in international competitions. One such means is the psychological preparation of an athlete, a method greatly underrated in the past but emphasized at present in the Soviet system of athletic training. The most striking aspect of contemporary Soviet sport psychology is the concentration on the applied nature of psychological research and on its connection with the work of Soviet physical culture and sport organizations.

This chapter gives a brief outline and analysis of the development of Soviet sport psychology in the last decade. Beginning by a discussion of the role of the psychologist attached to a Soviet national team, it then outlines the theoretical premises of Soviet sport psychology. The contemporary state of Soviet research in the field is then described, followed by a description of the various institutes where much of this research is carried out. The chapter continues with a discussion of the publication of research findings and then mentions recent developments in Soviet social psychology of sport. A brief conclusion sums up the discussion and emphasizes the differences between the working conditions of Soviet and western sport psychologists. Finally a few representative Soviet studies in sport psychology of recent years are appended to illustrate some of the points made in the paper.

SOVIET SPORT PSYCHOLOGY AND
THE SUPERIOR ATHLETE

Psychologists are regarded as increasingly important in the preparation of Soviet national teams, and new ways of using the psychologists' professional abilities are being sought. Hanin and Martens (1978) report that there are at present about 250 to 300 sport psychologists in the Soviet Union. Hanin asserts that about 50 to 60 work in a clinical capacity, that is, they are affiliated directly with Soviet republic and USSR national teams in different sports. Of this number 20 are physicians, most of them former psychiatrists. However, the number of those involved in the study of different psychological aspects of motor activity and sport is probably much greater than these figures suggest. Smirnov (1975) reports that there are in the Soviet Union 23 institutes for physical culture and 91 faculties of physical education attached to pedagogical institutes and universities, all of them training specialists with higher education in physical culture and sport, as well as a number of scientific-research institutes undertaking studies in sport psychology. Many staff members of these scientific-research institutes are attached to different Soviet national teams, conducting research and trying to implement the findings of experimental and field studies into everyday practice. A staff member attached to a team usually stays in this position for several years at least. As a rule, it is preferred that the psychologist have practical experience in the sport concerned, as well as coaching experience if possible. It is considered important for the psychologist to become well acquainted with the members of the team and to gain their confidence. In addition, he is required to establish a good working relationship with other staff members, in particular with the coaching staff and the team physician. In the USSR it is presumed that the main psychologist of a team should be its head coach, a specialist who has mastered the basics of applied psychology. Despite the fact that many Soviet leading coaches have advanced academic degrees, few have the time and the professional qualifications to do serious psychological work on a national team.

According to Khudadov (1978), psychologists attached to national teams could, in broad terms, be divided into three distinct groups. To the first group belong those who limit their activity to psychodiagnostic research and to compiling data on the psychological characteristics of athletes. In the second group are those who also make practical recommendations for the selection and psychological preparation of athletes. To the third group belong those who, with the permission of the head coach, work directly with the athletes.

The duty of a psychologist attached to a team is primarily to help the coach prepare the given team or individual for the forthcoming competition and to help them reach peak athletic condition at the right time. The team psychologist conducts psychodiagnostic investigations and makes personality assessments. On the basis of the psychological traits and qualities exhibited by the athletes in the process of year-round training and during the preparation for and participation in competition, he compiles psychological characteristics and makes recommendations on the psychological and teaching methods to be used in the preparation of a given athlete or team. The psychologist also must teach the athletes methods of self-control and psychoregulation. He is required to inform the head coach of all the information he gathers and to make any necessary recommendations. Usually such recommendations are implemented by the coaching staff; only when the psychologist has coaching experience himself, and has the permission of the head coach, can he approach an athlete to discuss his personal psychological problems. In such cases the psychologist could discuss with the athlete the psychological reasons for the lack of success; he could attempt to improve the athlete's motivation and his attitude to other members of the team, to change his daily regimen, to alter his self-evaluation, to teach the athlete methods of diversion, concentration, desensitization, etc. If the psychologist is qualified he can also teach athletes self-control, psychoregulation, autogenic and ideo-motor training, and auto-suggestion.

The duty of a psychologist attached to a team is primarily to help the coach prepare the given team or individual for the forthcoming competition and to help them reach peak athletic condition at the right time. The Soviet National Hockey Team achieved such a peak in the final game of the three-game Challenge Cup Series (winter, 1979) routing the NHL All-stars 6-0 and leaving all Canada in shock. The illustration shows defenseman Vasiliev and captain Mikhailov, who scored the winning goal, hoisting the Cup in triumph.

The problem of how best to prepare and guide a team psychologically is closely connected to that of the most appropriate way to select the members of such a team. It is claimed that one of the tasks of contemporary Soviet sport psychology is to compile lists of the most important psychological traits and characteristics that have been scientifically substantiated and tested in practice for different sports (psychograms), and on the basis of them to establish models of "ideal" athletes for each sport discipline (Rodionov, 1978). It is presumed that it is useful to have such a model, which combines the traits and qualities of the leading athletes in a given sport, before attempting to influence a superior athlete of that sport. Such a model should include psychological, medical-biological, and educational components and it should be based on the psychological profiles of the leading athletes in the country as well as on the professional characteristics and peculiarities of the sport discipline in question (sportprofessiograms).

The model of the "ideal" superior athlete should project a proper correlation of the basic traits and peculiarities of an individual, his psychophysiological qualities, and psychic conditions which are important for high results in important competitions. The model should also contain a most probable combination of psychic qualities, and the lack of a certain important psychic quality could be compensated for by other appropriate comparable qualities. The psychologist attached to a Soviet national team is responsible for compiling psychological profiles of leading athletes and members of national teams and supplying data for the information of a model of an "ideal" athlete.

One of the important problems with which Soviet national team psychologists are at present concerned is related to the recommendations which a psychologist can and should make for the selection of the most qualified and reliable candidates for the national team, and, in particular, for participation in one given competition. Davydov (1975) suggests that in general terms selection is made on the basis of three distinct components: (1) long-range potential for growth, (2) dependability, and (3) readiness to perform at the required level. In most cases the athlete must have a combination of the above qualities to be selected. It must be added, however, that no system of practical psychological recommendations for the selection of the best possible athletes for participation in Soviet national teams has yet been devised. A number of Soviet sport psychologists recommend the selection of athletes for national youth teams on the basis of the mobility and adaptability of the nervous system and whether its response to stimulation is a balanced one. They suggest that future athletic performance can be predicted with a certain degree of reliability from an evaluation of all such characteristics. It appears, however, from Soviet experience that this approach is only relevant and useful in selecting athletes on the intermediate level, where individual psychological traits are not as important as with those who perform on the highest level. Therefore, this method is little used in picking the best athletes from members of Soviet national teams for participation in a given competition. In practice most psychological recommendations for the selection of these athletes (a decision usually reached at training camp immediately prior to competition) are based on the observation of the behavior of an athlete, on his dependability, and on the confidence of the coaches that he will perform at the given competition better than any other available athlete (Khudadov, 1978).

The daily clinical duties of a psychologist with a Soviet national team include a number of responsibilities that are determined by the stage of training and competition. Psychotherapy occupies an important place in his work. Soviet psychologists are not supposed to administer any medical treatment, such as, for example, medication for relaxation, but a Soviet national team always has a team physician in attendance who works closely with the psychologist and the coach and who will readily assist the psychologist to solve his problem.

The difficulties in guiding the training of superior athletes are at present stressed in the Soviet Union time and again. It is claimed that a specialist in one single area cannot resolve all the technical, physical, and psychological problems connected with guiding an athlete to world records and Olympic championships. Thus the preparation of Soviet national teams has become a cooperative effort in which the sport psychologist has an important contribution to make.

GENERAL THEORETICAL PREMISES
OF SOVIET SPORT PSYCHOLOGY

Soviet sport psychology is a part of Soviet general psychology and is based on the theoretical premises of Marxist-Leninist philosophy, in particular, of dialectical and historical materialism. Therefore, it has in the past often been subject to the vacillations and pressures to which general Marxist dogma has been exposed in the Soviet Union (Smirnov, 1975).

All Soviet psychologists currently subscribe, at least in public, to the view that the product of the psychic function of the brain is a reflection of objective reality, that there is a strict determinism in psychic activity, that man's consciousness is socially conditioned, and that there is a unity between man's consciousness and his activity. It is therefore presumed that the analysis of sport activity should be based on the analysis of general human activity, and that any sport activity is socially determined and motivated.

The dean of Soviet sport psychologists, Professor P.A. Rudik (1973), has defined and subdivided the psychological structure of sport activity into the following areas:

1. Ideological directions of sport activity and its social significance.
2. Technical means and practical operations during activity.
3. Motor skills which are of special importance in the structure of sport activity.
4. The level of development and qualitative peculiarities of various psychic functions, in particular sensory and motor functions.
5. Special knowledge relevant to the given activity.
6. The emotional condition of sport activity.
7. The dynamic character of sport activity.
8. Behavioral aspects of sport activity.

Rudik suggests that the means and methods of psychological preparation could include a cycle of special exercises for the development of the psychological processes and individual qualities required by an athlete. These exercises could be applied during athletic training proper as well as separately without connection to the individual's motor activity. Rudik subdivides these exercises into three broad groups:

1. Exercises for the development of visual, muscular-motor, and vestibular sensations and perceptions, their speed and accuracy.
2. Ideo-motor exercises aimed at the formation and the perfection of motor notions.
3. Exercises for the self-regulation of emotional states.

According to Rudik his psychological structure of sport activity should assist in reaching the immediate goals of Soviet sport psychology which include solving problems such as: the meaning of sport activity; orientation in a changing sport environment; differentiation of sensory and motor processes and the coordination of motor activity; will power required to overcome obstacles; competitive emotions, their qualitative peculiarities and regulation; individual psychological traits and their formation during sport activity; psychological peculiarities of the sport group (team) and the interaction of the members within that group; and socio-psychological investigations.

CURRENT RESEARCH STUDIES
IN SOVIET SPORT PSYCHOLOGY

Although Soviet sport psychology adheres to the general theoretical premises of the Soviet sciences, in practice it is called upon to research motor activity from all possible angles and to produce results which could be useful and helpful to Soviet athletes and teams in their struggle for world records and Olympic championships.

Soviet sport psychology is a growing field and a number of studies by the leading Soviet scholars, A.Ts. Puni and P.A. Rudik and their pupils, are well known in the west (Vanek and Cratty, 1970). Soviet studies of the psychological parameters of various sports, of the pre-start and post-start tensions in athletes, of different psychological aspects of will power, and many others have been utilized by Soviet theorists of physical education and incorporated in one form or another in Soviet programs of athletic training. Vanek and Cratty's (1970) publication gives a good overview of the development of Soviet sport psychology up to the late 1960s. The only shortcoming of this book is the lack of social perspective, making it often appear that there is no difference in the way athletes are conditioned and motivated in countries with different social systems.

Valeriy Borzov, known as the "manufactured sprinter," *arrived on time* at the Munich Olympics and won both sprint events. Reportedly he was a product of a six-year development program.

The aims and objectives outlined by Rudik, in the early 1970s, form a broad framework for the development of Soviet sport psychology. It is possible, however, to suggest that this framework is a reflection of past accomplishments rather than a blueprint for the requirements of the 1970s. It has by now become obvious that in general terms, Soviet research in sport psychology until the 1970s, has been of little use to the individual athlete aspiring to improve his athletic proficiency at the highest level. Practical Soviet research findings were important and useful, but they mainly benefitted the average athlete, while the superior sportsman, in need of personal attention and individual help in coping with his problems, was left to himself. This situation was aggravated by the fact that experimental research findings in one sport were often applied indiscriminately to problems in other sports, often bearing most unexpected negative results. This circumstance and the ever increasing demand for the superior athlete to improve his performance forced Soviet psychologists in the late 1970s to seek new directions for psychological research.

One of the leading Soviet sport psychologists, A.V. Rodionov (1978), suggests that contemporary research in sport psychology should put equal emphasis on two distinct components of sport. On the one hand research would concentrate on the subject, the individual athlete with all his personal traits and qualities, and on the other, the object would be studied, that is, the particular sport activity including all its peculiar manifestations and rules. This approach is, however, not a simple one because it requires the psychologist to be familiar not only with the subject of his study, the athlete, but also with the sport discipline in question. Indeed, many Soviet sport psychologists, who are graduates of Soviet institutes for physical culture, have in the past been highly qualified sportsmen, and yet they know only the sport in which they have specialized intimately and they may tend to relate research findings to personal experience and suggest the application of results received in experiments with athletes in one sport to athletes in other sport disciplines.

SOVIET INSTITUTES AND THEIR
PRIMARY RESEARCH ORIENTATION*

General and sport psychology are compulsory subjects in most of the institutes and faculties training specialists in physical education referred to earlier, and many staff members, particularly in the centrally located institutes, are involved in some kind of research work. In addition, there are in the USSR several scientific-research institutes for physical culture which are under the direct jurisdiction of the Committee of Physical Culture and Sport of the USSR Council of Ministers. Research in sport psychology is also conducted in institutions such as the Moscow Scientific-Research Institute of General and Pedagogical Psychology of the USSR Academy of Pedagogical Sciences, the Kiev Scientific-Research Institute for the Study of Medical Problems of Physical

---

* For a discussion of specialist training in physical education and motor activity, see: N. Norman Shneidman, *The Soviet Road to Olympus: Theory and Practice of Soviet Physical Culture and Sport.* Toronto: OISE, pp. 73-88.

Culture of the Ukrainian SSR Ministry of Health, and many other institutions.

Psychologists in institutes for physical culture carry a heavy teaching load, but those attached to scientific-research institutes, which are essentially institutions dedicated to the development of new knowledge, are not required to teach and devote all their time to research. The Moscow All-Union Scientific-Research Institute for Physical Culture, for example, has departments of sport psycho hygiene, higher sport mastery, scientific-methodological information, the medical supervision of national teams, the physiological foundations of the guidance of movement, and many others in which advanced research in physical education and motor activity is conducted.

Soviet scientific-research and educational institutions usually have long term plans for scholarly investigation, which are approved by higher standing bodies and financed by the state. In most cases a psychology department of such an institution receives a research assignment in which most staff members participate, generally under the supervision and guidance of a senior staff member. Rodionov (1978) outlined a number of different aspects of sport psychology that are currently under investigation in the following Soviet institutions:

The psychic reliability of athletes in different conditions of sport activity and the mechanics of self-control during technical training are being studied at the Moscow All-Union Scientific-Research Institute for Physical Culture.

The psychological factor of optimum conditions and motivational factors in sport activity are under investigation at the Moscow Central State Institute for Physical Culture.

Psychographic characteristics of different sports and the factors which determine readiness for sport activity on the superior level are being studied at the Leningrad State Institute for Physical Culture.

The psychological foundations of technical and physical preparation and the tolerance of psychic tension are being researched at the Leningrad Scientific-Research Institute for Physical Culture.

At the Kiev State Institute for Physical Culture the psychological foundation of technical training and rehabilitation after heavy workloads are under study.

At the Armenian State Institute for Physical Culture in the city of Erevan the psychological conditions of coaches' activity are being studied.

Problems of selecting athletes are being studied at the Cheliabinsk State Institute for Physical Culture and at the

Scientific-Research Institute of General and Pedagogical Psychology of the USSR Academy of Pedagogical Sciences.

Problems of ideo-motor training are being investigated at the Volgograd State Institute for Physical Culture.

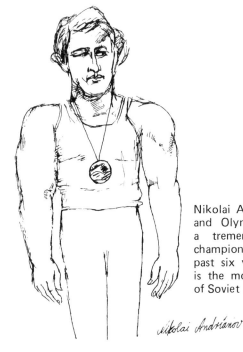

Nikolai Andrianov, the reigning world and Olympic champion, has shown a tremendous consistency in his championship performances over the past six years. This kind of stability is the most important characteristics of Soviet athletes.

Nikolai Andrianov

PUBLICATION OF IMPORTANT FINDINGS

The results of experimental research and field studies in sport psychology are usually published in professional periodical publications. The most important journal of that kind, published in the Soviet Union, is the monthly *Teoriia i praktika fizicheskoi kul'tury* (Theory and practice of physical culture). In addition, research papers often appear in monographs, such as *Psikhologiia i sovremennyi sport* (Psychology and contemporary sport) (1973), edited by P.A. Rudik, or in booklets published by educational institutions which include only works by staff members of these institutions. *Important findings of practical relevance are not published but distributed in the form of methodological letters to those who can benefit directly from such information.* Research findings directly related to the preparation and performance of

Soviet national teams are seldom publicized at all because they are viewed as important weapons in the combat of Soviet athletes and teams against representatives of other countries.

Reports of most psychological research published in the Soviet Union in the last decade, therefore, are of a general nature and, with rare exceptions, say little about the psychological preparation of superior athletes, in particular those who participate in the international struggle for world records and Olympic championships. Several examples of characteristic studies in sport psychology published in the USSR in the 1970s are given at the end of this paper as an illustration of this point.

These examples show that Soviet sport psychologists use advanced methods and equipment in their research and experiments. They also utilize western research techniques extensively and often quote western sources in their studies. In general terms all scientific research in sport psychology conducted in the Soviet Union could be divided into three groups:

1. Research studies of general theoretical and methodological importance which are, however, of little practical significance.
2. Research studies and experiments that are of practical relevance to the Soviet theory of physical culture and to the theory of athletic training. The results of such studies are often incorporated in educational programs and are used in planning training programs for athletes at different levels of proficiency.
3. Research studies which have immediate practical importance for the superior athlete. Studies that help to select the best possible athlete for a given athletic task and guide him to victory. The number of such studies is in all probability limited, and the results have so far not been made public.

DEVELOPMENTS IN SOVIET
SOCIAL PSYCHOLOGY OF SPORT

Social psychology as well as sociology are relatively young disciplines in the Soviet Union. Soviet psychologists and sociologists tackle serious social problems in a very careful manner, because according to Marxist dogma human cognition is unlimited and man is essentially regarded as a rational creature. According to Lenin's theory of perception only the perception which appears in its unity of irrational sensation and rational reflection can be regarded as valuable. Emotions aroused by the heat of athletic competition are, however, often irrational and difficult to control. A study by a leading theorist of Soviet social sport psychology (Goncharov, 1976) defines the discipline as a part of Marxist materialistic social psychology and asserts that among the most important principles of Soviet sport psychology one should include historicism, determinism, development, communication, relative independence, social importance, and the activity of consciousness.

Studies on intra-personal, intra-group, and intra-team conflicts are currently being carried out by a number of Soviet sport psychologists, including Khanin from the Leningrad Scientific-Research Institute for Physical Culture (1976, 1977) and the Romanins from the Moscow All-Union Scientific-Research Institute for Physical Culture (1976). Soviet social psychologists of sport discuss in their works problems of leadership, status, and social motivation, but there are few studies which analyze the social behavior of the Soviet athletes in relation to the general patterns of behavior in contemporary Soviet society. No studies have been published recently in which the relationship of the personal and social components in the motivation of Soviet athletes are analyzed, or the psychological aspects of participation in international competitions discussed. Such studies would be of immense interest to western psychologists because they would help western athletes to understand their Soviet opponents better. One can only surmise that the results of such studies would often contradict the accepted premises of Soviet social psychology and that, therefore, they are not publicized.

CONCLUSION

In conclusion it would be worthwhile to comment in brief on the working conditions of Soviet sport psychologists, which are very different from those in the west, and on the distinction between the North American system of athletic training and the Soviet system of organized athletics; only by appreciating the differences will we be able to understand, and make use of, the research findings of Soviet psychologists. First of all it is necessary to remember that a Soviet sport psychologist attached to a national team is a state employee assigned an important task of national significance. Similarly the subjects of his study and care, the athletes, are individuals assembled and supported by the state for what is considered an important social, national, and ideological pursuit, and their cooperation is always assured. The composition of Soviet national teams is stable and changes slowly, and the psychologist usually has enough time to study the athletes and to establish a good working relationship with them. In addition, most team psychologists have coaching qualifications and a good understanding of the sport concerned. Important also is the fact that the psychologist usually works with a highly qualified coach. Most Soviet national team coaches are themselves professional specialists, often with advanced academic degrees, who are able to utilize the contributions of the psychologists and physicians and work with them as a team.

Finally it should be added that western students of Soviet sport psychology and of Soviet sport in general should always remember the differences in motivational factors, social pressures, and the relationship between the personal and social components in the athletes' behavior when comparing Soviet and western athletes. It is necessary to bear in mind that because the social makeup of individuals representing different social systems is not the same the psychological ramifications of their performance in the same sport activity or competition could be diverse.

APPENDIX: FOUR STUDIES OF ELITE ATHLETES

1. Nguen Zui Fat and O.V. Dashkevich (1973) from the Moscow Central State Institute for Physical Culture have produced a study on the effect psychic tension has on the performance of shooters.

Thirty highly qualified athletes participated in the experiment which was conducted during both training and competition and whose objective was to determine the state of emotional tension at which shooters achieve their best results. The shooters' heart rate and hand tremor were registered by means of a two-channel electrocardiograph connected to seismic monitoring devices attached over the athlete's heart and to the middle finger on his right hand. The experiment established that the heart rate and hand tremor are higher before competition than during training; that the heart rate and hand tremor are higher before shooting on the first day of competition than on subsequent days; that there is a positive correlation between the heart rate and the hand tremor; and that the shooters' achievements are related to their level of emotional tension. Thus it was concluded (on the basis of the above) that there is an optimal level of emotional tension at which shooters are able to achieve their best results. If the emotional tension increases beyond this level, however, performance declines. Tables 1 and 2 illustrate statistically significant changes in average heart rate and average hand tremor of subjects in different stages of training and competition.

Table 1. Changes in average heart rate and average hand tremor of shooters.

Measurements	Before training session	Before competition	t value	After training session	After competition	t value
Heart rate (beat/min)	87.18	93.07	$t=2.46$**	79.85	86.36	$t=2.55$**
Amplitude of tremor (in mm)	5.52	6.36	$t=2.10$*	5.70	6.65	$t=2.11$*
Frequency of tremor (vibrations/sec)	12.65	13.48	$t=2.07$*	13.18	13.98	$t=2.10$*

*$p < .05$; **$p < .02$

Table 2. The change in average heart rate and average hand tremor before different days of competition.

Measurements	June 15, 1972	June 17, 1972	June 19, 1972
Heart rate (beat/min)	99.27	91.20	88.38
Amplitude of tremor (in mm)	6.75	6.02	5.93

2. M.A. Matova (1976) from the Institute of General and Pedagogical Psychology of the USSR Academy of Pedagogical Sciences produced a study on the psychic state of athletes during extreme muscular exertion.

The objective of the experiment was to study the psychic state created during an all-out physical performance and in connection with it. Particular attention was devoted to the question of to what extent is it possible to combine extreme physical activity with a high degree of mental alertness. It also studied the stage of maximum muscular activity at which man's reasoning powers may fail. The group investigated consisted of 31 superior athletes, 19 men and 12 women, 25 of them members of the figure skating and swimming national teams, and the experiment involved physical work of increasing intensity, divided into six levels of three minutes each and performed on a special Monarch bicycle ergometer. While working at the different levels the athletes were given simple mathematical questions, and the answers were recorded automatically. Their mental and physical states at the time of the experiment were assessed using various indices, such as exterior breathing, electrocardiography, electromyograms, bio-chemical tests, etc. Before and after the experiment the athletes underwent a medical examination and answered a questionnaire.

The experiment revealed a number of psychic conditions which are normally difficult to detect. On the first and second levels of physical intensity the athletes were mainly calm and confident. At the end of the second level and the beginning of the third level for women, and at the third and fourth levels for men, signs of failure of certain functional systems were appearing and were expressed in unexpected changes in the rhythm of muscular work, in mental errors, and in confusion. On the fifth and sixth levels of physical intensity the athletes reached a state of total exhaustion. Psychic failure was revealed through errors of judgement—in answering the mathematical questions—of which the athletes were not aware at the time of the experiment and which usually occurred at least 40-20 seconds before total physical exhaustion.

Matova suggests that the results of her study could be used to help the psychological preparation of athletes for activities in which intense physical work needs to be accompanied by high psychic capabilities.

3.   V.A. Kanygin and E.G. Kozlov (1978) researched at the Moscow Regional State Institute for Physical Culture the factor of psychic tension for weightlifters in competition.

The experiment was conducted on a group of weightlifters, students of the physical culture institute, and its objectives were the following: (1) to check the validity of methods of measuring electroskin resistance (ESR) for the study of psychic tension, (2) to interpret the results of the ESR test administered during

ESR

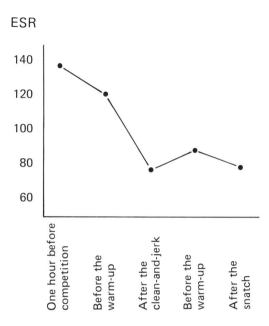

Figure 1. The dynamics of the ESR indices based on the group average during competition.

competition, and (3) to use the ESR test to evaluate psychic tension in visualization exercises and in conditions of ideo-motor practice.

In the first stage of the experiment (objective 1) the relationship of ESR to psychic tension was studied during students' examinations at the institute. In the second stage ESR dynamics were studied during weightlifting competitions. And in the third stage the possibilities of projecting competition conditions during ideo-motor practice were studied. Figure 1 illustrates the dynamics of the ESR indices during competition, while Figure 2 illustrates the dynamics of the ESR indices during the ideo-motor training of an advanced weightlifter.

4. S.A. Razumov and P.S. Saburov (1978) from the Leningrad State Institute for Physical Culture studied the psychophysiological basis of pre-competition training regimens for ski jumpers.

Thirty ski jumpers were divided into two groups according to whether they were introverts or extroverts. Psychological, psychophysiological, and pedagogical methods of testing were used. A questionnaire of 56 questions adapted by H. Botteher, was dis-

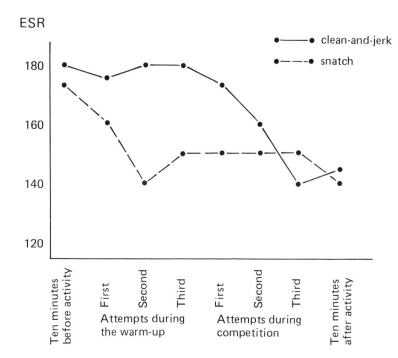

ESR

Figure 2. The dynamics of the ESR indices based on the group average during ideo-motor training.

tributed. Psychophysiological reactions were studied by monitoring the time, speed, and accuracy of different reactions; the heart rate during jumping was measured through radiotelemetric and tape recording equipment. Urine samples were taken daily during training, competition, and periods of rest.

The study concluded that extroverts and introverts peaked for a given competition in different ways. The extroverts lowered their state of emotional tension prior to competition, alternated with special physical exercise, and rested before competition. The introverts, on the other hand, reached their peak by systematically increasing the number of ski jumps, and as competition approached, by alternating jumps with general and special physical exercises. Thus different and specialized pre-competition training regimens for ski jumpers increase their tolerance of emotional stress, strengthen their psychological defence mechanisms, and increase their readiness for competition.

the scandinavian practice of sport psychology

Willi S. Railo
Lars-Eric V. Unestahl

PART ONE*

In Scandinavia, and especially in Sweden, advanced research has been done in the field of sport psychology during the last decade. We have also been greatly interested in the physiological aspects of sport. During the last few years in all the Scandinavian countries we have established relatively good research centres in sport physiology, and our coaches are fairly well educated in this field. The coaches' interest in sport physiology remains high in Scandinavia, but during the last seven or so years, their interest in sport psychology has increased dramatically. In some respects I would say that the interest is sometimes too great. I think this development is caused by three factors: (1) the ever increasing level of performance means that marginal (psychological) effects are to a great extent defining the winner; (2) the other aspects of sport (physiological, technical, tactical, and so on) are fairly well understood, and accordingly interest has turned to "new" areas; and (3) the establishment of the new sport college in Norway with a more behavior-scientific orientation compared to the established traditional colleges elsewhere in Scandinavia, made it possible to develop sport psychology and to educate students and coaches in this field. In this chapter I will try to present the main topics with practical applications for top athletes, on which sport psychology is working in Scandinavia. I limit my discussion to different applied psychological training techniques, but this does not mean that different general psychological approaches, like conversation "therapy" for example, are excluded. In addition, sport psychology in Scandinavia includes a variety of topics that are not concerned with top athletes: planning of sport for all, psychological development within the sport for children and youth, the effect of different sport programs for different handicapped groups, and so on. Professor Unestahl is describing some of these approaches in the second section of this chapter.

* This part was written by Willi S. Railo, Norway.

DEVELOPMENT TRENDS IN SCANDINAVIA

When I wrote a book on the practical application of sport psychology in 1972, the interest in and discussion about sport psychology had clearly increased, especially in Norway and Sweden (later even in Denmark and Finland). Because of this interest, the Norwegian as well as the Swedish National Sport Federations included the book in their educational programs for coaches. Then a more systematic education in sport psychology started within both federations.

Since that time more psychologists and teachers in Scandinavia are engaged in this educational program. Since 1972 I have given a lot of courses for coaches, psychologists, and teachers. I think it is correct to say that even among athletes the interest in practical sport psychology has increased remarkably.

Thus far in Scandinavia the sports governing bodies, the coaches, and the athletes are all extremely interested in sport psychology. However, our main problem is our ability to bring the knowledge in a practical way to the coaches and athletes. In Scandinavia only the exceptional and very talented athlete can count on direct help from a sport psychologist. Although many psychologists are interested in the field of sport, they are generally unsuccessful if they lack a background in sport. It seems that it is easier to teach applied sport psychology to an interested coach than to teach knowledge of sport to an inexperienced psychologist. To reach most athletes, therefore, our method has been to educate coaches so that they can work directly with their own athletes.

The trend in Scandinavia is increasingly to work through the coaches, using the following method. First they are taught the theory and practice of sport psychology. A practical period then follows during which the coaches try only the simplest methods on their athletes and gain experience; they are able to contact a psychologist for advice. After this stage they return for further education and more advanced procedures. This method is working quite well in Norway, but I should stress that it is important that the coaches be supervised by a skilled psychologist.

REGULATION OF
PSYCHOPHYSIOLOGICAL TENSION

The main theory behind the psychic regulation of an athlete is the well-known inverted-U relationship between the athlete's arousal/

activation and his performance which is discussed by Peter Klavora in chapter 15. (The term "tension" is used in Europe to describe what is known as "activation" or "arousal" in North America.) In attempting to apply regulation it is important to take into account: (1) the basic anxiety of the individual athlete and his specific psychic reaction to tension in the competitive situation, (2) the type of sport, (3) the skill level of the athlete's technique, and (4) the cause of the tension.

Basic Anxiety Level

To measure the basic level of anxiety, one can, of course, use different psychometric tests. This I have done in several cases. My experience is, however, that such tests are not too good at predicting what an athlete's reactions may be in competitive situations. If you have little or no knowledge of the athlete, such tests can be informative. But when you have personal contact with the athlete, the tests in most cases give little additional knowledge of practical value.

A practical alternative to these tests is to discuss with the athlete his psychological reactions, observe his behavior in competitive situations of differing importance, learn his typical emotional reactions, and compare them to the performances.

Another important approach is to make the athletes conscious of their own emotional reactions and give them tasks to help them discover the relationship between their own psyche and their performance. This can be done, not only in respect to the tension level, but even in relationship to other significant psychological reactions. The crucial point is to work with the athlete to find the beneficial pre-competition feeling. We frequently speak of the "winning feeling." This is a feeling that many athletes associate (often on an unconscious or preconscious level) with their readiness to perform well.

To make the athletes more conscious of the desired psychological states we use a combination of conversation and systematic observation by the coach (and if possible, a psychologist) and systematic self-evaluation by the athlete himself. The self-evaluation schemes will differ, but the table on page 251 provides an example.

Type of Sport

Before deciding in what way to regulate tension, we divide all sports into groups depending on whether they tolerate (or require

Table 1. Self-evaluation table.

Psychological reaction	Subjective scores					Personal remarks
	low	low+	medium	high-	high	
Heart frequency				✓		
Nervousness			✓			
Flight reaction			✓			
Fight reaction	✓					
Motivation			✓			
Concentration	✓					
Self-confidence		✓				
Fear of losing					✓	
Social expectations			✓			
Goal-setting				✓		
Feeling as favorite		✓				
Feeling as underdog				✓		
etc.						

for good performance) a low, medium, or high level of tension or arousal. High tension is usually beneficial to the pure mobilization of muscular strength and endurance, but as soon as technique is required, tension can be disruptive, because it affects general co-ordination and concentration. Sports where maximum strength and endurance are involved, such as running, skiing, weight lifting, and cycling, will need and can tolerate a high level of tension in the athlete. On the opposite end of the scale, sports involving complicated technique with little need for strength and endurance such as shooting, archery, bowling, table tennis, and tennis, will tolerate only a low level of tension. In the middle group we have sports that depend on both complicated techniques and strength or endurance; examples here are football, soccer, hockey, basketball, and handball.

Level of Automatic Skill Execution

It should be mentioned that tolerance of tension will vary within a sport depending on the extent to which the athlete's technique has become automatic: the more automatic the execution of the skill, the more tension the athlete can tolerate. In addition, the tension tolerance of an individual athlete will also vary depending on whether the skill being executed is a dominant one for that athlete. For example, a tennis player may have a high tension

tolerance on a highly skilled and automatic (and dominant) fore-
hand and much less tolerance on a less skilled (not dominant)
backhand.

Cause of Tension

Furthermore, it should be stressed that we cannot just look at the
tension *level*: the cause of the tension must be taken into consideration. The cases are quite different if the tension level is caused
by nervousness, for example, rather than by motivation. For a
detailed description of various causes of increased levels of pre-
competitive anxiety of athletes see chapter 20 prepared by Walter
Kroll. Tension has accordingly both a quantitative and a qualitative aspect that should be evaluated.

TECHNIQUES FOR
REGULATING TENSION

Because there are so many factors to take into consideration, I
have found it inappropriate in practice to define the psychological
preparation needs of a certain athlete from test information. You
have to evaluate the individual athlete in definite and concrete
situations within his sport.

There are a lot of techniques to choose from when it comes to
psychoregulatory training techniques (tension regulation). The
technique used most is a special adaptation of "autogenic training." Other techniques that are used a lot are progressive relaxation (an adaptation of Jacobson) and a simple breathing technique. I will not describe these techniques in detail, but just say
that I have found a combination of these techniques most effective. I use training sessions of approximately 15 minutes, where
I first alternate between slow and deep breathing and maximum
muscular tension (in many gross muscles simultaneously) and de-
tension. I then go into concentration on, for example, both arms
heavy, and so on. My experience is that you achieve much better
results if you have longer training sessions (15 minutes) than
originally and go straight to both arms, both legs, stomach, and so
forth.

Normally, I meet the athletes for group training and conversation once a week. In addition, the athletes train at home daily for
approximately two months by listening to my cassettes. Generally
athletes have to train for six months to be able to apply the techniques in situations of serious stress. At the beginning of the train-

A session showing Willi Railo teaching a famous Scandinavian soccer player self-regulation of pre-competitive tension.

ing, say for two months, we train without any disturbances. After this we gradually introduce different disturbing effects (noise, talking, etc.) into the training sessions.

In my experience athletes have to be motivated to complete such a training program. Furthermore, it is important to inform the athletes that the effect does not come "overnight" but as a result of systematic training. It is also important to inform the athletes that the initial effects can be quite the opposite to the final effects: often the athletes are tired and lack concentration during and after the training.

In many cases the psychoregulatory training takes place in connection with the physical training sessions, under the leadership of an educated coach. (It should be mentioned that deep relaxation *can,* but seldom does, lead to some negative effects on the athletes, for example anxiety, that skilled coaches can easily prevent.)

Other relaxation techniques, such as transcendental meditation, yoga, psychomotor training, biofeedback, and so on, are applied much less in Scandinavian sport psychology.

Many other factors are taken into consideration when we try to regulate the tension level of athletes. These include: physical activity (longer and harder physical warm-up program), massage, warm showers, lowering the pressure of social expectations, and reducing performance anxiety by avoiding negative sanctions of bad performances, and so on. We try in different ways to strengthen the athlete's positive achievement motivation and his self-confidence.

ENERGY REGULATION

Athletes must have sufficient psychological energy to put into the competition itself. Often we find (1) that athletes have not built up their energy resources during the training sessions, (2) that athletes consume too much energy before the competition, and (3) that they waste their energy during the competition. When we turn to the question of how to build up energy potential, we base our reasoning on the fact that training basically involves the body's adapting (physically as well as psychologically) to stressors or more generally, to stimulation of athletic training and competition.

Often we find that athletes in training mobilize 70 to 80 per cent of their maximum, while in competition they must mobilize 100 per cent. This kind of training does not build up (adapt) the body's potential to mobilize 100 per cent. Accordingly, we try to have maximum psychic mobilization in many, but not all, training sessions. In many sports we recommend quite often that athletes train less but with a higher mobilization of energy. When the competitive season approaches, we try to regulate the amount and intensity of training and plan the program of competition so that athletes have maximum psychological energy for the important competitions. The *psyche* of the athlete, not just his physical state, should have an important place in determining his training program. Scandinavian coaches do not yet take the psyche sufficiently into account.

When mobilizing energy one should keep in mind that athletes consume energy. Athletes often consume too much energy before competition in the following ways: (1) they are too nervous for too long before the competition, (2) they overconcentrate on the competition, and (3) they are exposed in a competition to too much stimulation or too many new situations.

I normally give the following advice. Save energy before the competition (control nervousness, concentrate intensively but for limited times, and activate the athletes with familiar things) and mobilize just before the competition (say one or two hours before). The mobilization consists of self-mobilization through concentration and social mobilization through "pep talks" and so on. I also advise building up energy by sufficient sleep, deep and relatively long relaxation sessions (adapted "autogenic training"), using humor and pleasant activities in the preparation. Too often the preparation is too serious with little pleasure and high tension.

In sports where competition takes a long time (tennis, bowling, shooting, etc.) it is important that athletes conserve their energy, which is important both to the releasing of physical resources and to concentration. Mobilize when necessary and relax when mobilization is not necessary. Do not try to mobilize all the time.

FIGHT AND FLIGHT REGULATION

When a human being is exposed to a stress situation, the reaction is often flight or fight. Thus in competitive sports we see the athlete who cannot stand the stress level without choosing a flight reaction. By a flight reaction we mean that the athlete becomes defensive in his attitude. Often this leads to a loss of self-confidence, a lowering of goals, and an application of different defense mechanisms. The defense mechanism that most coaches recognize is rationalization. (The athlete may say: "I'm in bad form," "I'm hurt," "I have trained too little," "I don't care about this competition," "I don't like the lane, the wind," etc., etc.) Normally the flight reaction gives a bad base for a good performance, compared to the fight reaction, in which the athlete is offensive, keeps his self-confidence, keeps his goals, and does not care about his own psychological defense.

An important part of psychological preparation is to promote the fight reaction in the athlete. But how? First, it is important to underline that there is an interaction between the personality of the athlete and the stress level: some athletes can stand very little stress before they are forced into a flight reaction, while others can stand a high stress level and still choose a fight reaction. Thus we find athletes' reactions changing from one competition to another, because of the changing stress level.

Because the main problem is that the personality cannot stand the stress level and because the flight reaction often is so effectively "defended" by the athlete, we generally advise the following procedures: control stress level by relaxation techniques, work with the athletes to make them aware of their flight reaction (recognize the symptoms), lower the pressure of expectations on the athlete, try to reduce the athlete's performance anxiety, for example by strengthening the cohesiveness of the group, eliminate negative emotional sanctions of bad performances, and train the flight reaction away systematically by symbol training.

MODEL TRAINING

I have already mentioned that all training involves adapting the organisms to stressors/stimulation. Expressed negatively we could say that you will have no training effect without stimulation. This is the basic principle of model training, which is very common in Scandinavia. First, working with the athletes, we try to find out what factors or what situations they find difficult to control psychologically. Having defined these factors or situations, we try to introduce (copy or modulate) these factors into training situations, or we try to find competitive situations where these models will probably occur. It is important here to motivate the athlete to want to solve the problems.

In my work with athletes I have commonly found that they like and are attracted to situations that they already control, and that they avoid situations in which they have problems. Many hold the opinion that the important routine comes with age. It does not come with age but with training (adaptation to the situation).

Here it should be emphasized that *concentration* is developed according to the following principles. When we are working on concentration endurance, we have not found any method other than stressing long-lasting concentration in the training sessions (thus the body will adapt to the actual concentration intensity and length). When we turn to concentration stability, we try to reduce the "orientation reflex" by introducing the kinds of stressors or disturbances that may occur in competition.

Depending on the sport, we use tapes from competitive situations, introduce stress elements in training, find training conditions that the athletes do not normally like, for example windy weather, bad lanes, strange light, false judging, high expectations, and so on. It is important not to overdo this kind of training, to have a gradual adaptation, and it is important that the athletes are motivated to overcome any problems that may occur.

It should be unnecessary to say that competing in real and tough competitions is good model training. Within this area we find a clear tendency: we try to copy or model a real competition many times before the competition itself occurs, for example, copying of lanes, cross-country (terrain) profiles, etc. This is done to have a physical and psychological adaptation to that specific situation.

DESENSITIZATION

In many cases it is, of course, practically impossible or difficult to model or copy a real competitive situation. We then apply a simple and effective mental technique called "desensitization," that is, training the athletes to be less sensitive to stress situations.

The training procedure again starts with an analysis of the problems that the individual athlete has in the competitive situation. Every ambitious athlete should have a list of his own "stress situations." When the different situations have been defined, the crucial point is to link or associate the stress situations to a relaxed and safe feeling. The simplest method is to sit or lie down with eyes closed and just relax for one minute. When feeling calm and relaxed, the athlete mentally goes into the stress situation and stays there for 30 seconds to a minute. Then the athlete leaves the situation and just relaxes for 30 seconds or so. He then repeats the procedure.

A somewhat more advanced procedure that we apply quite a lot in Scandinavia is a combination of a deep relaxation technique and the mental rehearsal of being in the stress situation. The effect of this combination seems to be better. I think the reasons for the greater effectiveness are the following:

1. Deep relaxation gives a clearer relaxation (destressed) association to the original stress situation—relaxation is much more exposed.
2. The body's unconscious ability to learn seems to increase in the state of deep relaxation (probably because of the lowered defense mechanisms).

The technique could be described like this:

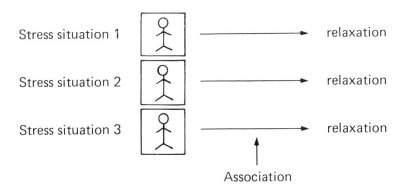

How much training is enough? This is a difficult question to answer because it depends on the number of stress situations and their seriousness for the athlete, as well as his ability to learn, and his ambition.

The *number* of repetitions is more important than the length of each. It should be made quite clear to the athlete that the effect does not come overnight but slowly and gradually. As an average I recommend to top athletes to train for five minutes a day, four days a week, over most of the training period. I further recommend that they start with the simplest situations and proceed to the more serious ones. More than two situations should not be included in the same training session. Be aware of the fact that the athletes have to train for approximately two to four weeks to have sufficient concentration to be able to get *into* (and not remain outside) the situations.

In addition to year-round general training, we often work the same way for a specific important competition and the stress or problem situations that may occur there. The athletes then are mentally adapted to that competition and its surroundings. We may bring in films, slides, photos, and verbal descriptions of the competition arena, so that the athletes can familiarize themselves with competition conditions.

SYMBOL AND ANTI-SYMBOL TRAINING

This training is based on the premise that human behavior and reactions are to a great extent determined by unconscious factors. The training aims to (1) reduce or eliminate negative reactions stored in the unconscious and (2) "program" the unconscious with positive steering impulses.

Reducing negative reactions. Many athletes have learned and stored different negative reactions in the unconscious, for example, a flight attitude or defensive attitude, or different psychological blocks such as against certain goals ("I can't reach that high level," "I can't beat that competitor," "I can't win that game," etc.), blocks against certain competitors, lanes, weather, wind, terrain, special elements in the performance ("My backhand never works in that situation"), and so on.

A central problem for many athletes is that their self-confidence is too low before and during the competitive situation. Here it should be mentioned that to achieve one's physical and technical potential, high goals (*accepted* by the unconscious) must be combined with a high level of self-confidence. One could divide self-confidence into general self-confidence and situation-specific self-confidence. My experience is that the situation-specific self-confidence to a great extent can be trained by symbols.

Coaches are fully aware of the athlete who is superior in practice but some-how never does well in competition. Many variables are different in the real tournament, race, meet, and so on. Physical variables may differ, as may psychological ones. The rule is that practice makes perfect, the more similar the practice demands are to the game demands.

Programming the unconscious. It should be mentioned that the athletes can use the same technique for self-motivation before important competitions, by systematically applying formulas to promote motivation. The same could be said about "form." Form normally has a physical and a psychological component, although of course, many factors are involved here. But one should be especially aware of the fact that the athletes themselves can in-fluence their form development by systematic concentration. The athletes should not wonder *if* they will come into form for a certain important competition, they should decide to come into form, and store this "opinion" or "program" in the unconscious, from which it often works when the real situation occurs. Here, too, we can divide the application into a simple and a more ad-vanced (and more effective) version: the first does not use deep relaxation and the second includes the deep relaxation state.

We often use this procedure to train away different negative reactions. After having defined the actual "problem situation" in which the athlete has undesired reactions, the athlete first closes his eyes, rehearses the situation and is asked to try as many nega-tive associations, thoughts, and reactions on himself as possible (for example, "feel defensive," "feel tense," "lose self-confi-dence," "feel afraid not to succeed," and so on). It is important here to convert the athlete's negative reactions into adequate (for the athlete) symbols (words, sentences, pictures).

Having established the athlete's negative symbols in the problem situation, the next step is to define the anti-symbols (the opposite of the negative symbols). Then it is important to find anti-symbols that can evoke adequate psychological reactions in the athlete. (It should be stressed that negations should never be used in the anti-symbols.) The whole idea with the technique is to replace the negative reactions/symbols in the actual situation with positive reactions/anti-symbols. The athlete has to work so long with the anti-symbols that they become *stronger* than the problem symbols. After having trained on pure relaxation for about two months, I introduce this anti-symbol training into the relaxed state. In most cases it is effective when the athlete works systematically.

When we have no special problem situation to overcome, but just want to prepare desired reactions (for example, form, self-confidence, and so on), we use the same method but omit the analysis of the problem reactions. In my experience, it is still preferable to link the symbols as much as possible to concrete situations.

MENTAL PRACTICE

Mental practice is a well-known technique. The procedure is theoretically fairly simple but is often difficult to apply in practice. In this technique the athlete is asked to close his eyes and rehearse a correct technique mentally. We have even applied the technique for the training of reaction speed (primarily in complex reactions) and for tactics.

We can divide mental rehearsal into two main categories:
1. Mental rehearsal of a film-like picture, in which the athlete sees himself performing the correct act. (This technique is fairly simple and is appropriate at the beginning of training.)
2. Mental rehearsal of being *in* the situation in which the athlete sees and feels himself going through the correct performance. (This is fairly difficult for many athletes and often requires a lot of training.)

This training is being applied more and more in Scandinavia, and is usually independent of the technical/physical training. However, certain combinations seem helpful:
1. Teach the athletes to stop immediately after a successful performance and rehearse it mentally several times before doing anything else—to reinforce and strengthen the memory of the good performance. It seems to help the athletes in

their mental rehearsal at home.

2. Alternate the physical/technical training with mental practice. Here we sometimes use videotapes showing the correct performance in training. The athletes look at the videotapes, have a period of mental rehearsal of that performance, and then try the activity physically before going back to the videotapes. In most cases this technique seems to work effectively.

Normally I recommend training periods at home, five days a week for five or ten minutes. If motivation is high, it is of course preferable to have more training sessions, but longer sessions are not required. It seems that the mental rehearsal at home combined with deep relaxation is very effective. In these cases we use two to three minutes to get into the relaxed position and then we alternate between one-minute periods of mental rehearsal and thirty-second periods of relaxation. It is important that the coach ensure that the rehearsal is correct. In some cases the coach might verbally lead the rehearsal and underline the crucial points in the actual performance. Normally I record cassette tapes that the athlete can listen to at home. Some of the tapes are of a general character and some are made specially for the individual athlete.

CONCLUSION

Finally, I have to mention that coaches must understand the importance of speaking about psychological factors with their athletes; they should not just use these factors to try to manipulate their athletes. Open conversation about different psychological reactions among the athletes as a group or a team often brings good results. Let the athletes speak of their psychological reactions and be careful not to give negative reactions/sanctions.

Some coaches begin with regular conversations and then go a bit further with different group dynamic exercises. The effect of such an approach will, of course, vary with the insight of the coach. Many of the coaches that I have had the opportunity of supervising have achieved good results from both a performance and a humanistic point of view.

PART TWO*

Most people nowadays recognize that psychological factors play a significant part in sports, particularly in competitive sports. An athlete can judge himself to be in the best physical condition and yet perform badly. Sometimes his main opponent seems to be himself. Psychic or mental training should therefore be as natural a part of a training program as physical or technical training.

In spite of steadily increasing awareness of this need, few athletes have until now started any regular and methodical psychological training. The reason is obvious. There is little literature about psychic training and almost nothing is written in a practical vein. For that reason I have been working for some years developing and testing various programs for psychic training. As an example I will describe here in brief a basic three-month training program, which is intended to be used by athletes from all different sports. I will then discuss the application of the program to competitive sports, before going on to discuss its application to other areas of life.

PSYCHIC TRAINING PROGRAM

The program covers three months of training on five days per week. The daily training lasts between 10 and 25 minutes and can be done individually or in a group. Descriptions of 14 elements of the program have been recorded and are available on three cassettes, and the book providing the background information and the principles behind the methods should be read before training begins.** The program consists of the following sections:

Weeks 1-2—Muscular Relaxation

Since relaxation is contradictory to any voluntary effort, it has to be learned in such a way that it will come automatically. A common program for systematic, progressive, and differential

---

* This part was written by Lars-Eric Unestahl, Sweden.

** Unestahl, Lars-Eric. *Inner Control by Mental Training: Applications in Sports.* Orebro, Sweden: Veje Publ., 1979. Available only in Swedish. Will be published in English during 1979. The cassettes are also in Swedish and will be translated into English during 1979. The cassettes in Swedish can be purchased from Veje Publ., Box 106017, 70016 Orebro, Sweden. Price: $30 for three cassettes.

relaxation is used. To increase the induction speed of and the control over the relaxation effects, these effects are conditioned to a concrete and practical trigger.

Scandinavian coaches have long recognized the fact that often the athlete's main opponent seems to be the athlete himself. Psychic or mental training should therefore be as natural a part of his training program as is physical or technical training.

Weeks 3-4—Mental Relaxation

The first two weeks of training in muscular relaxation have given the athlete a concrete understanding of the notion of relaxation and also increased the effects. The purpose of the mental relaxation training is: (a) to teach the athlete to induce relaxation through mental triggers, and (b) to change the attention from the muscular effects to the mental effects, for example, feelings of calmness and confidence. The athlete also learns to differentiate between the two kinds of effects. He is given additional triggers to enable him to induce the mental effects directly without any reduction of muscular tonus. An additional purpose of the mental relaxation training is to deepen the relaxation and to introduce a *mental room.* The athlete learns to find this room in a fast and easy way. He learns to use it for effective rest and quicker recovery.

Week 5—Supplementary Training

There are significant differences between individuals, not in their basic ability to learn muscular and mental relaxation, but in the length of time required to do so. This week gives athletes a chance to work in those areas that need supplementary training.

Week 6—Dissociation and Detachment Training

The training thus far usually increases the athlete's ability to dissociate and detach himself from his surroundings or to produce an altered state of consciousness. The purpose of this week is to teach a kind of selective dissociation, a learning of how to eliminate distractions. This training occurs in an environment with many disturbances, much noise, and so on. A new method of handling these distrubances is introduced to the athlete each day, such as concentration/distraction, emotional dissociation, changing the experience, changing the attitude, mental wall, and so on.

Week 7—Goal Programming Training

The learned relaxation and dissociation seem to bring about a hemispheric shift, an activation of the non-dominant or right side of the brain, and a deactivation of the dominant or left side. This shift brings a reduction of certain functions such as the reality testing, critical logical thought processes, verbal abilities, and the defense mechanism system. At the same time other functions seem to increase, such as the imaginative and creative powers, suggestibility and holistic ability. Because voluntary effort often fails and can even produce the opposite effect, an alternative method of controlling the psychic processes is needed. The training during the first six weeks has created the prerequisite conditions to replace voluntary control with a kind of cognitive or imaginary control. When a person's images and expectations (short- and long-term goal programming) are controlled his inner resources will be directed to the goals. The athlete can then just *let it happen* without any conscious voluntary effort. During this week the athlete learns ways of goal programming. On a screen in his mental room he can produce films (images) and on a blackboard he can see different key words being written (suggestions). He also learns to induce the state of letting it happen, a state of detachment, singlemindedness, and blankness—the winning feeling.

Week 8—Ideo-Motor Training

During this week the athlete has the opportunity to apply the principles of goal programming in an area where the effects are seen immediately. By exercises such as "the pendulum" or "arm levitation" he learns to master these principles. He also learns to apply ideo-motor training to the process of motor learning and motor automation. Experiments by myself and many others have shown that such mental practice may be as effective as physical training, and that a combination of both seems to be most effective. Through imagery, the athlete can focus on kinesthetic and proprioceptive feedback which is essential to good performance.

Weeks 9-10—Problem Solving

All athletes experience situations in which a poor performance has created an awareness of problems, and this awareness can easily fix the negative performance in the mind. A vicious circle is created which must be broken in some way; negative expectations have to be replaced by positive ones. The methods used are based on the assumption that our nervous system has difficulty in knowing the difference between a situation that is imagined in a relaxed state in a lively and intensive fashion and the corresponding real situation. Thus it is possible to create new experiences and memories.

During the first week the training concentrates on the poor performances. The program starts with a regression back to a time before the problem started. The athlete relives a similar event where he had the winning feeling. The activated winning feeling is then transferred to the problem situation and combined with an imaginary future good performance. Besides, problems of behavior or achievement difficulties can often arise because of negative emotions. For that reason the second week is devoted to phobia training, where a common program for systematic desensitization is used.

Week 11—Assertive Training

Self-confidence can be regarded as a general goal, a standing order which in turn gives rise to a number of specific and automatic expectations. Low self-confidence creates low expectations which impede and block the individual's potential resources. Poor results further reinforce the negative self-image. The athletes in this week work on ego strengthening; specific and general suggestions and images are given in a deep relaxed state during which the decreased reality testing powers cannot block the information.

Week 12—Concentration Training

If concentration is characterized by an intensive attention in a small area, then it is accompanied by inattention (or detachment) from what is going on outside this area. Concentration is also contradictory to voluntary effort; it is a passive process. The ability to concentrate varies from one individual to another both in intensity and duration. Few athletes have a "Nicklaus concentration" which can last for hours. However a "Trevino concentration," which disappears as soon as the ball has been hit, presupposes effective triggers to re-establish the concentration immediately when needed.

To establish such triggers post-hypnotic suggestions are used. I have found it useful to divide post-hypnotic suggestions into different types depending on their content and how they are put into effect. There are two main types in terms of content: (a) suggestions for a specific response, often a certain act, and (b) suggestions for a general state, for instance, a certain mood, emotion, activation level, or attitude. Both types of suggestions can be released through: (1) awakening, (2) establishment of a later time for the suggestion to take effect, and (3) stimuli given signal value under hypnosis. The effect of a post-hypnotic suggestion for an act limited in time ceases when the suggested act has been executed. Suggestions of type (b), on the other hand, continue to work until the effect spontaneously ceases or until a new signal is given which abolishes the effect. However, every time the signal is given, the suggestions are activated. Textbooks on hypnosis state that post-hypnotic suggestions can last for months or years but this is not true. However, the signal can keep its value for years and elicit the suggested response again and again. Any stimulus can be used as a signal: words, sounds, motor acts, patterns of behavior, or even situations.

Before starting this part of the training the athlete chooses some situation or pattern of behavior to serve as a signal or trigger. This pattern of behavior or situation will then receive signal value during deep relaxation. To maintain concentration during performance a kind of "Gallwey-technique" is introduced; the athlete is taught to let himself be caught by something interesting in the sport itself, like the geometric form of the path of a ball. This technique prevents thoughts and emotions from disturbing the body and enhances the ability to live in the present. To block disturbing thoughts and feelings in any pauses, concentration is shifted from this external mechanism to an internal one—to breathing. At this point the basic training program has been completed.

MENTAL PREPARATION FOR COMPETITION

After finishing the three-month mental training the athlete is allowed to apply what he has learned—before and during competitions. This program consists of four parts:

1. Activation Training

In the same way as the athlete earlier learned methods for tension reduction he will now receive triggers for getting psyched up.

2. Going Through the Competition

The main purposes are to establish positive attitudes and expectations and to lower the level of negative feelings. The program starts with a reactivation of the winning feeling. This feeling, a kind of rhythm or trance, in which everything runs smoothly of its own accord, implies direction by a lower level of consciousness. Performance is automatic and afterwards memories are faint; sometimes there is no conscious memory at all. If the athlete is in an altered state of consciousness and successfully reactivates a former winning feeling (another altered state of consciousness) he will be more likely to gain control over this ideal state of mind. The athletes themselves choose when to start this program. Let me quote our best swimmer: "Mentally I start swimming an important race eight months in advance. I increase the intensity as time goes on until I reach a maximum two to three weeks before the race. In the training I often achieve the winning feeling. However, if I do not feel happy and satisfied in general, it is more difficult to reach this state. In my mental swimming, I impress intermediate times, turns, start, strategy, and so on, on my mind, which makes me believe that the times I have set as goals are becoming more and more realistic."

3. Getting Psyched Up

This part is to be followed two to eight hours before the competition. It consists of alternating between relaxation and activation with three periods of four minutes' relaxation interrupted by three periods of 30 seconds' activation. In many athletes this creates a raised level of adrenalin and a feeling of being ready for the competition.

4. Competition Suggestions

The earlier programming of images is here supplemented by suggestions. This is especially helpful for those athletes who have not yet learned how to program themselves. The main aim of this part is to induce the winning feeling at the competition.

Up to this moment the training has been the same for all sports. After this point the athlete can continue with a program for mental training which is worked out specifically for his sport.

EVALUATION OF THE PROGRAM

The development of these programs started in 1975 after some years spent investigating problems in many different sports. The first program was used by the Swedish Track and Field Team before the Montreal Olympic Games. Since then 1200 athletes have been practicing the different programs, among them the Swedish national teams in eight different sports. The programs have been changed and modified continually according to the points of view and experiences of these athletes and will continue to be adjusted in the future.

APPLICATIONS IN OTHER AREAS

The type of problem an athlete encounters is not unique. Many people have problems with tension, nervousness, and anxiety or suffer from experience phobias. The athlete and the man in the street have the same kind of problems, even though they may turn up in different situations. Thus the techniques and programs described can also be applied outside of sports, and the mental training can be beneficial to an athlete even after he has finished competing.

I will give two examples of how the principles of mental training can be applied. The first one deals with recreational sport and the second with relaxation in school.

Meditative Running

Despite all the campaigns for sports for everyone, there are surprisingly few Swedes who exercise regularly, even once a week. The reason for this is cause for speculation. Some claim that the old school gymnastics turned them off exercise. I do not believe this is the only or even the main reason. An exercise study in Northern Sweden showed that as long as people were part of the study with its well thought-out program and good social relationships, the motivation was high. A follow-up a year later showed, however, that few had continued on their own. How then do we get people interested in physical activity? One possibility would be to stress other effects of exercise than the actual conditioning. Everyone knows that you have a higher oxygen consumption through physical effort, but how many know anything about the mental effects that come with regular exercise?

For a while now jogging has been very popular in the United States. You see pictures of people jogging along Fifth Avenue in New York and patients jogging with their therapists. It is pointed out that this apparently is as effective as any other psychotherapy. It's been long known that physical activity has a tension reducing effect. In the old days you were sent out to chop wood when you were irritable. In the same way jogging a few miles reduces irritation and tension. I have met injured hockey players, who describe how irritation builds up with each day of inactivity.

For a while now I've been conducting a project at the College of Gymnastics and Sports, which we call "meditative running." We try to combine running and meditation by running in a meditative way. One of the main principles of meditation is a passive concentration on something that is constantly repeated. The something can be a mantra, a mandala, a bodily function, or a physical activity. The expression LSD-running (long, slow, distance running) is in Sweden called even-tempo running, since the most important element in meditative running is the even tempo. You start the body at a certain pace and then let it continue at the same pace for about 20 minutes.

We have added various tasks in order to focus on the consciousness. Some days the test people have concentrated on the movements of their feet; some days on the movements of their arms, and other days on the breathing. And some days the people have run without any of these tasks. The study is not yet quite evaluated, but it looks as if you do not need such extra tasks. The monotony of the running itself apparently results in a kind of cognitive relaxation.

When the thoughts are less governed, they start wandering more freely. The activity of the left side of the brain is reduced in favor of the right side. You become less logical and more creative, and people have reported on this increased creativity. You get ideas while running. Unfortunately, you forget many of these ideas afterwards—a problem we're trying to solve. These effects are not new. I know journalists who for a long time have used jogging to get ideas for articles. In addition, when you run meditatively you do not feel the same fatigue you normally do. The relaxation screens out feelings of pain and fatigue.

As I mentioned, the meditative effects in running and other physical activity are not new. It could, however, be interesting to examine how and if these effects could be increased. It may also be important to use them to motivate more people to exercise more.

Relaxation in School

A certain control of activation and tension is necessary for people to survive. Relaxation is practiced more or less successfully by all people. Some have not lost the natural ability to relax—others are forced to relearn. Results from studies show an optimum ability to learn at age eight to twelve. There are many advantages in learning relaxation at an early age. The natural relaxation that a child has from birth, but which is reduced or disappears as he grows up, can more easily be learned again at a young age. Learning to relax is then not tied to special problems such as phobias, pain, and anxiety, which later in life are the motivation for practicing relaxation. Relaxation seems to be nature's own calming medicine, but it also brings a number of other positive effects: it provides rest and recovery, saves energy, provides greater possibility for self-control and self-influence, adds to an increased body awareness, and counteracts stress.

Little research is documented regarding children and relaxation. Systematic experiments in schools are almost completely lacking. Relaxation is practiced sporadically at some nursery schools, for instance, in connection with creative movement and other creative activity. At the elementary and middle school levels some teachers use relaxation both in physical education and classroom situations. At the high school and junior college levels relaxation exercises are used in physical education, in drama, and in art classes. Students should have a chance to practice relaxation in school. In physical education classes the relaxation exercises can be advantageous almost any time but especially after a strong physical effort and preferably at the end of the class.

In the fall of 1975 an experimental study was undertaken at the elementary school level in a town in Sweden to see how relaxation could be added to the school's curriculum in a natural and systematic way. All students in grades 4, 5, and 6 (about 300)

In Sweden we found that school children generally liked the relaxation program, that the program increased their concentration abilities, and that over half of the children became generally happier, calmer, and more secure.

participated in the experiment, which lasted six weeks. The gym period finished with five minutes' relaxation, and content and presentation were varied. The purpose of the experiment was among other things to see to what extent you can teach relaxation to elementary school children, to measure their experience and interest in relaxation as well as to try out the most suitable program for these age groups (Setterlind and Unestahl, 1977).

The general attitude towards the relaxation training turned out to be very positive. Between 80 and 90 per cent found it pleasant and comfortable. Three-quarters of the students also wanted to expand it to other subjects. Almost half the students reported that school work became easier and the ability to concentrate increased. Over half stated that they became generally happier, calmer, and more secure. More than 60 per cent have tried to practice relaxation at home, and one in four practices regularly.

CONCLUSION

The benefits of psychic training for the athlete are soon apparent, and the training principles and techniques are the same for all sports. These principles can be applied to many other endeavors. The aim of the training techniques is to stimulate the resources of the individual. I have given but two examples of other applications, but anyone can learn to apply the principles of mental training to areas in which he has special needs.

the canadian approach to /port p/ychology

Vietta E. Wilson
Harold A. Minden

PSYCHOLOGICAL SERVICES FOR AN AMATEUR SPORT*

INTRODUCTION

The Canadian Gymnastic Federation is an amateur sport organization which has implemented a long-range plan for gymnastic development across the nation. Included within the framework of the plan are an extensive talent identification program, fitness testing, basic motor skill testing, and gymnastic skill testing. The competitions and training camps are designed for the particular skill level of each gymnastic group. The federation has used physical education and psychology consultants in the past but not on an extended basis. A few years ago the executive committee decided to add a psychological program to complement their existing programs. The relationship established between the federation and Harold Minden and myself began with our presenting a working philosophy to the executive committee.

> The psychological consultants see their prime role as professional support personnel to the coaches and athletes.
> Their function, goal, and concern would be for the full actualization of each athlete's potential in a harmonious climate that would not only foster excellence in skill performance but would attend to and be sensitive to mental and emotional well-being.

We then identified the following major areas we wished to investigate without obligating ourselves to a predetermined focus:

1. assessing, understanding, and developing motivational styles;
2. developing strategies to cope with emotional problems that result from stress, anxiety, and the fatigue of training and pre- and post-competition;
3. the assessment of individual differences in learning styles; and
4. interpersonal and communication problems between administration, coaches, athletes, and parents.

* This part was written by Vietta E. (Sue) Wilson.

It was believed essential that we study the gymnastic process for one competitive time period (18 months), which would allow us an opportunity to observe which problems or areas were most important to those in the gymnastic process and lessen the possibility of our focusing on non-questions.

The value of a psychological team approach was also presented.

> Our plan as a consultant team would be to take advantage of the opportunities to check, on a continual basis, our individual perceptions of situation and problems and to be able to draw on our different experiences, expertise, and professional association for the solution of problems and the development of programmes.

The confidentiality of any information about an individual was made clear from our first conversations and was included in the contract.

> We are conscious and will be protective of our professional responsibility for the mental health of the individuals with whom we will be involved. Questions of confidentiality are critical and must be left to the discretion of the psychological consultants.

"Observation of the gymnastic process took place at every gymnasium, at competitions, and at training camps. Interviews were held with gymnasts, coaches, judges, administrators, and parents," says Wilson.

SCOPE ASSESSMENT

The primary groups for assessment were the twenty to twenty-five elite female gymnasts, eight to ten elite coaches, and related officials and administrators. The scope of the assessment included attending administrative meetings regarding organization, finances, operation, and team selection. All correspondence from the national office was available to us (minutes, travel reports, and so on). Judges' meetings, coaches' meetings, and team meetings were also open for us to expand our working knowledge of the organization.

Observation of the "gymnastic process" took place at every gymnasium which had a level 3 gymnast, at local, provincial, national, and international competitions, at training camps, and during local and foreign travel. Interviews, small group sessions, and counseling sessions were held with gymnasts, former gymnasts, coaches, judges, administrators, and parents. Behavioral charting, standardized psychological testing, questionnaires, and videotapes were occasionally used to aid our assessment.

PSYCHOLOGICAL PROGRAMS

During the course of our assessment a three-pronged stress management program was initiated during the training camps. Relaxation training (modified Jacobson and autogenic), behavior modification training (modified Meichenbaum), and modelling were presented to the gymnasts and coaches. Electromyographic biofeedback was also used for stress demonstrations and later incorporated into flexibility training for selected gymnasts. A major weakness of our presentations was in not supplying coaches with resource tapes and written procedural manuals for the techniques to be used during training at their own clubs. In his section of this chapter Harold Minden has given further information about the on-going programs.

GYMNASTS

It takes a special effort and talent to obtain national and international ranking in a sport and the gymnasts showed that "specialness" in many ways. While standardized psychological testing revealed no stereotypic personality, it did suggest that as a group gymnasts had above average scores on the Cattell High School Personality Questionnaire on the traits of emotional stability (C), conscientiousness (G), self-sufficiency (Q_2), and control or self-discipline (Q_3). These are essentially the same traits identified in a sample of elite gymnasts in 1973 (Wilson, 1973).

They also showed dedication and self-discipline by devoting four to six hours per day to training while still attending school and maintaining above average grades. Because of their exceptional skills and experience, we had to remind ourselves occasionally that the gymnasts were young teenagers who retained many of the traits and turbulences of their age group.

The gymnasts all expressed a desire to have their coaches view them as individuals, and they wanted coaches who were understanding and had a positive outlook. A sense of humor was a definite plus for a coach and being a positive model during stress was another asset often mentioned by the gymnasts.

Frustration was expressed by the gymnasts when time conflicts between school work and gymnastic training required that they perform in both school and gymnastics to a standard below what they expected of themselves. Another frustrating time was when

Elfi Schlegel, the 1978 Canadian all around champion and double gold medal winner at the Edmonton Commonwealth Games, belongs to the recent crop of very young Canadian gymnasts who devote four to six hours per day to training while still attending school and maintaining above average grades.

the learning or performance of skills either was slower or was not accomplished. They either were unaware of plateaus in learning or performance or were unwilling to accept plateaus. They revealed that it was during these times that they might doubt their abilities and question their potential for future performance. It is logical that we should investigate "drop outs" to determine if it is plateaus rather than loss of interest, "burn outs," or too much stress which contribute to leaving. This frustration drop-out possibility is further supported by the fact that every gymnast (including former gymnasts) thought the main element keeping them in the sport was the learning of a new skill. The overwhelming affirmation and intensity of this finding has critical implications for teachers, coaches, and sport psychologists.

The second most important force motivating gymnasts was the interaction with coaches and other gymnasts who, obviously, were the dominant influence in their social lives. The adventure of travel and national/international status were strong motivators not only for those who travelled but also for those who were not in the top group (rank 10 to 25). Although some gymnasts in the latter group thought it unlikely that they would make a national team, they kept working in the hope of being selected for foreign travel and the related rewards.

Concern was expressed by some gymnasts about the financial, time, and life style burdens that their families had to endure. Most gymnasts felt there was too much competitiveness among the coaches but did not feel that it seriously affected the relationship between gymnasts.

Although sacrifices may have been made during the course of her life as an elite gymnast, every former gymnast contacted claimed that gymnastics had been the most enjoyable, worthwhile event in her life and that she would do it all over again. Alumnae did express disappointment in not being effectively involved in gymnastics at the elite level upon their retirement (as assistant coaches, demonstrators, and so on).

COACHES

It was more difficult for coaches to say what motivated them to continue their heavy time commitment to gymnastics. However, satisfaction at seeing a gymnast succeed was often mentioned, with travel, ego fulfilment, and social interactions also reported as motives. Frustration was expressed by some regarding the total time, emotion, and energy commitment necessary to remain competent and competitive. (The majority of coaches do not receive financial remuneration.) During our club visits coaches most often requested information for helping "problem" gymnasts, predictors of success, training motivators, and psychological preparation for competition. The sheer number of responsibilities undertaken by the coach created internally and externally imposed stress. Some coaches reported they ignored or delegated some aspects of the gymnastic training in order to cope with the stress.

ADMINISTRATORS

The health and growth of the sport depends upon the philosophy, and its implementation, of the administration. Open communication is essential for developing a framework in which coaches, athletes, and officials can function at their best. It is essential that the everyday in-house tasks are completed quickly and efficiently since most in the sport system are volunteers and have little time for administrative chores. At the elite level, it is helpful if the administration is knowledgeable about the politics of sport.

PARENTS

The life of the gymnast's family is just as hectic as that of the gymnast. Family routines are disrupted and the entire family usually has to adjust its schedule to accommodate an elite athlete (or coach). Parents noted that the fine line between encouraging excellence and pushing can cause much soul-searching and anxiety. More specific information on how to be a parent of an elite athlete and the stages of development to expect from a competitive daughter might be beneficial.

CONSIDERATIONS FOR
SPORT PSYCHOLOGY CONSULTANTS

Based upon the aforementioned assessment and many years as a sport psychology consultant, the following suggestions are presented for your consideration:

1. The sport psychology consultant should be an integrated part of the sport process at the local field, gymnasium, or pool. It is at this level that significant assistance will be rendered and relevant data collected.
2. Much public relations work needs to be done as there is still a common belief among athletes, coaches, administrators, and the lay public that sport psychology consultants are only for "psyched out" athletes. Few members of these groups know how sport psychology can be applied to improve skill performance or to aid in self-management techniques.
3. Certification and coordination of consultants seems essential as many groups (sport psychology associations, medical associations, psychology associations, therapy associations,

physiological associations, and commercial groups) are offering their services. Leaving qualifications aside, the sheer number of "helpers" will leave the athlete no time for practice or performance!

4. It may be useful to distinguish between the sport psychology clinician and the sport psychology researcher. The researcher would be responsible to the sport governing body or for advancing the body of knowledge while the clinician would be responsible for helping the individual athlete or coach. In the sport process there are times when these two objectives are mutually exclusive and professional ethics dictate that one's responsibility be known (Ogilvie, 1977).

5. Sport psychology conferences of the future should deal with a code of ethics, certification, legal liability, and related topics. Practical sessions on contracts, conflict resolutions, and media relations would be beneficial for those working with elite athletes.

6. The time to organize an effective method for the delivery of psychological services to amateur sport is now. One method might be to organize sport psychology consultants in a city or region who can then collectively offer a wide range of sport and psychology expertise and availability to sport groups or individuals. Another method might be to have those knowledgeable in a particular sport work together. In either case, the national sport psychology association, as well as the local sport psychology group, could aid communication by notifying sport governing bodies, sport medical associations, and appropriate government and civic associations about the existence of the consulting group.

Sport psychology consultants have much to offer the sport process, but we need to focus our energies into some logical plan if we really want to maximize our usefulness.

REFLECTIONS ON AN ENLIGHTENED MANDATE*

INTRODUCTION

One of the factors that influenced the contract that Vietta Wilson and I signed with the Canadian Gymnastic Federation was a concern that a number of sport psychologists were not taking the time or were not allowed the time to understand the unique problems and questions that exist within a specific sport. Often their questions were preconceived, their hypotheses established, and the relevance of the findings to the realities and needs of that specific sport was minimal. An additional concern with some of the investigations was that sport psychologists were not attempting to translate the findings of experimental and clinical studies in learning, performance, personality, motivation, and emotion into applied programs for athletes and coaches. Finally, our greatest concern had to do with the many psychological studies of isolated variables which were conducted without any attempt to relate the findings in terms of the total, complex equation of athletic performance. Many of the studies are neat, short-term, unreplicated, irrelevant, and self-serving. This "hit and run phenomenon" abuses the confidence, trust, and time of our athletes and coaches who subject themselves to experimentation with great hope and expectation. There is a need for pure research but it must be honest, and it must declare itself without hiding behind vague suggestion and promise such as "the practical implication of this study is . . ."

The state of the art and science of sport psychology suggests a need for a commitment, (a) to in-depth, long-term applied research and applied programs, and (b) to accountability. This proposal may be threatening to many of our colleagues, but it is critical that we recognize that "we owe our supporters." By not taking the time to observe, to question, and to learn the uniqueness and needs of a specific sport we may impose faulty assumptions, biases, and findings on a trusting constituency and preclude our usefulness.

* This part was written by Harold A. Minden.

AN ENLIGHTENED MANDATE

Our contract with the Canadian Gymnastic Federation (CGF) was an open mandate to explore the psychological needs of the Women's Gymnastic Program. Vietta Wilson has described above how we travelled, studied, discussed, and learned. Our learning took place in selection meetings, in technical meetings, in seminars, in demonstrations, and, perhaps most instructive, in informal "rap sessions." Our goals were to assist in the actualization of peak performance and to ensure that no psychological damage was incurred by this very vulnerable age group. Though we agreed on the goals, the choice of procedure was left to our judgement. Our exposure could not have been more complete. We were allowed tremendous freedom to explore, to question, and to test procedures, and as we did, we became more aware of the complexity of the equation of peak performance.

A CHANGE IN FOCUS

On the basis of our observations it became apparent that we would have to change our central focus from the athlete to include the critical agents in the athletes' surround. Much of what was happening to the athlete was a function of the behavior of these critical agents, the coaches, parents, technical committee, and administrators. Professionals were being presumptuous and myopic in attempting to assist and remedy a situation without the inclusion of these critical agents; they were not considering the other affecting and infecting environments and the fact that perhaps success could be achieved only with a program that strengthened and supported these agents rather than just an intervention program for athletes.

As we probed, questioned, observed, and tested it became evident that the primary strategy in this high powered scene should be the development of programs to assist the coach *directly* and that we needed to think in terms of the maintenance of their good "psychological health" as well as the psychological health of all the critical agents involved in the athletes' environment.

TOUGH DATA

What we found in our explorations were problems, factors causing stress, and patterns of behavior that were not being dealt with in the literature of sport psychology, sport medicine, or motor learn-

Problems that affect young female athletes include failure and harm anxiety, training satiation, fatigue, cyclical moods, personality differences between coach and athlete, academic, social, and familial difficulties because of the heavy demands of training and competition, and so on.

ing. They were patterns demonstrating that the athletic scene was but a small microcosm, which mirrored the whole but more intensely.

We saw incidents of fear, anxiety, insecurity, misunderstanding, suspicion, and the distress and pain they caused. We also saw demonstrations of affection, fairness, support, understanding, empathy, faith, caring, and great sacrifice. We saw an amalgam of superb technical expertise and sometimes not such superb expertise in problem-solving and human relations.

These data are tough to work with but are part of the equation of human performance. I can understand our researchers wishing to avoid such messy variables as suspicion, insecurity, and empathy and concentrating on studies of reaction time and the effects of induced tension on tension. However, the messy variables have to be dealt with because they affect the functioning and lives of all involved.

SPECIFIC PROBLEMS

Among the specific questions and problems that surfaced were those that specifically affected the athlete, those that specifically affected the coach, and some that affected the parents, technical personnel, and judges.

A sample of problems that affected young female athletes would include:

1. failure anxiety;
2. harm anxiety;
3. self-confidence;
4. injuries;

5. training satiation, fatigue, and performance plateaus;
6. cyclical moods and cyclical motivational levels;
7. concerns about weight and changes in body configurations with onset of menses, problems of adjustment to the dramatic physical and emotional changes that take place in puberty;
8. personality differences between coach and athlete;
9. conflict of motives and needs peculiar to this age group;
10. academic, social, and familial difficulties because of the heavy demands of training and competition;
11. the painful experience of an exit from the elite program which can be self-imposed or imposed by others and its affect on self-esteem;
12. parent-athlete problems such as differences in expectations and motivation; and
13. preoccupation with self rather than with the task.

A sample of the problems that affect the coach would include:

1. the overwhelming demands of time, commitment, and energy (many of the coaches at the elite level are not paid and are involved in another vocation to support themselves and this dual involvement and pressure can create personal and family strains);
2. dependence on financial support of the club by others and the consequence of this dependence;
3. differences in motivational styles and needs between coach and athlete;
4. high anxiety level and low threshold of frustration, which also affect the athlete since it becomes infectious in training and competition;
5. the difficult decisions that have to be made because of injuries, the possibility of irreversible damage to the athlete;
6. lack of a vehicle or set to discuss and resolve differences; and
7. adjustment (for coach and athlete) to the realities of political judging on the international scene.

These are but a sample of the problems with which we became involved. In some ways the experiences and problems loomed as indigestible and insoluble chunks.

PSYCHOLOGICAL PROGRAMS

Our training as clinicians helped us deal with the immediate crises, and as researchers we began to develop models and programs to prevent the crises and to facilitate maximum performance. Currently we are working on the following programs:

1. A stress management model that includes: (a) the learning of techniques to reduce the stress reaction (relaxation procedures and biofeedback), (b) modification or elimination of the stressor, (c) modification of the perception of the stressor, and (d) strategies to cope with the stressor. Items b, c, and d are preventive rather than reactive procedures. This stress management program is being developed for the athlete, coach, parents, technical personnel, and judges.

2. Development of an assessment battery of psychological tests measuring learning styles, anxiety, motivation, and other personality dimensions which will be specific to the needs of this age group and sport.

3. Self-instructional cognitive modification for the development of control and self-confidence.

4. Programs for parents emphasizing the critical role of the parent as a partner in the enterprise. Assisting the parent to develop skills and understanding so that they may assist their athlete.

5. An exit program for athletes who are leaving or have been asked to leave the program. The aims of this program are to assist the athlete in understanding, exploring alternatives, and maintaining self-esteem.

6. Interpersonal contracts.

One of the most interesting programs suggested by the problems encountered deals with interpersonal contracts. The notion of a contract recognizes that in all our interpersonal relationships there exists, as Rousseau indicated, a contract, agreement, or understanding. A contract is sometimes explicit, sometimes implicit and many problems develop because of differences in perception of the contract or ignorance of its terms.

A contract exists between husband and wife, between parent and child, between friends, between coach and athlete, between athlete and athlete, between coach and federation, and between coach and parents. Some may react against the notion of contract in interpersonal relationships and see it as too formal an arrangement, but it is a reality. It is the author's conviction that many of the problems encountered would not have existed had there been a clearer understanding of expectations and the rules in the relationships.

On the basis of discussion with coaches and athletes and from an analysis of some of the problems in interpersonal relationships, I have isolated the following elements of a contract for consideration: philosophy, expectations, level of commitment, responsibilities, rules, fairness, clarity, communication, dynamic, flexibility, temporal dimension, consequences of breach, procedures for evaluation, procedures and opportunity for ventilation, and procedures for renegotiation. A good understanding and a good relationship seemed to be predicated on the inclusion and consideration of all the above elements.

We have discussed these elements and have clinically tested various models of interpersonal contracts with some of our coaches. Our initial feedback indicates a diminution of misunderstandings, improved morale, and a feeling among the athletes that they are part or can be part of the decisions that affect their lives. Our next step is to develop valid and reliable measures to test the effectiveness of alternative models of contracts.

In addition to the development of the above programs we have been available to our coaches for the wide variety of problems that surface during competition and training. We have attempted to put out some fires and calm turbulence. The coaches have been patient with us, taught us, included us, shared with us their inner thoughts and feelings and have clearly delineated the questions, problems, and areas in which they needed assistance. The above programs are products of their direction.

CONCLUSION

After two years of intense involvement in every aspect of the sport, I am convinced that there is a role for sport psychologists in amateur sport as clinicians and as researchers. To insure that sport and the role of the sport psychologist are not endangered we must put our house in order with regard to our credentials to conduct research or to treat psychological problems clinically, as Vietta Wilson has discussed above at greater length. We have an important obligation to sport governing bodies, coaches, and athletes as they engage the services of psychologists. We must make them aware of the type of training, expertise, and certification that a psychologist in sport needs.

Finally, there are few content areas in psychological study in practice that are as exciting as sport psychology. It has magic moments and desperate moments and every human emotion is exposed. Few can stand back with distance and scientific objectivity while enveloped in this arena of ultimate effort. It has its own special intrinsic rewards, and it is a privilege to be able to assist in the psychological preparation of its members.

behavioral applications of psychology to u.s.a. world class competitors

Richard M. Suinn

This chapter is based on the work I have done in the last ten years or so in sport psychology with U.S. athletes. A brief personal history might help to establish the perspective leading to my current interests and involvement. My own field in clinical psychology is behavior-modification, with its philosophy of retraining as opposed to that of treatment, its emphasis on action-prescriptions as opposed to talking, and its concern with immediacy of results as opposed to long-term time commitments. It was natural, then, to agree to work with the Colorado State University's Alpine Ski Racing Team, since they were looking for some psychological training approach which would have performance results in the short time that they had before the competitive season began. While they were initially interested in the management of tension, as a result of a recent case (Suinn, 1976a) I was more interested in the use of mental rehearsal or imagery for skill-training. So, we came to an understanding: I would provide desensitization for pre-competition tensions, if they would allow me to try imagery training for other competitive goals. In reporting on this imagery training plus relaxation for skill development, I labeled the approach by the grandiose title of *Visuo-Motor Behavior Rehearsal* or VMBR (Suinn, 1972, 1973). And this was how I became involved in athletics: I was subsequently contacted by the U.S. Nordic Ski Team, went as the psychologist to the 1976 Winter Olympics for this team and the U.S. Olympic Biathlon Team, worked with three other national teams in the pentathlon, marksmanship, and track and field, and I am now feeling that a simple avocation is becoming an almost full-time responsibility . . . but it has been fun.

I would like to summarize the types of activities and approaches I have taken over the past years, showing the behavioral approach, giving some examples, and devoting some attention to the VMBR approach. I believe very strongly that the contribution of psychology to sports increases to the degree that psychology can understand the specific needs of athletics, translate those sometimes ambiguously stated concerns into psychological principles, and then translate these principles into recommendations for immediate action. We have been fortunate in having a number of psychological training techniques available, such as relaxation, imagery rehearsal, biofeedback, cognitive strategies, attentional methods, and autogenic training. To avoid the problems of wholesale, helter-skelter exposure of competitors to training, simply because the training is there and without regard for the appropriateness of the training for the individual athlete, it is important to recognize first the importance of assessment. And I would like to start briefly with this topic.

THE BEHAVIORAL ASSESSMENT

Every so often I receive a telephone call or a letter, requesting a prescription for an athlete. These requests are expressed in terms such as "I want to be the very best goalie on the ice rink," or "I'm in a slump, I am losing confidence, and instead I want to be able to win the next meet," or "I want to stay in control, especially when I'm shooting a perfect score during the early part of the match." These are *goal* statements, not statements that permit defining a program of training. These statements are a good starting point since it puts you in the right ballpark, even though it does not tell you who's at bat or what the score is. It is important to know, for example, that the coach who called me during the Olympic tryouts had the goal of helping a competitor, who was going to be disappointed at not qualifying for the Olympic team, stay with racing. This is a very different goal from the same coach's request that I help another athlete who could make it, if he could substantially improve his second day's performance in the next day's race. However, to actually design a program of action requires more assessment information. I would like to describe how I approach assessment from scratch, that is, from the point of first contact by a group for consulting help.

My typical approach starts first with interviewing coaching staff and athletes on the basics of their sport (if I have no direct experience with that particular sport). My questions start with the behavioral realm: "What are you required to do? what cues trigger off a change in response? how is what you do scored in the competition?" Next, I am interested in learning about the environmental conditions as cue conditions, for example, "is there a mass start? is

Billy Koch

I believe very strongly that psychology can understand the specific needs of athletics, translate those sometimes ambiguously stated concerns into psychological principles, and then translate these principles into recommendations for immediate action.

crowd involvement a factor that affects performance? what limits are set on what you can do or is maximum self-control permitted? is presence of other athletes an important variable? does wind or sun create a problem?'' I also want to know something about the factors that the coach or athlete believes to be important in distinguishing the successful competitor from the also-ran. At this point, an open-ended interviewing style is important, since my concern is their perceptions, without worrying about the clarity of the terms used to express them. Many coaches use psychological terms that have a general meaning, such as confidence or intensity or will to win, but which have no clear, direct behavioral referents. But at least it is possible to obtain a kind of listing of possible variables. During this segment of the assessment, it is also helpful to discuss what the coaches and athletes feel to be problems on which a psychologist might be asked to consult. Finally, the interview needs to guide the discussion towards operationalizing the information, for example, ''When you speak of confidence, could you give me a specific example that illustrates this during competition?" I tend to use a behavioral interviewing technique that relies upon themes, and use of examples, and identifies the behaviors occurring, what preceded and followed these behaviors. For example, the theme may be how to deal with negative thoughts, but specifically during a race. The example given could be that the actual response is the thought, "Suppose I don't have enough in me to ski up that hill? suppose I'm too tired." The condition just prior to this thought might be the cue of the sight of a hill on the cross-country course. The event which follows this negative thought is the skier *trying too hard*, forcing the tempo, and expending more energy than is necessary, thereby losing time, and leading to further panic. There are a variety of possible sources for the problem. Elsewhere, I have presented a conceptual model (Suinn, 1978) identifying possible categories of target behaviors, ranging from deficits in the skill required (e.g., poor physical training so that this skier lacked the endurance) to inadequate transfer from training to competition (e.g., if the problem turned out to be negative thoughts prompted by the anxiety of the competition) to negative cognitive responses (whereby the focal point is the thought itself, and hence a change in the thought would lead to a change in performance). In this case, the thought itself was deemed to be the key problem, and a method for shifting attentional focus was recommended, using the principle that it is impossible to attend to two thought-tasks at the same time. The athlete was instructed to "look for the highest tree on the hill" and to keep attending to skiing for that tree. (This is not unlike the Gallwey *Inner Tennis* notion of looking for the seam on the ball; as Braden points out, "no one can actually see the seam," but it does shift one's attention.)

The advantages of the behavioral assessment approach have been discussed by Rushall (1977). The approach aims at making concrete the conditions that affect the performance, by emphasizing describing action, cue conditions, and the sequence of events that form the behavioral chain. It tries to operationalize terms that we normally accept as meaningful, but which are fraught with assumptions and ambiguity, such as *anxiety, confidence, concentration, fear of failure, motivation.* I hasten to add, however, that these terms may still have use as starting points, perhaps as traditional psychometric personality trait tests. One profile I obtained suggested that a biathlete (an athlete who skis cross-country and shoots on a rifle range in this double event) was emotionally volatile. In terms of applying this trait information behaviorally, I suggested that he use a cueing technique of yelling while skiing to trigger off an activated emotional level, which in turn might offer a more aggressive skiing style. The next day he could be heard yodeling and yelling all over the forest, and he placed second in a challenging field! A member of the modern pentathlon team deliberately reviews all the reasons that he dislikes his competitors as a means of cueing off anger, which in turn increases his reflexes during the fencing matches. Of course, it would be desirable to have psychometric scales that are behaviorally oriented, rather than the traditional personality measurements. Such scales have been recommended by others (Horsfall, Fisher, and Morris, 1975; Rushall, 1975; Nideffer, 1976) and are beginning to appear. We (Youngblood and Suinn, 1978), have just recently put together what we hope will be a measure of motivation whereby motivation is so defined that the coach can immediately determine how he might respond in a way that will increase the athlete's motivation. Items represent such categories as coach approval, tangible rewards, family support, self-mastery. Given a particular athlete's profile of motivating factors, a training program can be instituted which uses material appropriate to these factors. An interesting early finding in our research is that the variables associated with high motivation early in the season differ from those apparent after the team has been selected, and at the time of Regionals. Thus, the athlete who is most sensitive to the coach's evaluation is more likely to be performing in a way suggesting high motivation prior to team selection. On the other hand, the factors most predictive of the level of motivation, when assessed immediately after the Regionals, involve responsiveness to crowd support and competitive cues.

Of course, it is possible and often even desirable to have a referral where the athlete directly specifies the problem in behaviors, without using psychological terms. For example, I once received a telephone call from a Masters swimmer in another state who wanted help, because although she won in the 50-, 100-, and 400-meter events as a matter of routine, in the 200-meter event she so much lost control that she would swim out of her lane into the wall. The behavioral assessment in this case involved having her describe what was happening prior to hitting the wall, then prior to that, then prior to that, until we had backed up to the moments immediately after coming off the starting block. Here she described responses such as "feeling my mind was separated from my body, feeling that I did not control what I was doing". . . all reports of behaviors common to athletes reacting to stress. We used a type of desensitization, some attentional focusing activities, and VMBR in one afternoon session. She subsequently won a gold, three silver, and one bronze in one competitive meet, and more recently she won at the Nationals. As an aside, we used VMBR to enable her to practice a flip turn, a turn she has not used in years following a neck injury in an accident because of residual physical damage. She now uses flip turns. (This suggests one use of imagery rehearsal techniques which I will elaborate on later.)

THE MANAGEMENT OF STRESS TECHNIQUES

The first point, then, is the importance of doing behavioral assessments to identify the target behavior, conditions preventing its appearance, or cue conditions which might prompt its appearance, before arriving at any recommendations for psychological training. I would now like to explain some specific techniques which we have used to accomplish particular objectives, starting with the management of stress.

Desensitization

Desensitization or the use of relaxation during graduated imagery is a straightforward behavioral method for anxieties that are specifically associated with competitive cues, such as standing in the starting gate. On the other hand, another approach is needed where the types and numbers of cues are diverse or unpredictable, such as where the stimulus for tension may be the score, how far into the match you are, changing crowd conditions, or where the match environment changes from locale to locale.

Anxiety Management Training

Around 1970 (the published report appeared in 1971, see Suinn and Richardson, 1971), I put together a behavioral technique which I called *Anxiety Management Training* (AMT). In this approach, the client is trained in recognizing early signs of bodily stress and taught to use relaxation to abort the stress response and regain control. The stress stimuli can differ since AMT training is not dependent upon a graduated stimulus hierarchy in the way desensitization is. AMT also utilizes a deep breath as a cue controlled stimulus for relaxation, and is particularly suited to athletic competitors who frequently use deep breathing as part of their training histories. A good example of this was a pentathlete whom I saw the day before his pistol match. He was first trained to relax through a brief Jacobson deep muscle relaxation exercise, then introduced to imagery in which he was in a competitive scene that aroused high stress. The AMT approach then instructs the athlete to permit the stress responses to build, using the scene to prompt the tension. Then the athlete is guided in reducing the muscle stress reaction by returning to muscle relaxation. AMT, of course, involves a few more steps, and these are described elsewhere (Suinn, 1975, 1977). Following the afternoon's training, the pentathlete shot his personal best and went on to win the overall trophy against a field comprising members of the U.S. Olympic Team, and the Canadian and Mexican Teams. AMT seems to have some impact on physiological responses. One alpine ski racer was trained to use AMT, and then had his heart rate monitored during a VMBR session. In this session he was asked to race a course. As Figure 1 shows, this racer's heart rate began to increase when he was "in the starting gate," and rose dramatically during the scenes of being on the course. He was then instructed to reduce his heart rate by reducing the stress, and apparently was able to accomplish some changes as seen in the recordings. With such information, and with the corollary research on AMT with other studies of anxiety control among non-athletes (Suinn, 1975), I am convinced that it is possible for athletes to learn stress management.

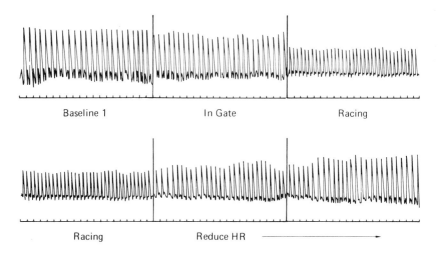

Figure 1. Athletic imagery and heart rate.

Visuo-Motor Behavioral Rehearsal

The second major area in which I have spent a great deal of time is the application of imagery rehearsal or *Visuo-Motor Behavioral Rehearsal* (VMBR). By this approach, the athlete is taught deep muscle relaxation, and then instructed to imagine a scene involving competition. The exact nature of the scene depends upon the objectives. For example, if the objective is motor skill development, then the scene would involve rehearsing the particular moves or sequence of moves desired. In the earlier case of the swimmer, she practiced the flip turn. For this person with her fear of aggravating an injury, VMBR permitted her to safely try out a new movement. Such a use of VMBR might be similarly applicable for gymnasts and divers in trying out a new high risk routine. VMBR has also been used to enhance transfer of the motor skill from practice to competition conditions. A problem for many coaches is the athlete who does well in practice, but poorly in competition. A principle from learning theory proposes that transfer is a function of the degree of similarity between the practice conditions and the testing conditions. VMBR experiences are so realistic that they enable the athlete to practice performing under conditions nearly exactly comparable to the competition. One swimmer reported in her first VMBR experience that she suddenly felt the cold slap of water as she entered the pool in her imagery. Another skier re-experienced the irritability and emotions she had felt during a qualifying race when she repeated the scene in her mind. Once again with a skier, electromyographic (EMG) recordings were obtained from the leg muscles during a VMBR session. He was asked to ski a race, first by thinking about skiing the race, and then later using VMBR to visualize skiing the race. Under the "think" condition, no recordings were observed, suggesting no muscle activity. Under the VMBR condition, several spurts of muscle activity were evident. At the end of the session, the racer was asked to describe the course that he had raced in his imagery. It was a downhill course, and the muscle bursts matched the terrain he raced over, the two jumps, for example, showing up clearly (Figure 2). Thus, it would seem that VMBR can replicate competition conditions and hence could be used to enhance transfer of practice. In fact, one of the major parts of my program at the Winter Olympic Games was having the competitors skiing the Olympic courses through VMBR to prepare themselves. Another use of VMBR is to practice for the unexpected. In a study by Mahoney and Avener (1977), the difference between the successful Olympic Tryouts competitors and those

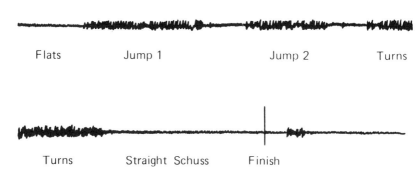

Figure 2. EMG for downhill racer.

who did not win a position on the team was in their response to errors. The successful ones used the error as a cue for what needed to be done next, rather than as a source of distraction from the routine. I have used VMBR with a scene of "in a moment something unexpected will happen" in order to have the athlete practice quickly adjusting to the circumstance.

Finally, VMBR has been applied as a diagnostic method. Occasionally, neither a coach nor an athlete can determine what went wrong during an event, for example, when a gate was missed, or a disqualification occurred. By using VMBR to repeat that part of the event, and with the instruction to "pay attention" to what went wrong, it has been possible to identify the flaw, and to correct it with another VMBR scene. To what degree VMBR works is partly suggested by the EMG study. However, there is also one controlled research study done on eight basketball teams. Kolonay (1977) used audio tape recordings for VMBR training, with the scenes developed after a luncheon consultation we had together. Her data showed a significant increase in the foul-shooting percentage for the VMBR trained athletes, but no such changes for the relaxation-only subjects or the imagery-without-relaxation subjects. Finally, in a recent survey we completed of professional alpine ski racers (Suinn and Andrews, 1978), we discovered that both successful and unsuccessful racers used mental rehearsal, but the successful skiers had more vivid imagery. In fact, the worst racer described the imagery as more equivalent to "thinking" about skiing.

I cannot resist discussing one case study in terms of its use of VMBR. *Concentration* was the major goal of a football coach in referring his place-kicker to us. In reviewing this player's previous season's record, the head coach felt that three more games might have been won, based upon either a field goal or a conversion attempt, including a major upset. In specifying examples of concentration, the coach spoke of a particular game in which crowd noise was high, a time-out was called before the field goal by the opposing team, there was confusion about how much time was left in the game, and referees' whistles were blowing like runaway trains. One of my faculty members determined that the desirable format would be to have the athlete over-learn the routine of setting-up, taking practice swings, and focusing on these actions rather than on crowd noises or other distractions (Titley, 1976). In fact, VMBR was used to train in *not* attending to distracting cues as well as to attending to the appropriate cues, such as ball placement, head position, or follow-through. By the end of the season this athlete went on to establish 14 school records and an NCAA field goal record of 63 yards.

I would like to end by briefly mentioning some other techniques I have applied, and some research we are involved in at the moment. One of the approaches we sometimes forget is the integration of the psychological training into the competitive routine. Frequently, the training provided takes place away from the competition site or even the practice field, if one is using relaxation training, VMBR, stress management training, and so on. (Of course, operant based programs are more likely to be implemented directly on the field.) It is important to include transfer of the program to the practice field, through, for example, assigning to competitors the task of using some of the psychological methods and of reporting back at the next psychological training session. In addition, if the psychologist travels with the team to the competition site, he can call for a session on the field. At the Olympics, I had Bill Koch go through VMBR outside the warming hut, in the snow, for about three minutes, just before the relay race. I have also used a modified relaxation strategy with alpine racers on site just before being called into the starting gate. Finally, it is possible to actually program the use of VMBR into a schedule prior to, the night before, the morning of, and minutes before the competitive event (Suinn, 1976a).

Lest I give the impression that relaxation and imagery are the only approaches I have taken in working with competitors, I should quickly mention that these only form a part. I think most sport psychologists are faced with two types of service, the first being a general program approach, and the second an individual problem-solving approach. In the former, one presents a series of training sessions to all team members in a group, with the training reflecting the objectives, for example, stress management, practicing starts, and working on course memorization. In the problem-solving approach, a particular athlete wants to work on a specific problem, such as breaking out of a slump. In this case, behavior learning principles are again applied with behavior assessment, leading to the design of a particular program of action for that individual. The tailor-made program can range from applying an operant model with emphasis on response features, to working on the stimulus control dimension via new cue prompts, to cognitive strategies. I refer you to the *Psychology Today* article for some specific examples (Suinn, 1976b).

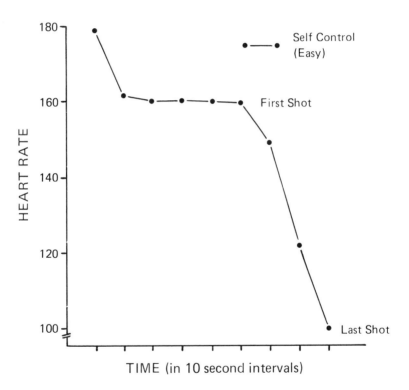

Figure 3. A biathlete's heart rate as he skied into position to fire at the first target.

Regarding our research, we certainly hope to expand our work with the motivation measuring instrument. Also, the survey of the professional alpine skiers involves a study of the psychological training methods that separates the better ones from the poorer ones, as well as describing their response profiles, that is, cognitive, behavioral, emotional, during competition. We are currently in the middle of a laboratory study through a U.S. Olympic Development Fund grant. We have selected and matched distance runners from the track team. I am using VMBR to determine if we can affect physical variables, specifically efficiency as measured, for example, through oxygen usage. This was originally encouraged by some data we obtained on a biathlete whose heart rate we monitored by telemetry, and who apparently showed a decrease in heart rate as he skied into position to fire at the first target (Figure 3). This was an athlete with whom I had worked for some time, and the psychological training may or may not have been the crucial variable in this type of self-control.

CONCLUSION

The field of sport psychology is growing at a dramatic rate, as competitive teams are recognizing that psychology can be meaningful rather than mystical, useful rather than threatening. The major issue now is the integration of the various techniques so that there is some conceptual consistency, and so that we avoid the serious problems of becoming technicians. There can be nothing more damaging than to use a single or even a group of techniques without careful behavioral assessment, and without clearly seeing the relationship between the program offered and the objectives to be reached. On the other hand, we are at a time in history when athletic programs, both competitive and recreational, are most receptive to what we can offer.

where to from here?

Peter Klavora

The major objective of this book was to illuminate the psychological methods sport psychologists across the world have used with considerable success in sport practice. In other words, the book stands to answer the question "What is the state of the art on the brink of 1980s?" However, there was a second objective behind the publication, namely, to indicate the status of applied psychology in sport practice on the North American continent and to present some comparisons with European countries, notably Scandinavia and the Soviet Union. In these concluding notes I intend to summarize the book under two subtitles and at the end suggest some possibilities and implications of applied psychology for sport practice in Canada. My remarks will be based mainly upon the materials presented in this volume. Furthermore, although my comments will be directly related to the Canadian situation, I believe they will be relevant to sport psychologists, coaches, athletes, and sport consultants in other western countries as well.

The Status of Applied Sport Psychology

The reader will agree that, by inference, Part One and certain sections of Part Two are almost a perfect replica of my experiences described in the introductory chapter. In various ways these sections of the book reveal the enormous dichotomy between the offerings of those scientists who call themselves "sport psychologists" on the one hand and the real needs of the practitioner, the coach and the athlete, on the other. With only a few exceptions, the North American sport psychologists have eliminated themselves completely from the reality of sport practice. Locked between the walls of their laboratories, they have been busy testing theories and isolated laboratory behavior, and formulating complicated research paradigms which at best have been under-

297

stood only by themselves. By following this route they have been rewarded by publications in scientific journals and they have, according to Martens in chapter 7, successfully played the vital "academic game" of scHolarship. In the process, however, they have entirely forgotten the most important thing—sport. Those psychologists who did show a genuine concern for sport practice and became deeply involved with coaches, athletes, and teams, were scorned by their colleagues and regarded as inferior scholars. Since it began in the early 1960s, applied work in sport has been considered unacceptable as scholarship even by undergraduate programs, let alone the graduate schools and various psychological societies.

In comparison, European applied sport psychology, notably that of the Soviet Union, has made great strides and has developed a high level of usefulness for athletic training and competition. According to Shneidman (chapter 22), the Soviet model of total development and preparation of the athlete is complete. The international calibre athlete is entrusted to a team of applied scientists, in most cases headed by the coach, who is a highly educated individual himself. In addition, these efforts of the applied scientists and practitioners are supplemented by the research activities of their colleagues employed at sport institutes and colleges of physical culture who are advancing the theoretical aspects of sport psychology.

Thus, in preparation for international sport combat, in the Soviet Union little is left to chance. This is reflected in remarkably stable and superior performances of Soviet athletes and teams. Sport psychologists, permanently attached to sport teams, have been making significant contributions to this cooperative effort for years.

In Canada there is also an enormous demand for psychological services by sportspeople. This is indicated by the fact that they have listed (chapter 1) psychology as the number one item on their shopping list, clearly showing the need for scientific support services. However, their requests have generally not been met by the sport psychologists. The work of Rushall, and Wilson and Minden between 1976 and 1978 are only isolated instances of permanency being achieved in psychological assistance to Canadian national teams. Furthermore, Pulos' appointment as the psychologist to the 1978 Canadian National Commonwealth Team marks a surprising breakthrough in attitudes of the Canadian sport administrators. However, it should be noted that at the present time, only Minden has continued his assistance to the Canadian Women's Gymnastic Team.

In the U.S.A. the picture is even worse. To my knowledge, Suinn is the only psychologist who has recently assisted U.S. athletes on the Olympic site. Morgan's work with Olympic rowers and wrestlers is significant but it has not been continuous. Ogilvie and Tutko, pioneer U.S. sport psychologists, have been deeply involved with sport practice since the early 1960s. However, their work has concentrated mainly on college and professional levels.

Perhaps the efforts of many other psychologists who have tried to work with athletes and coaches in Canada and in the U.S. should be mentioned at this point. Their efforts were in most cases shotgun arrangements. Therefore they were short-lived. Unfortunately, the approaches and methods they used led to significant abuses particularly of athletes who did not take long to slam the door behind them as noted by Kidd in chapter 4. This, by the way, has adversely affected the credibility of the field and of the work by all those psychologists who have been able to enhance sport training and competition.

The State of the Art

The state of the art of applied sport psychology is presented comprehensively in Parts Three, Four, and Five by authors all of whom have had a commitment to the application of psychology to sport. These psychologists are generally recognized as leaders in their special fields. Because they have practiced their techniques judiciously and selectively, they have rendered invaluable assistance to athletes and coaches. Their work is regarded as epitomizing the state of the art of today's applied sport psychology. The methods these psychologists have developed to date can be summarized under the following headings: (1) clinical counseling, (2) techniques for self-control, (3) psychometrics, (4) hypnosis and self-hypnosis, (5) motivational techniques, and (6) learning or coaching techniques. A thorough mastery of techniques such as hypnosis and psychometrics requires a high level of expertise based on extensive graduate and post graduate training as well as years of experience. Other techniques, however, such as those for self-control, motivation, and coaching can be learned by all if taught properly. The importance and applicability of these techniques to sport practice at the international level of training and competition needs to be emphasized.

Clinical counseling in sport. I consider the clinical counseling of athletes and teams the most important responsibility of sport psychology. Without doubt, it is the most time-consuming aspect of psychological work in sport and clearly requires the psychologist-in-residence approach if it is to be applied effectively to athletics. A resident psychologist, working intimately with athletes and teams in training camps away from the home environment for months and years in order to prepare for international competition, is a must. Furthermore, a psychologist trained in clinical counseling should accompany travelling national teams on the road, which will often be for weeks and months. This is imperative in sports such as swimming and women's gymnastics, where the average age of the participants seldom reaches beyond teen years.

In my view, when psychological problems develop as a result of prolonged hard training or competition, a psychologist trained in clinical counseling is the only person who can handle them effectively. Many coaches and managers of teams have demonstrated excellent abilities to counsel their athletes. However, because of their own vested interests in training and competition, they cannot remain sufficiently impartial in their treatments, and furthermore, many psychological problems are simply beyond their general counseling abilities.

Techniques for self-control. Of the several psychological techniques for improving self-control found to be effective in sport practice, the ones most often discussed in this book are: desensitization, meditation, psychical self-regulation, mental practice, visuo-motor behavior rehearsal, symbol and anti-symbol training, biofeedback, combining the elements, and verbal formulas. By improving attention and enabling the athlete to monitor his own arousal and anxiety levels, these techniques are designed first to increase overall well-being, and second to stimulate maximum performance.

With serious training athletes can master most of these techniques and apply them according to need. It is the sport psychologist's duty to provide the introduction to these methods. Later, when the coach becomes familiar with them he can, if he wishes, continue the teaching of these techniques. The psychologist's services continue only in a supervisory capacity.

Psychometrics. The application of various psychological inventories to athletes and the interpretation of their results is the sport psychologist's domain. It is his domain because he alone possesses such skills as the ability to select appropriate tests, to understand the crucial methodological aspects of such tests, to use computer analyses, and to intepret personality profiles.

However, there are a number of simple tests that coaches and athletes can use themselves in everyday training and competition. These tests assess the athlete's moods, anxiety levels, motivation levels, aggression, and so on. Scoring and interpretation of these tests are simple and the information obtained useful. Therefore, I would recommend that coaches in consultation with a sport psychologist become familiar with some of these tests and integrate them into their training procedures.

Hypnosis and self-hypnosis. There seems to be much promise in the use of hypnosis for elite athletes. Only experts, psychologists and psychiatrists trained in hypnotic techniques and psychodynamics, should be permitted to apply this method in sport practice. At the present time, more practical research is needed before a valid assessment of the usefulness of hypnosis in sport can be made.

On the other hand, athletes can be taught self-hypnosis. Self-hypnosis coupled with mental rehearsal and visualization training has great merit in sport practice and athletes should be taught this technique. It can be used effectively for the elevation of motivation to practice, improvement in relaxation and sleep, reduction of interfering aspects of stress upon concentration, and so on.

Motivational techniques. Motivational and coaching techniques are the bread and butter aspects of coaching. The sport psychologist can assist the coach immensely, but it is mainly the coach who must apply them in sport practice. The two, the coach and the psychologist, work closely together in continuously developing new motivational patterns which are to stimulate the athlete to habits of sustained practice and competition on high levels.

Where to from Here?

New developments in sport psychology will have to take place in Canada if the field is going to realize its potential in sport practice. Excellent models are available from Scandinavia and the Soviet Union from which we can learn. Over the past few years, albeit on a small scale, we have developed our own models with a moderate success. It is now up to all of us, the Canadian sport psychologists, practitioners, and sport administrators to find a scheme which would integrate these experiences into a model which would satisfy the needs of all involved and particularly the needs of the competitor. In these concluding notes I will present some of my personal views which may be more of a wish than a vision. They are offered as a reflection of my dual experience as a practitioner and a scholar; they are offered by a person who believes that the sport psychologist's place in the 1980s will be the sports arena just as the laboratory has been up to now. However, this is not to say that we should abandon the basic research. What I am advocating is a balance between applied and basic research activities, with the applied side having much catching up to do.

Responsibilities of the CSPLSP. The Canadian Society for Psychomotor Learning and Sport Psychology should take on a strong leadership role and first of all identify all those members of the society who have a geniune interest in the applied work in sport. These members should establish their own subgroup within the society whose main responsibility would be to regulate and guide all professional activities of its members. Other related sub-tasks would include: (1) to suggest an adequate training and preparation of its members; (2) to certify its members based on their training; (3) to determine the psychometric batteries and psychological programs to be implemented to various sport groups; (4) to promote the development of new psychological programs and psychometric inventories; (5) to clearly define objectives of psychological services and the realistic expectations of these services to the sport groups; (6) to establish a code of ethics for testing and interpretation of results and implementation of psychological programs; (7) to sponsor applied symposia and workshops; (8) to establish and maintain an active liaison with national and provincial sport governing bodies; and (9) to maintain a close liaison with the support services groups of Commonwealth, Pan American, and Olympic Games committees.

Responsibilities of the sport psychologist. It should be the responsibility of the sport psychologist (1) to practice only those psychological techniques which he is trained to use and perhaps "retool" if his training background is in other areas of expertise; (2) to become familiar with the sport with which he intends to work and to become involved in the planning and training procedures of competitors; (3) to work closely with other scientists also involved in preparation of the same sport group; and (4) to promote the profession and share the information with colleagues and students.

Responsibilities of the practitioner. The coach and the athlete should generally be modest in their expectations of the offerings of sport psychology at the present time, particularly in the area of selection of athletes and prediction of performance based on psychometric testing. However, they should begin to cooperate fully with the sport psychologists in their attempts to generate a valid data bank on athletes in training and competition which would in turn enhance their prediction abilities. Furthermore, the coach and the athlete should allow enough time in their schedules for practice of the various psychological techniques. Much like physical training, it takes time, strong commitment, and continuous practice to master these techniques to the point when they become useful.

Responsibilities of sport governing bodies. All sport governing bodies should develop research committees to assist in searching out the information they need to improve their programs. These committees must identify and categorize the most urgent needs and secure funding from private sources and government agencies to adequately fund the desired scientific support services.

Responsibilities of the universities. It is the responsibility of every university to respond to the needs of the society. For several years now the federal government in Canada has publicly voiced its support for sport excellence. It has backed this emphasis with considerable funding, particularly in coaching development areas. The universities should (1) develop undergraduate and graduate programs aimed at training coaching personnel in which sport psychologists could play an important role; (2) offer new—or change the existent—courses in sport psychology reflecting the specific needs of applied psychology of sport; (3) develop new programs for training graduates on master's and doctoral levels of expertise in applied psychology; (4) tolerate long-term commitment of sport psychologists to sport teams often characterized by prolonged absenteeism; and (5) recognize the applied dimension of psychological research in physical education and sport as a respectable scholarly activity.

Responsibilities of government and other sport agencies. Sport Canada, Coaching Association of Canada, Canadian Olympic Association, and the Commonwealth and Pan American Games committees should (1) support the scientific needs of sport governing bodies; (2) adopt policy of ensuring that the scientific support personnel accompany the Canadian national teams to major international events and to future training camps; (3) provide incentives to scientists who are involved in sport practice; and (4) to ensure sufficient funds for applied research in sport.

WHERE TO FROM HERE? IT IS OUR JOINT RESPONSIBILITY!

bibliography

Adams, J.A. "A Close-loop Theory of Motor Performance." *Journal of Motor Behavior* 3 (1971).

Alderman, R.B. "Sports Psychology: Past, Present, and Future Dilemmas." In P. Klavora and K.A.W. Wipper (eds.). *Psychological and Sociological Factors in Human Performance.* Toronto: School of Physical and Health Education, University of Toronto, 1979.

Alderman, R.B., and Wood, N.L. "An Analysis of Incentive Motivation in Young Canadian Athletes." *Canadian Journal of Applied Sports Sciences* 1, No. 2 (1976).

Alexander, F.M. *The Resurrection of the Body.* New York: Delta Books, 1969.

Asinof, E. *Seven Days to Sunday.* New York: Simon and Schuster, 1968.

Atkinson, J. W. and Raynor, J.O. *Motivation and Achievement.* New York: Wiley, 1974.

Bard, C., Fleury, M., and Salmela, J.H. (eds.) *Actes du Septième Symposium canadien de l'Apprentissage Moteur et de la Psychologie du Sport-Mouvement.* Québec: A.P.A.P.Q., 1975.

Basmajian, J.V. *Muscles Alive: Their Functions Revealed by Electromyography.* Baltimore: Williams and Williams, 1962.

Bell, M. "Hypnosis in Sports." *Sport,* March 1974.

Bertherat, T. and Bernstein, C. *The Body Has Its Reasons: Anti-Exercise and Self-Awareness.* New York: Pantheon Books, 1977.

Birch, D., and Veroff, J. *Motivation: A Study of Motivation.* Belmont, Ca.: Brooks/Cole, 1966.

Birk, L., and Brinkley-Birk, A.W. "Psychoanalysis and Behavior Therapy." *American Journal of Psychiatry* 131, No. 5 (May 1974).

Botterill, C. "The Psychology of Coaching." *Coaching Review* 1, No. 4 (1978).

Brady, J.P. "Behavioral Therapy." *American Journal of Psychoanalysis* 133 (1976).

Brenner, D., *et al.* "Somatically Evoked Magnetic Fields of the Human Brain." *Science* 199 (January 6, 1978).

Brooks, C. *Sensory Awareness: The Rediscovery of Experience.* New York: Viking, 1974.

Butt, D.S. "Aggression, Neuroticism, and Competence: Theoretical Models for the Study of Sports Motivation." *International Journal of Sports Psychology* 4 (1973).

Butt, D.S., *Psychology of Sport.* Toronto: Van Nostrand Reinhold, 1976.

Butt, D.S., "Short Scales for the Measurement of Sports Motivation." Manuscript, 1978.

Campagnolo, I. *Towards a National Policy on Amateur Sport* (The Green Paper on Sport). Ottawa: Health and Welfare, 1977.

Christina, R.W., and Landers, D.M. *Psychology of Motor Behavior and Sport 1976.* Champaign, Ill.: Human Kinetics, 1977.

Cooper, K. *The Aerobics Way.* New York: M. Evans, 1977.

"Coué, E." *New Encyclopedia Britannica.* 15th ed. Chicago: Encyclopedia Britannica, 1974.

Cousins, N. "The Mysterious Placebo: How Mind Helps Medicine Work." *Saturday Review,* October 1, 1977.

Crase, D. "Has Physical Education Achieved a Scholarly Dimension?" *Journal of Physical Education and Recreation* 49 (October, 1978).

Cratty, B.J. *Psychology in Contemporary Sport.* Englewood Cliffs, N.J.: Prentice-Hall, Inc., 1973.

Crossman, E.R.F.W. "A Theory of Acquisition of Speed-skill." *Ergonomics* 2 (1959).

Davydov, V.V. "Sovremennaia Obshchaia Psikhologiia i Psikhologiia Sporta" (Contemporary General Psychology and the Psychology of Sport). *Teoriia i Praktika Fizicheskoi Kul'tury* No. 2 (1975).

deCharms, R. *Personal Causation.* New York: Academic Press, 1968.

Dembo, A.G. "O Nekotorykh Aktual'nykh Voprosakh Sportivnoi Meditsiny" (On Certain Important Problems of Contemporary Sport Medicine). *Teoriia i Praktika Fizicheskoi Kul'tury* No. 10 (1972).

DePalma, D.M., and Nideffer, R.M. "Relationships between the Test of Attentional and Interpersonal Style and Psychiatric Subclassification." *Journal of Personality Assessment* 41 (1977).

Downey, L.W. *et al. Report of an Inquiry into the Rights of Individuals in Amateur Sports (Hockey).* Edmonton: Alberta Department of Culture, Youth and Recreation, 1973.

Ebeze, S. "Psychological Inventories for Competitive Soccer." Unpublished Master's thesis, Dalhousie University, Halifax, 1975.

Endler, N.S., and Hunt, J.M. "Generalizability of Contributions from Sources of Variance in the S-R Inventories of Anxiousness." *Journal of Personality* 37 (1969).

Endler, N.S., Hunt, J.M., and Rosenstein, A.J. "An S-R Inventory of Anxiousness." *Psychological Monographs* 76, No. 17, whole No. 536 (1962).

Eysenck, H.J., and Eysenck, S.B.G. *Manual for the Eysenck Personality Inventory.* San Diego, Ca.: Educational and Industrial Testing Service, 1968.

Feather, B.W., and Rhoades, J.M. "Psychodynamic Behaviour Therapy." *Archives of General Psychiatry* 26 (1972).

Feldenkreis, M. *Awareness Through Movement: Health Exercises for Personal Growth.* New York: Harper and Row, 1972.

Fixx, J. *The Complete Book of Running.* New York: Random House, 1977.

Fox, R.G. "The Construction of an Achievement Motivation Scale for Use in Sporting Environments." Unpublished Master's thesis, Lakehead University, Thunder Bay, Ont., 1977.

Freud, S. "The Ego and the Id." In James Strachey (ed.). *The Standard Edition of Complete Works of Sigmund Freud.* Vol. 19. London: Hogarth, 1961.

Gallwey, W.T. *Inner Tennis.* New York: Random House, 1976.

Gergen, K.J. "Social Psychology as History." *Journal of Personality and Social Psychology* 26 (1973).

Gergen, K.J. "Social Psychology, Science and History." *Personality and Social Psychology Bulletin* 2 (1976).

Goncharov, V.D. "Metodologicheskie Problemy Sotsial'noi Psikhologii Fizicheskoi Kul'tury" (Methodological Problems of the Social Psychology of Physical Culture). *Teoriia i Praktika Fizicheskoi Kul'tury* No. 6 (1976).

Green, E. and Green, A. *Beyond Biofeedback.* New York: Delacorte Press, 1977.

Groves, D.L., Heekin, R., and Banks, C. "Content Analysis: International Journal of Sport Psychology." *International Journal of Sport Psychology* 9 (1978).

Gruneau, R.S. "Conflicting Standards and Problems of Personal Action in the Sociology of Sport." *Quest* 30 (Summer 1978).

Hanin, Y., and Martens, R. "Sport Psychology in the USSR." *Coaching Review* 1, No. 5 (September 1978).

Hargreaves, J. "The Political Economy of Mass Sport." In Stanley Parker *et al.* (eds.). *Sport and Leisure in Contemporary Society.* London: School of the Environment, Polytechnic of Central London, 1975.

Harrison, B. and Reilly, E. *Visiondynamics Baseball Method.* Laguna Niguel, Ca., 1975.

Helmreich, R. "Applied Social Psychology: The Unfulfilled Promise." *Personality and Social Psychology Bulletin* 1 (1975).

Hickman, J.L., Murphy, M., and Spino, M. "Psychophysical Transformation through Meditation and Sport." *Simulations and Games* 8, No. 1 (March, 1977).

Horsfall, J.S., *et al.* "Sport Personality Assessment: A Methodological Re-examination." In D.M. Landers (ed.). *Psychology of Sport and Motor Behavior II.* Penn State HPER Series, No. 10. College Station: Pennsylvania State University, 1975.

Ikai, M., and Steinhaus, A. "Some Factors Modifying the Expression of Human Strength." *Journal of Applied Physiology* 16 (1961).

Jacobson, E. *Progressive Relaxation.* 1938; rpt. Chicago: University of Chicago Press, 1942.

Jacobson, E. *The Self and Object World.* New York: International Universities Press, 1964.

Jamieson, J., Rushall, B.S., and Talbot, D. *Psychological and Performance Factors of Canadian Olympic Games Swimmers — 1976.* Research report. Ottawa: Canadian Amateur Swimming Association, 1976.

Jenner, B. and Finch, P. *Decathlon Challenge: Bruce Jenner's Story.* Englewood Cliffs, N.J.: Prentice-Hall, 1977.

Johnson, R., and Barber, T.X. "Hypnotic Suggestions for Blister Formation: Subjective and Physiological Effects." *The American Journal of Clinical Hypnosis* 18 (1976).

Kanygin, V.A., and Kozlov, E.G. "Faktor Psikhicheskoi Napravlennosti v Sorevnovatel'noi Deiatel'nosti Tiazheloatletov" (The Factor of Psychic Tension in Competition Activity of Weightlifters). *Teoriia i Praktika Fizicheskoi Kul'tury* No. 8 (1978).

Kerr, B.A. *Human Performance and Behavior.* Calgary: University of Calgary, 1977.

Kessler, L., and Rothstein, A.L. "Videotape Replay and the Learning of Skills in Open and Closed Environments." *Research Quarterly,* in press.

Khanin, Iu.L. "Mezhlichnostnye Konflikty v Sportivnoigrovoi Deiatel'nosti" (Inter-personal Conflicts in Sport-Game Activity). *Teoriia i Praktika Fizicheskoi Kul'tury* No. 7 (1976).

Khanin, Iu.L. "O Srochnoi Diagnostike Sostoianiia Lichnosti v Gruppe" (On the Diagnostics of the Individual's Condition in a Group). *Teoriia i Praktika Fizicheskoi Kul'tury* No. 8 (1977).

Khudadov, N.A. "Nauchno-prakticheskie Voprosy Psikhologicheskogo Obespecheniia Podgotovki Sportsmenov Vysokogo Klassa" (Scientific and Practical Problems of the Psychological Preparation of Superior Athletes). Paper presented at the 1978 Congress of the Canadian Society for Psychomotor Learning and Sport Psychology, November 2-5, 1978, at Toronto.

Kidd, Bruce. "The Coach Grew a Beard for Credibility." *Weekend Magazine,* May 5, 1971.

Klavora, P. "State Anxiety and Athletic Competition." Unpublished doctoral dissertation, University of Alberta, Edmonton, Alberta, 1974.

Klavora, P. "Application of the Spielberger Trait-State Anxiety Theory and STAI in Pre-competitive Anxiety Research." In D.M. Landers (ed.). *Psychology of Sport and Motor Behavior II.* Penn State HPER Series, No. 10. College Station: Pennsylvania State University, 1975. (a)

Klavora, P. "Emotional Arousal in Athletics: New Considerations." *Actes du Septieme Symposium Canadien de l'Apprentissage Moteur et de la Psychologie du Sport-Mouvement.* Quebec: A.P.A.P.Q., 1975. (b)

Klavora, P. "An Attempt to Derive Inverted-U Curves Based on the Relationship Between Anxiety and Athletic Performance." In D.M. Landers (ed.).

Psychology of Motor Behavior and Sport. Champaign, Ill.: Human Kinetics, 1978.

Klavora, P. "Psychological Behavior of Oarsmen Before, During, and After a Championship Rowing Regatta." A paper to be presented at the Fifth European Congress of Sport Psychology, September 16-21, 1979, at Varna, Bulgaria. (a)

Klavora, P. "State Anxiety of Young Hockey Players During a Three-Week Trial Period." A paper to be presented at the Fifth European Congress of Sport Psychology, September 16-21, 1979, at Varna, Bulgaria. (b)

Kotonay, B.J. "The Effects of Visuo-Motor Behavior Rehearsal on Athletic Performance." Unpublished Master's thesis, Hunter College, The City University of New York, 1977.

Krippner, S., and Rubin, D. (eds.). *The Energies of Consciousness.* New York: Gordon and Breach, 1975.

Kroger, W.S. *Clinical and Experimental Hypnosis.* 2nd ed. Philadelphia: Lippincott, 1977.

Kroger, W.S., and Fezler, W.D. *Hypnosis and Behavior Modification: Imagery Conditioning.* Philadelphia: Lippincott, 1976.

Landers, D.M. (ed.). *Psychology of Sport and Motor Behavior II.* Penn State HPER Series, No. 10. College Station: Pennsylvania State University,1975.

Landers, D.M., and Christina, R.W. *Psychology of Motor Behavior and Sport.* Champaign, Ill.: Human Kinetics, 1978.

Landry, R., and Orban, W.A.R. *Motor Learning, Sport Psychology, Pedagogy and Didactics of Physical Activity.* Miami: Symposia Specialists, 1978.

Landy, F.J. and Stern, R.M. "Factor Analysis of a Somatic Perception Questionnaire." *Journal of Psychosomatic Research* 15 (1971).

Layman, E.M. "Psychological Effects of Physical Activity." In J.H. Wilmore (ed.). *Exercise and Sport Sciences Review.* Vol. 2. New York: Academic Press, 1974.

Le Cron, L. *Self-Hypnotism.* Englewood Cliffs, N.J.: Prentice-Hall, 1964.

Leonard, G. *The Ultimate Athlete.* New York: Viking, 1975.

Leonard, G. *The Silent Pulse.* New York: Dutton, 1978.

Lewis, A.J. *A Report by A.J. Lewis.* Los Angeles: Garret AiResearch Corp., 1976.

Lewis, A.J. "Psychic Self-Regulation." Paper presented at the Fourth Annual Western Regional Association for Humanistic Psychology Conference, 1977, at San Diego, Ca.

L'Heureux, W.L. "Morality, Sport and the Athlete." Paper presented to the Canadian Congress for the Multi-Disciplinary Study of Sport and Physical Activity, October 12-14, 1973, at Montreal.

Liepmann, L. *Your Child's Sensory World.* Baltimore: Penguin Books, 1973.

Lorenz, K. *On Aggression.* 1963, rpt. New York: Harcourt, Brace, and World, 1966.

Loy, J., McPherson, B., and Kenyon, G. *Sport and Social Systems.* Don Mills, Ont.: Addison-Wesley, 1978.

Lubin, B. *Manual for the Depression Adjective Checklist.* San Diego, Ca.: Educational and Industrial Testing Service, 1967.

Mahoney, M.J., and Aveer, M. "Psychology of the Elite Athlete: An Exploratory Study." *Cognitive Therapy and Research* 1, No. 2 (1977).

Marliana, B. "Psychological Readiness for Maximum Performance." *Scholastic Coach,* April, 1977.

Martens, R. "Anxiety and Motor Behavior: A Review." *Journal of Motor Behavior* 3 (1971).

Martens, R. *Sport Competition Anxiety Test.* Champaign, Ill.: Human Kinetics, 1977.

Matova, M.A. "Psikhicheskie Sostoianiia Sportsmenov Pri Krainikh Myshechnykh Napriazheniiakh" (Psychic Conditions of Athletes during Extreme Muscular Tension). *Teoriia i Praktika Fizicheskoi Kul'tury* No. 3 (1976).

McCluggage, D. *The Centered Skier.* Vermont Crossroads: Vermont Crossroads Press, 1977.

McGuire, W.J. "The Yin and Yang of Progress in Social Psychology: Seven Koans." *Journal of Personality and Social Psychology* 26 (1973).

McNair, D.M., Lorr, M., and Droppleman, L.F. *Profile of Mood States Manual.* San Diego, Ca.: Educational and Industrial Testing Service, 1971.

Mill, J.S. *On Liberty.* In *Great Books of the Western World.* Vol. 43. Chicago: Encyclopedia Britannica, 1952.

Miller, R.B. *Handbook on Training Equipment Design,* U.S. Airforce, W.A.D.C. Technical Report, 1953.

Mitchell, W.M. *The Use of Hypnosis in Athletes.* Stockton, Ca.: Valley Oaks Printers, 1972.

Moore, K. "Watching Their Steps." *Sports Illustrated,* May 3, 1976.

Morgan, W.P. "Efficacy of Psychobiologic Inquiry in the Exercise and Sport Sciences." *Quest* 20 (1973).

Morgan, W.P. "Psychological Factors Influencing Perceived Exertion." *Medicine and Science in Sports* 5 (1973).

Morgan, W.P. "Sport Personology: The Credulous-Skeptical Argument in Perspective." In W. Straub (ed.). *Psychology of Athlete Behavior.* Ithaca, N.Y.: Mouvement Press, 1978.

Morgan, W.P., and Horstman, D.H. "Psychometric Correlates of Pain Responsivity. *Journal of Perceptual and Motor Skills* 46 (1978).

Morgan, W.P., and Johnson, R.W. "Psychologic Characterization of the Elite Wrestler: A Mental Health Model." Paper presented at the Annual Meeting of the American College of Sports Medicine, 1977, at Chicago.

Morgan, W.P., and Johnson R.W. "Personality Characteristics of Successful and Unsuccessful Oarsmen." *International Journal of Sport Psychology* 9 (1978).

Morgan, W.P., and Pollock, M.L. "Psychologic Characterization of the Elite

Distance Runner." In P. Milvy (ed.). *Annals of the New York Academy of Sciences.* Vol. 301. 1977.

Morgan, W.P., and Vogel, J. "Psychometric Covariates of Rapid Translocation Across Twelve Time Zones." Unpublished report. U.S. Army Research Institute of Environmental Medicine, Natick, Ma., 1975.

Morris, F. *Self-Hypnosis in Two Days.* Berkeley, Ca.: Intergalactic, 1974.

Murphy, M. and White, R. *The Psychic Side of Sports.* Redding, Mass.: Addison-Wesley, 1978.

Nagle, F.J., *et al.* "Spotting Success Traits in Olympic Contenders." *Physical and Sports Medicine* 3 (1975).

National Coaching Development Program. *Coach's Manual Level 2.* Toronto: Ontario Ministry of Culture and Recreation, 1976.

Nguen Zui Fat, and Dashkevich, O.V. "Psikhocheskaia Naprizhennost' Sportsmena kak Faktor Rezul'tativnosti Strel'by" (Psychic Tension as a Factor in the High Performance of Shooters). *Teoriia i Praktika Fizicheskoi Kul'tury* No. 4 (1973).

Nicklaus, J., and Bowden, K. *Golf My Way.* New York: Simon and Schuster, 1974.

Nideffer, R.M. *The Inner Athlete: Mind Plus Muscle for Winning.* New York: Crowell, 1976. (a)

Nideffer, R.M. *The Test of Attentional and Interpersonal Style: An Interpreter's Manual.* Rochester, N.Y.: BRAG, 1976. (b)

Nideffer, R.M. "The Test of Attentional and Interpersonal Style." *Journal of Personality and Social Psychology* 34, No. 3 (1976). (c)

Nideffer, R.M. "A Comparison of Self-report and Performance Measures of Attention: A Second Look." *Journal of Perceptual and Motor Skills* 45 (1977).

Nideffer, R.M., and Sharpe, R. *A.C.T.: Attention Control Training.* New York: Wyden Books, 1978. (a)

Nideffer, R.M., and Sharpe, R. *How to Put Anxiety Behind You.* New York: Stein and Day, 1978. (b)

Ogilvie, B.C. "Walking the Perilous Path of the Team Psychologist." *The Physician and Sports Medicine* 5, No. 4 (April, 1977).

Ogilvie, B.C., and Tutkro, T.A. *Problem Athletes and How To Handle Them.* London: Pelham, 1966.

Ornstein, Robert. *The Psychology of Consciousness.* New York: Pelican Books, 1975.

Ostrander, S., Schroeder, S., and Ostrander, N. *Super-Learning.* New York: Delacorte/Confucian, 1979.

Oxendine, J.B. "Emotional Arousal and Motor Performance." *Quest* 13 (1970).

Pound, S. "Psychological Inventories for Basketball Players." Unpublished Master's thesis, Dalhousie University, Halifax, 1977.

Razumov, S.A., and Saburov, P.S. "Psikhofiziologicheskoe Obosnovanie Rezhimov Predsorevnovatel'noi podgotovki Prygunov na Lyzhakh s Tramplina" (Psychophysiological Basis of Precompetition Training Regimens for Ski Jumpers). *Teoriia i Praktika Fizicheskoi Kul'tury* No. 9, (1978).

Roberts, G.C., and Newell, K.M. *Psychology of Motor Behavior and Sport — 1978.* Champaign, Ill.: Human Kinetics, 1979.

Rodionov, A.V., (ed.). *Psikhologiia Sportivnoi Deiatel'nosti* (The Psychology of Sport Activity). Moscow, 1978.

Romanina, E.V., and Romanin, A.N. "Sootnoshenie Individual'no-Tipicheskogo i Sotsial'no-Psikhologicheskogo Povedenii Sportsmenov" (The Relationship between the Individual-Typical and the Socio-Psychological in the Behavior of Athletes). *Teoriia i Praktika Fizicheskoi Kul'tury* No. 12 (1976).

Romen, A., *et al.* (eds.). *Psychical Self-Regulation.* Vol. 2. Alma Ata, USSR: Kazakh University Press, 1974.

Rotter, J.B. "Generalized Expectancies for Internal versus External Control of Reinforcement." *Psychological Monographs* 80, whole No. 609 (1966).

Rudik, P.A. "Psikhologicheskie Aspekty Sportivnoi Deiatel'nosti" (Psychological Aspects of Sport Activity). In P.A. Rudik, V.V. Medvedev, and A.V. Rodionov (eds.). *Psikhologiia i Sovremennyi Sport* (Psychology and Contemporary Sport). Moscow, 1973.

Rushall, B.S. "Consultation Procedures for Sport Psychologists." In *Proceedings of the Third International Congress of Sport Psychology.* Vol. 1. Madrid: INEF, 1973.

Rushall, B.S. "The Status of Sport Psychology in Canada." Paper presented at the Fifth Canadian Symposium for Psychomotor Learning and Sport Psychology, 1973, at Montreal.

Rushall, B.S. "A Tool for New Directions in Sport Personality Research: Behavior Inventories for Swimmers." Paper presented at the Sixth Canadian Symposium for Psychomotor Learning and Sport Psychology, 1974, at Halifax.

Rushall, B.S. (ed.). *The Status of Psychomotor Learning and Sport Psychology Research.* Halifax: Sport Science Associates, 1975. (a)

Rushall, B.S. "Applied Psychology of Sports." In B.S. Rushall (ed.). *The Status of Psychomotor Learning and Sport Psychology Research.* Halifax: Sport Science Associates, 1975. (b)

Rushall, B.S. "Alternative Dependent Variables for the Study of Behavior in Sport." In D.M. Landers (ed.). *Psychology of Sport and Motor Behavior II.* Penn State HPER Series, No. 10. College Station: Pennsylvania State University, 1975. (c)

Rushall, B.S. "Environmental Specific Behavior Inventories: Developmental Procedures." Proceedings of Fourth European Congress of Sport Psychology, September 4-9, 1975, at Edinburgh. (d)

Rushall, B.S. "The Team Approach to Coaching." In J. Taylor (ed.). *1976 Post Olympic Games Symposium.* Ottawa: Coaching Association of Canada, 1977.

Rushall, B.S. "Applied Behavior Analysis as a Psychology for Practitioners." Paper presented at the Annual Conference of the North American Society for the Psychology of Sport and Physical Activity, May 24, 1977, at Ithaca College, N.Y.

Rushall, B.S. "Environment Specific Behavior Inventories: Developmental Procedures." *International Journal of Sport Psychology* 9 (1978). (a)

Rushall, B.S. *Team Identification Programs with the Canadian Commonwealth Games Swimming Teams.* Research report. Ottawa: Canadian Amateur Swimming Association, 1978. (b)

Rushall, B.S. "Sport Psychologist, Sport Organization and the Athlete." Paper presented at the 1978 Congress of the Canadian Society for Psychomotor Learning and Sport Psychology, November 2-5, 1978, at Toronto.

Salmela, J.H. "Application of a Psychological Taxonomy to Sport Performance." *Canadian Journal of Applied Sport Sciences* 1 (1976).

Salmela, J.H. "Skill learning in China." *Coaching Review,* in press.

Sarason, I.G. "Empirical Findings and Theoretical Problems in the Use of Anxiety Scales." *Psychological Bulletin* 57 (1960).

Schlenkar, B.R. "Social Psychology and Science." *Journal of Personality and Social Psychology* 29 (1974).

Schneck, J. "Hypnotherapy for Ichthyosis." *Psychosomatics* 7 (1966).

Schultz, J., and Luthe, W. *Autogenic Methods.* Vol. I. New York: Grune and Stratton, 1969.

Scott, Jack. *The Athletic Revolution.* New York: Free Press, 1970.

Setterlind, S., and Unestahl, L.-E. *Relaxation in School, Part I.* Orebro: Orebro University, Department of Sport Psychology, 1977.

Shelton, H.M. *Exercise.* Chicago: Natural Hygiene Press, 1971.

Shero, F. *Shero: The Man Behind The Bench.* Don Mills, Ont.: Nelson, 1975.

Simonton, C., Simonton, S., and Creighton, J. *Getting Well Again.* Los Angeles: Tarcher, 1978.

Slusher, H. *Man, Sport and Existence.* Philadelphia: Lea and Febiger, 1967.

Smirnov, V.G., "'Povyshat' Obrazovanie Spetsialistov po Fizicheskoi Kul'ture i Sportu" (Raise the Educational Level of Specialists in Physical Culture and Sport). *Teoriia i Praktika Fizicheskoi Kul'tury* No. 3 (1973).

Smirnov, A.A. (ed.). *Razvitie i Sovremennoe Sostoianie Psikhologicheskoi Nauki v SSSR* (The Development and the Contemporary State of the Psychological Sciences in the USSR). Moscow, 1975.

Spielberger, C.D., Gorsuch, R.L., and Lushene, R.E. *STAI Manual.* Palo Alto, Ca.: Consulting Psychologists Press, 1970.

Spielberger, C.D. "Tri-State Anxiety and Motor Behavior. *Journal of Motor Behavior* 3 (1971).

Spino, M. *Running Home.* Millbrae, Ca.: Celestial Arts, 1977.

Spino, M., and Hickman, L. "You Are What You Think." *Runner's World,* May 1977.

Spino, M. and Warren, J. *The Mike Spino Mind/Body Running Program.* New York: Bantam, 1979.

Strauss, J.M. "Source of Reinforcement as a Potential Factor in Women's Sport Involvement." Unpublished Master's thesis, University of North Carolina, Greensboro, 1975.

Suinn, R.M. "Behavior Rehearsal Training for Ski Races. Brief Report" *Behavior Therapy* 3 (1972).

Suinn, R.M. "Visuo-Motor Behavior Rehearsal for Athletes." *Sports Medicine Journal* 1, No. 6 (1973).

Suinn, R.M. "Anxiety Management Training for General Anxiety." In R.M. Suinn and R.G. Weigel (eds.). *The Innovative Pshychological Therapies: Critical and Creative Incidents.* New York: Harper and Row, 1975.

Suinn, R.M. "Visual Motor Behavior Rehearsal for Adaptive Behavior." In J. Krumboltz and C. Thoresen (eds.). *Counseling Methods.* New York: Holt, 1976. (a)

Suinn, R.M. "Body Thinking: Psychology for Olympic Champs." *Psychology Today* 10, No. 2 (July, 1976). (b)

Suinn, R.M. *Manual: Anxiety Management Training (AMT).* Fort Collins, Colorado: Rocky Mountain Behavioral Sciences Institute, 1977.

Suinn, R.M. "Psychology and Sports Performance: Principles and Applications." In R.M. Suinn (ed.). *Psychology in Sports: Methods and Applications.* Minnesota: Burgess, in preparation, 1978.

Suinn, R.M., and Andrews, F.A. "Psychological Strategies of Professional Competitors." Manuscript in preparation, 1978.

Suinn, R.M., and Richardson, F.C. "Anxiety Management Training: A Non-specific Behavior Therapy Program for Anxiety Control." *Behavior Therapy* 4 (1971).

Taylor, J.A. "A Personality Scale of Manifest Anxiety." *Journal of Abnormal and Social Psychology* 48 (1953).

Tharp, R.G., and Gallimore, R. "What a Coach Can Teach a Teacher." *Psychology Today* 9 (1976).

Thurston, H. *The Physical Phenomena of Mysticism.* London: Barnes, Oates and Washbourne, 1952.

Titley, R.W. "The Loneliness of a Long-distance Kicker." *The Athletic Journal* (1976).

Tutko, T.A., Lyon, L.P., and Ogilvie, B.C. *Athletic Motivation Inventory.* San Jose: Institute of Athletic Motivation, 1975.

Tutko, T.A., and Bruns, W. *Winning is Everything and Other American Myths.* New York: Macmillan, 1976.

Tutko, T.A., and Tosi, U. *Sports Psyching.* Los Angeles: Tarcher, 1976.

Vanek, M. and Cratty, B.J. *Psychology and the Superior Athlete.* New York: Macmillan, 1970.

Wade, M.G., and Martens, R. *Psychology of Motor Behavior and Sport.* Champaign, Ill.: Human Kinetics, 1974.

Watzlawick, P. *The Language of Change.* New York: Basic Books, 1978.

Weitzenhoffer, A. *Hypnotism: An Objective Study on Suggestibility.* New York: Wiley, 1963.

White, R.W. *Ego and Reality in Psychoanalytic Theory: A Proposal Regarding Independent Ego Energies.* New York: International Universities Press, 1963.

Whiting, H.T.A. "Subjective Probability in Sport." Paper presented at the NASPSPA conference, 1978, at Tallahassee, Fla.

Whitson, D. "Sociology, Psychology and Canadian Sport." *Canadian Journal of Applied Sports Sciences* 3, No. 2 (1978).

Williams, I.D., and Wankel, L.M. (eds.). *Proceedings of the Fourth Canadian Symposium for Psychomotor Learning and Sport Psychology.* Ottawa: Health and Welfare, 1973.

Wilson, V.E. "Personality Assessment of Elite Female Gymnasts." Unpublished paper, York University, Toronto, 1973.

Wolpe, J. *The Practice of Behavior Therapy.* New York: Pergamon Press, 1973.

Wooden, J.R. *They Call Me Coach.* New York: Bantam, 1972.

Youngblood, D. and Suinn, R.M. "A Behavioral Assessment of Motivation." In R.M. Suinn (ed.). *Psychology in Sports: Methods and Applications.* Minnesota: Burgess, in preparation.

Zander, A. "Motivation and Performance of Sport Groups." In D.M. Landers (ed.). *Psychology of Sport and Motor Behavior II.* Penn State HPER Series, No. 10. College Station: Pennsylvania State University, 1975.

About the Editors

Juri V. Daniel is professor and director, School of Physical and Health Education, University of Toronto. He holds degrees in physical and health education, psychology, exercise physiology, and he received his PhD in administrative theory and organizational behavior from the University of Illinois. A former national swimming champion, he was head coach of the Varsity Blues swim team of the University of Toronto in the 1960s. During his tenure as coach, the Blues won every OUAA and CIAU championship. He was chosen coach of the year of CIAU swimming in 1966. For close to a decade, Daniel has been director of the only residential life-style changes clinic for selected professions in Canada and has acted as consultant to numerous professional groups on the interrelationship of stress, fitness, and health. He has published in leadership theory, educational philosophy, fitness, and aquatics.

Peter Klavora has been teaching sport psychology, motor learning, and rowing activity courses in the School of Physical and Health Education, University of Toronto, since 1974. He completed his PhD at the University of Alberta. As an oarsman he competed internationally with considerable success and coached on amateur and professional levels in his native Yugoslavia and in Canada for over ten years. Among notable coaching successes are bronze medals at European championships and Pan American Games and fourth place at the 1964 Olympics. He published in sport psychology on the effects of anxiety and arousal of athletes on performance. He is the editor of two volumes of proceedings of the 1978 CSPLSP Congress, titled *Psychological and Sociological Factors in Physical Performance* and *Motor Learning and Biomechanical Factors in Physical Performance*. He is also president of the Canadian Society for Psychomotor Learning and Sport Psychology. Klavora has published two rowing books, over thirty articles on rowing activity, and he is technical editor of *Catch,* the Canadian rowing journal. He is also coordinator of the coaching development programs for the Canadian Amateur Rowing Association.